Politics in

THE REPUBLIC OF
SOUTH AFRICA

The Little, Brown Series
in Comparative Politics

Under the Editorship of

GABRIEL A. ALMOND

JAMES S. COLEMAN

LUCIAN W. PYE

A COUNTRY STUDY

Politics in
THE REPUBLIC OF
SOUTH AFRICA

Leonard M. Thompson
University of California
Los Angeles

Boston

 **LITTLE, BROWN AND COMPANY**

Foreword

THE Little, Brown Series in Comparative Politics has three main objectives. First, it will meet the need of teachers to deal with both western and non-western countries in their introductory course offerings. Second, by following a common approach in the analysis of individual political systems, it will make it possible for teachers to compare these countries systematically and cumulatively. And third, it will contribute toward re-establishing the classic relationship between comparative politics and political theory, a relationship which has been neglected in recent decades. In brief, the series seeks to be global in scope, genuinely introductory and comparative in character, and concerned with broadening and deepening our understanding of the nature and variety of political systems.

The series has two parts: the Country Studies and the Analytic Studies. The Country Studies deal with a set of problems and processes deriving from a functional, as against a purely structural, approach to the study of political systems. We are gratified that the participants, all of them mature scholars with original insights of their own, were willing to organize their discussions around a common set of functional topics in the interest of furthering comparisons. At the same time, each author has been urged to adapt the common framework to the special problems of the country he is discussing and to express his own theoretical point of view.

An introductory book, *Comparative Politics: A Developmental Approach,* written by Gabriel Almond and G. Bingham Powell, provides an analytic supplement to the Country Studies. It also will open our set of Analytic Studies, which will offer basic discussions of such topics as political change in the emerging nations, comparative analyses of interest groups, political socialization, political communication, political culture, and the like. We hope these books will prove to be useful and stimulating supplements to the Country Series as well as points of departure in more advanced courses.

Leonard Thompson's *Politics in the Republic of South Africa,* the third volume in the Country Series, is a thoughtful study of a unique political system. A racially stratified, plural society in which the dominant oligarchy has consolidated its position of absolute power, South Africa stands typologically alone, in many respects an anomaly among the polities of our time. The author's interpretation of this complex country not only reflects his own deep knowledge of its political evolution and present situation, but it also demonstrates how the imaginative use of the common functional categories of the Series can serve to illuminate the atypical as well as the generic features of different political systems.

Gabriel A. Almond
James S. Coleman
Lucian W. Pye

Preface

THE South African political system is unique; and its peculiar characteristics are likely to affect all of us. "White" people of European origin, numbering one-fifth of the total population, monopolize all the vital decision-making roles; and the rest of the population, most of whom are "black" people and are related to the inhabitants of the newly-independent states of tropical Africa, are restricted to subordinate roles and discriminated against in many aspects of their daily lives. South Africa is also by far the strongest state in Africa, and within the lifetime of most readers of this book its government is likely to possess atomic weapons. Consequently, South Africa is a crucial part — indeed, a major promoter — of the racial tensions that are bedevilling contemporary mankind.

The core of this book is a discussion of political power as it actually operates in the Republic of South Africa. There are also chapters on the context and the consequences of political actions. The analysis is necessarily cruder and more tentative than one possible when dealing with countries like the principal Western democracies. Not many aspects of the South African political system have been subjected to primary research; and since all the known revolutionary groups have been outlawed and broken up, one can only conjecture about the present state of such opposition within South Africa.

I have not included an elaborate discussion of the *theory*

of apartheid, which has been dealt with in many other places and which is not particularly germane to an understanding of the actual political process. The entire book, however, is a commentary on the *practice of apartheid.*

In the footnotes are detailed references to relevant literature. Through these it becomes evident that the student of contemporary South African affairs owes an immense debt to the South African Institute of Race Relations, Johannesburg, whose publications — especially the *Survey of Race Relations* compiled annually by Miss Muriel Horrell — collate and summarize much data from many sources. The reader who wants more background information is referred to *The Peoples and Policies of South Africa* (3rd ed., London: Oxford University Press, 1962), by Leo Marquard, whose emphasis differs from mine.

The staffs of the libraries I used during the preparation of this book — especially those at the University of California, Los Angeles, and the Royal Commonwealth Society, London — were most helpful in locating material and making it available. Dr. Leo Kuper, Professor of Sociology at U.C.L.A., generously placed at my disposal rare documents from his private collection. Miss Clodagh O'Dowd of the University of Cape Town made notes for me from the biographical files in the library of the *Cape Times.* Dr. John S. Galbraith, Chancellor of the University of California, San Diego, commented on the first draft of the early chapters. René M. de Villiers, sub-editor of the *Star,* Johannesburg, corrected errors in the Communications section in Chapter IV. Martin Legassick and William Lye read the proofs and made valuable suggestions. Mrs. Dorothy Modafferi typed the manuscript most efficiently.

My main debt is to Professor James S. Coleman. He persuaded me to write this book; and he went far beyond the obligations of an editor in sending me a battery of stimulating observations upon the first draft, based upon his incomparable insights into contemporary politics in tropical Africa. For the defects of the book, however, I alone am responsible.

Leonard M. Thompson
University of California, Los Angeles
August 1965

Table of Contents

CHAPTER I

Introduction

Less than a hundred years ago South Africa's sole significance to the outside world derived from its geographic location on the shortest sea route from Europe to Asia. This was the reason the Dutch founded a refreshment station at the Cape of Good Hope in 1652 and maintained it as long as they could; and this was why the British conquered the Cape in 1795 and reconquered it in 1806.

South Africa now has the added significance of being the one powerful industrial state in a generally undeveloped continent. It produces over half the world's supply of gold and also leads the world in the production of gem diamonds, platinum, and antimony; it is the second largest producer of chrome, vanadium, and vermiculite, and the third largest of uranium, manganese, and asbestos. The country has vast coal and iron resources and considerable supplies of copper, lead, zinc, tin, and sulphur. It produces three times as much steel and generates three times as much electricity as the rest of Africa. There are about as many automobiles and telephones in South Africa as in the rest of the continent. There is a wide range of manufacturing and agricultural industries. The communications system by road, rail, and air is efficient. The armed forces are the best equipped and probably the most disciplined in Africa. Thanks to gold exports, the balance of trade is favorable.

1

British, American, German, French, Italian, Japanese and other foreign groups have considerable investments in South Africa and are rapidly increasing them. Indeed, by all the recognized criteria, South Africa's economy is strong and self-sustaining and its rate of development is rapid — illustrated by a fourfold increase in the gross national product and a fivefold increase in gross industrial production between 1945 and 1963.[1]

The South African ports are still important links in intercontinental trade. A large volume of shipping rounds the Cape each year; and although the Suez route between Europe and Asia is the shorter, the Canal was closed to ships of many nations during World War II and during the 1956 crisis, and could be closed again. At present South Africa is a terminus rather than a stepping-stone in air travel, but with the development of south polar routes its importance may increase. It already has an American tracking station for space flights.

These geographical and economic factors do not in themselves make South Africa particularly significant for mankind as a whole; yet the country does crucially affect the destiny of man, and this is due almost entirely to its political system, which is unique in the modern world. In no other system in a sovereign state is overriding power exercised by a minority racial group. In no other system is the maintenance of racial stratification — systematic, undiluted and inescapable — the primary object of policy. In no other system are the leveling effects of urbanization effectively countered by political processes.

The population of South Africa is officially divided into four main racial groups: white, Coloured, Asian and African.[2] The whites form 19.3 percent, the Coloureds 9.4, the Asians 3.0, and the Africans 68.3 of the total population of sixteen million. The whites have a monopoly of political power. Only whites may be members of the South African Parliament and the South African Cabinet, which are sovereign over the entire Republic. Economic power, too, is vested to an overwhelming extent in the hands of whites who own most of the land and control all the major industries and businesses. But every appreciable enterprise in the country employs nonwhites who do

[1] See D. Hobart Houghton, *The South African Economy* (Cape Town: Oxford University Press, 1964), which contains a good, select bibliography.

[2] See p. 31, where these terms are discussed.

the unskilled work at low wages, as well as whites who do the skilled work at high wages. Thus, though members of all the racial groups participate in the modern sector of the economy, and are dependent on it, their opportunities and rewards are determined by their race.

South Africans rarely meet members of racial groups other than their own, except as white employers and nonwhite employees, or white officials and nonwhite subjects. Members of the racial groups live in different areas; they attend different schools and churches; they sit in different parts of buses, trains and aircraft; they use different post office counters and rest on different public benches; they eat in different cafes and join different clubs and trade unions. When they are ill they receive different medical treatment, and when they die they are carried in different hearses to different cemeteries. In practically every case the facilities for whites are greatly superior to the facilities for nonwhites. Most of this separation is embodied in laws enacted by the sovereign all-white Parliament on the initiative of the all-white Cabinet, applied by all-white courts and enforced by police under the orders of all-white officers.

South Africa is unique; and being unique, it is isolated and threatened. The threat comes from without as well as within, for it is the one glaring example of a national political system devoted to the perpetuation of white domination in a period of history when racial domination is generally considered to be morally indefensible; so long as it exists the independent governments of tropical Africa will regard their revolution as incomplete.

THE CASE FOR THE GOVERNMENT

The policy of the Nationalist Party which has ruled South Africa since May 1948 has been vigorously defended over the years, especially by Eric H. Louw, Foreign Minister from 1948 to 1963, and by Dr. H. F. Verwoerd, Minister of Native Affairs from 1950 to 1958 and Prime Minister since 1958.[3] The essence

---

[3] Several of Eric Louw's speeches have been republished in H. H. H. Biermann, ed., *The Case for South Africa* (New York: Macfadden Books, 1963). Major statements have been made by H. F. Verwoerd in the South African House of Assembly in debates on no-confidence motions moved by the Leader of the Opposition, e.g., *Debates of the House of Assembly,*

of the South African government's case may be summarized as follows:

The white South African nation has as much right to exist in South Africa as the American nation in North America. Both trace their origins to the 17th century, both are fundamentally Christian nations derived from Western Europe, both have struggled to become independent from Britain, and both have built up strong, prosperous countries in formerly primitive environments. Today South Africa is a country of remarkable stability and its prosperity is increasingly shared by all sections of the population:

> Per capita of our nonwhite populations, more schools, both primary and secondary, are available for the nonwhites than in the countries of most of [tropical Africa] . . . per capita of our nonwhite populations, more beds are available for nonwhites in our hospitals than in any other state on the continent of Africa . . . per capita of our nonwhite peoples more housing has been provided during the past years for nonwhite occupation than in many of the countries [of tropical Africa] . . . . So, also, as regards money spent on social services. In South Africa . . . there are more nonwhite students attending universities than in any other state in Africa. . . .[4]

White South Africa, under whose leadership these results are being achieved, has the right to survive as a nation. Its survival would be compromised by any policy which promoted the integration of the Bantu people into the white political society, because the Bantu are in a majority in the country; once the

---

January 23, 1962, cols. 60-99, and January 25, 1963, cols. 221-48. Authoritative statements of the policy of the government are in the annual speeches made by the State President to both Houses of Parliament at the beginning of each annual session, e.g., *ibid.*, January 19, 1962, cols. 6-13, and January 18, 1963, cols. 4-11. For a brief defense by S. Pienaar, foreign correspondent of the *Burger*, see S. Pienaar and Anthony Sampson, *South Africa: Two Views of Separate Development* (London: Oxford University Press, 1960) pp. 3-29. For a more elaborate statement by Afrikaner Nationalists see N. J. Rhoodie and H. J. Venter, *Apartheid: A Socio-historical Exposition of the Origin and Development of the Apartheid Idea* (Cape Town: HAUM, 1960). The full flavor of Afrikaner nationalism is to be found in the contemporary Afrikaans press, notably the *Burger* (Cape Town) and the *Transvaler* (Johannesburg).

[4] Eric H. Louw, speech to the General Assembly of the United Nations, November 6, 1962, cited in Biermann, *op. cit.*, pp. 142-43.

process of integration started, they would not be satisfied with anything short of majority rule, which would mean Bantu domination and the suicide of the white nation. The Liberal Party policy of universal suffrage, the Progressive Party policy of a limited color-blind suffrage, and even the United Party policy of "racial federation" would sooner or later lead to Bantu domination:

> This so-called multi-racial nation with one multi-racial Parliament, can, however, never become a unit. Such divergent elements would try to exterminate each other. True unity in a racial group can only develop amongst its own people, separated from the others. The only national unity for the whites is unity amongst the whites.[5]

But just as the whites have the right to national existence and self-fulfillment, so have the several nonwhite communities — and more particularly the Bantu communities, which are embryonic nations:

> We do not only seek and fight for a solution which will mean our survival as a white race, but we also seek a solution which will ensure survival and full development — political and economic — to each of the other racial groups, and we are even prepared to pay a high price out of our earnings to ensure their future. . . . We want each of our population groups to control and to govern themselves, as is the case with other Nations. Then they can cooperate as in a Commonwealth — in an economic association with the Republic and with each other. In the transition stage the guardian must teach and guide his ward. That is our policy of separate development. South Africa will proceed in all honesty and fairness to secure peace, prosperity and justice for all, by means of political independence coupled with economic interdependence.[6]

This is a realistic policy of gradual withdrawal of white control over the Bantu Areas. Being gradual, it will not repeat the faults of those European governments which, not being responsible to

[5] H. F. Verwoerd, election day statement, October 18, 1961, cited by Verwoerd in Parliament, January 25, 1963 in *House of Assembly Debates*, 1963, col. 231.

[6] H. F. Verwoerd, speech in London in May 1961, cited by Eric H. Louw in his speech to the U.N. General Assembly on November 6, 1962 in Biermann, *op. cit.*, p. 147.

electorates in Africa and not reaping the effects of their errors, abandoned their commitments in Africa with precipitate speed after World War II, leaving conglomerations of backward peoples, who had not been welded into nations, to be misruled by self-styled leaders, who lack the self-discipline, the experience and the training necessary for effective statesmanship.

The main problem facing South Africa is to prepare the Bantu nations (Xhosa, Zulu, Sotho, etc.) for self-government in their own areas. The problem of the future of the Coloured and Asiatic peoples is less urgent, for they are smaller communities and their national consciousness is less mature. However, provision will be made for a great deal of functional self-administration by the Coloureds and Asiatics under the general supervision of the republican authorities, and ultimately it is conceivable that Coloured and Asian nations will control Coloured and Asian states in areas yet to be determined.

We cannot expect that so complex a task should be completed in a few years; but already great advances have been made, with the creation of the Bantu Authorities system, the grant of internal autonomy to the Xhosa in the Transkei, and the establishment of a Coloured Representative Council, soon to be followed by a similar council for Asiatics.

All this is being done in the teeth of persistent and vicious criticism from inside and outside South Africa:

> Subversive Bantu organizations in South Africa, which enjoy the support of only a small percentage of the Bantu people with active encouragement from small, white Communist and ultra-liberalist groups, have realized that the active and progressive steps taken by the Government are having a favorable reaction among the Bantu and they have therefore been doing their utmost to undermine the Government's plans and to create discontent among the Bantu. Expatriate members of these subversive organizations are very active in carrying out an anti-South African campaign overseas, particularly in New York and London.[7]

Such expatriates have the support of the governments of the new Afro-Asian states, which are themselves guilty of discrimi-

[7] Eric H. Louw, speech of November 6, 1962 in Biermann, *op. cit.*, p. 148.

natory practices and of oppression of large sections of their own populations. A campaign of slander and vilification has been unleashed against South Africa at the United Nations. Out of ignorance, weakness, or opportunism, several Western governments, which should have known better, have joined in the criticism, and made South Africa the whipping-boy of the world.

Since the internal opposition has led to serious acts of sabotage, the government has been obliged to act with the utmost firmness to preserve law and order and national security. Subversive organizations like the Communist Party, the African National Congress and the Pan-Africanist Congress have been banned, and steps have necessarily been taken to prevent their resurrection under different names and to restrain their members from committing acts of sabotage.

In the course of time it is to be expected that South Africa's reputation will improve. Already many responsible nonwhites realize that their living conditions in South Africa are infinitely superior to those prevailing in the countries further north, and that the policy of separate development holds out the promise of complete satisfaction for all the peoples of South Africa. Already the sabotage movement is declining. Already foreigners of goodwill, especially American and European businessmen who have visited South Africa and seen the true state of affairs, are telling their fellow-countrymen and their governments what they have found. Already the excessive sentimentalism that used to prevail in Europe and especially in the United States towards the African nationalist movement is beginning to be dissipated by knowledge of the facts. As the years go by, it will become increasingly evident that the new regimes of tropical Africa are unstable, backward, and unpredictable, while the South African regime is strong and prosperous and the one reliable ally of the West in the African continent.

These are the arguments in the case given by the Nationalist Party ruling South Africa.

THE CASE AGAINST THE GOVERNMENT

Opposition to the ruling Nationalist Party from within South Africa covers a wide spectrum. There are three other parties which aspire to gain power by constitutional means — that is to say, by winning a parliamentary majority from the existing white electorate. The United Party, the official opposition, would, if successful, try to preserve white "leadership" throughout the Republic by milder means than those adopted by the Nationalists, and would provide some limited representation in Parliament for all the nonwhite groups. The Progressive Party, which won one seat in the 1961 election, would introduce radical constitutional reforms, giving full political rights to all adults who meet a test of "civilization," creating safeguards against group domination, and guaranteeing the fundamental rights of all individuals. The Liberal Party, which has held no seats in Parliament since 1960, would extend the franchise to all adults after a brief interim period, and would also guarantee fundamental human rights. Before they were banned in 1960 there were also several congress organizations which, consisting for the most part of unenfranchised nonwhites, sought to gain power by extra-constitutional means and, having done so, to inaugurate a non-racial democratic state "based on the will of the people." That remains the professed objective of African nationalists and their allies in other ethnic groups. Among several other extra-parliamentary political organizations that have existed in recent years, there was a small, multi-racial Communist Party of South Africa, which was banned in 1950, but which was apparently revived as an underground organization in 1960.[8]

---

[8] For documents illustrating the principles and programs of South African political organizations see Gwendolen M. Carter, *The Politics of Inequality: South Africa since 1948* (London: Thames and Hudson, 1958) appendix iv; and D. W. Krüger, ed., *South African Parties and Politics 1910-1960: A Select Source Book* (Cape Town: Human and Rousseau, 1960). For South African political personalities see Ronald Segal, *Political Africa: A Who's Who of Personalities and Parties* (London: Stevens and Sons, 1961), and *African Profiles* (Harmondsworth: Penguin Books, 1962). For the United Party see also speeches by Sir D. de Villiers Graaff, the party leader, moving motions of no-confidence in the government in *House of Assembly Debates*, January 23, 1962, cols. 39-60, and January 22, 1963, cols. 22-41. For the Progressive Party see speeches by Helen Suzman in the no-confidence debates, *ibid.*, January 25, 1962, cols. 198-207, and January 23, 1963, cols. 102-10; also Z. J. de Beer, *Multi-Racial South Africa: The Reconciliation of Forces* (London: Oxford University Press, 1961); and Donald B. Molteno, *The Molteno Report: A Report Prepared for the Progressive Party of South Africa by a Commission of Experts* (2 vols., Johannesburg: Progressive Party, 1960-62). For the Liberal Party see

Though these South African opponents of the government vary in many respects, all except the United Party criticize not merely the performance of the Nationalist government within the framework of the existing political system, but the system itself. The common essence of their criticisms of the system may be stated as follows:

The Afrikaner Nationalists have a distorted view of the nature of South African society. Whatever their antecedents may have been, the peoples of South Africa are not now separate nations which happen to have become temporarily and partially intermingled. Nearly all South Africans participate in one modern economic system controlled by one sovereign government, with the result that they have been molded into a single society and are irrevocably interdependent. That the Afrikaner Nationalist view of South African society is false is proved beyond all reasonable doubt by the fact that since 1948, while the government has been enacting and applying all sorts of separatist laws, the number and the proportion of South Africans of each racial group which live in the industrial towns and contribute to the modern sector of the economy have persistently increased. Apartheid, in the sense of the separate development of separate races in separate areas, is therefore the very antithesis of what is happening in South Africa. The task of statesmanship is to accept, not to deny, these basic facts of South African life. Afrikaner nationalism, or any other nationalism which excludes masses of fellow South Africans, is a sectional and disruptive force; and there is no justification for discriminating against nonwhites in seven-eighths of South Africa. The Bantustan policy is fraudulent for the additional reason that the "Bantu Areas," forming the remaining eighth of South Africa, are small, scattered territories which could not conceivably become viable national homelands for anyone, let alone for eleven mil-

---

the journal *Contact*. On the African National Congress see Mary Benson, *The African Patriots: The Story of the African National Congress of South Africa* (London: Faber and Faber, 1963); Edward Feit, *South Africa: The Dynamics of the African National Congress* (London: Oxford University Press, 1962); and Albert Luthuli, *Let My People Go* (London: Collins, 1962). For the Communist Party see the *African Communist* (London, 1960ff.).

lion Africans, even if they were given complete political independence. At no stage has the government genuinely consulted freely chosen representatives of the Coloured, Asian, and African communities. When the government has made a show of consultation, it has done so with carefully selected individuals and it has taken pains to manipulate the situation to its own advantage. Except for those who have succumbed to official patronage and intimidation — and they are remarkably few in the circumstances — nearly all nonwhite South Africans reject the entire political system as one which enables one-fifth of the inhabitants of South Africa to dominate the rest. This rejection is almost universal among the most highly educated and skilled nonwhites, who would be the national leaders of South Africa, given conditions of freedom.

The withdrawal of moral allegiance from the existing political order was explicitly stated by Nelson Mandela, a leader of the banned African National Congress, in 1962 when he was on trial for inciting people to strike and for leaving the Republic without permission:

> Your Worship, I would say that the whole life of any thinking African in this country drives him continuously to a conflict peculiar to this country. The law as it is applied, the law as it has been developed over a long period of history, and especially the law as it is written and designed by the Nationalist government, is a law which, in our view, *is immoral, unjust and intolerable.* Our consciences dictate that we must protest against it, that we must oppose it and that we must attempt to alter it. . . .
>
> We have been conditioned by the history of white Government in this country to accept the fact that Africans, when they make their demands strongly and powerfully enough for those demands to have some chance of success, will be met by force and terror on the part of the government. This is not something we have taught the African people, this is something the African people have learned from their own bitter experience. *Government violence can do only one thing and that is to breed counterviolence.* . . .
>
> I hate the practice of race discrimination, and in doing so, in my hatred, I am sustained by the fact that the overwhelming majority of mankind hates it equally. . . . I hate the racial

arrogance which decrees that the good things of life shall be retained as the exclusive right of a minority of the population, and which reduces the majority of the population to a subservience and inferiority, and maintains them as voteless chattels to work where they are told and behave as they are told by the ruling minority. Nothing that this Court can do will change in any way that hatred in me, which can only be removed by the removal of the injustice and the inhumanity which I have sought to remove from the political, social and economic life of this country.[9]

INTERNATIONAL EFFECTS OF SOUTH AFRICAN POLICY

From a very early stage South Africa has been the subject of criticism in the United Nations; and as the intensity of apartheid legislation has stiffened and the number of Afro-Asian members of the United Nations has increased, the criticisms have become more severe and the demands for active intervention more urgent.

In 1962, by a vote of 67 to 16 with 23 abstentions, the United Nations General Assembly recommended that member states break off diplomatic relations (if they had any) with South Africa, deny the use of their ports and air space to South African ships and aircraft, boycott South African goods and refrain from exporting goods to South Africa; asked the Security Council to consider the expulsion of South Africa from the United Nations; and called for the establishment of a special committee to keep South Africa's racial policies under continuous review. This resolution was not mandatory and it has not been strictly observed by some of the Afro-Asian countries which initiated it, while it has been ignored by the countries which opposed it, including Britain, the United States and South Africa's other principal trading partners. Nevertheless, boycotts of varying completeness have been imposed by many nonwhite countries, the South African Airways has had to re-route its flights to Europe via Angola, the Cape Verde Islands and Portugal, and South Africa's trading potential with tropical Africa is not being realized. That is not all. In 1960 the International Commission of Jurists, in an elaborate review entitled *South Africa and*

[9] *The Observer* (London), November 18, 1962. Italics from *The Observer*.

the Rule of Law, declared that the South African government
had denied to a vast majority of the population those opportunities without which the legitimate aspirations and dignity
of a human being could not be realized, contrary to generally
accepted concepts of justice and principles of human rights,
thereby creating a potentially explosive situation. And in December 1962 the International Court of Justice decided that it
was competent to hear a complaint by Ethiopia and Liberia
that South Africa has violated its mandate over South-West
Africa.[10]

By 1965 South Africa was perilously isolated. The country
left UNESCO in 1956, and resigned from the British Commonwealth in 1961, following scathing criticisms at a prime ministers' conference. It ceased participating in the ILO and
WHO and left FAO,[11] the Economic Commission for Africa,
the Council for Technical Cooperation in Africa and the
Council for Science in Africa. Its athletes were unable to take
part in the 1964 Olympic Games. And in 1963 thirty heads
of independent African states, meeting in conference at Addis
Ababa, set up an African Liberation Committee consisting of
representatives of nine states, with offices in Dar es Salaam, for
the purpose of organizing the overthrow of the present regimes
in Angola, Mozambique and South Africa.

Viewed from the government offices in Pretoria, the tide of
African nationalism is now at its peak, and will soon begin to
ebb. The repeated collapse of law and order in the Congo, the
fragility of the new regimes in East Africa, the revolution in
Zanzibar, the trend towards totalitarianism in Ghana, and the
pervasive economic weakness of tropical Africa are taken as
welcome manifestations of African division, impotence and un-
reliability. It is believed that Americans, Europeans and other
"civilized" foreigners have been suffering from a temporary de-
lusion about black Africans and that, as time goes by, they will

[10] Peter Calvocoressi, *South Africa and World Opinion* (London: Ox-
ford University Press, 1961); Muriel Horrell, compiler, *A Survey of Race
Relations in South Africa* (Johannesburg: South African Institute of Race
Relations, annual); Vernon McKay, *Africa in World Politics* (New York:
Harper and Row, 1963).

[11] International Labor Organization, World Health Organization, and
Food and Agricultural Organization of the United Nations.

lose confidence in the new African states and increasingly respect South Africa's strength, appreciate South Africa's anti-Communism, invest in South African industries, and value South Africa's friendship, regardless of its political system. Meanwhile, the South African government has been trying to destroy the African nationalist movement within the Republic and to preserve a belt of colonial territory between the Republic and the area under African control, by keeping a firm hold over South-West Africa, by encouraging the Portuguese to stamp out the rebellion in Angola, by supporting the white Rhodesians, and by prompting Britain to stop short of giving full independence to Lesotho, Bechuanaland and Swaziland.

The new African states, however, despite their teething troubles, are not likely to lose influence in the world; and despite rigorous suppression, African nationalism is still very much alive in the Republic and likely to remain so, even if, being outlawed, it can only make its presence felt by violence. Furthermore, the International Court may rule that the United Nations, as the heir to the League of Nations, has the right and the duty to intervene in South-West Africa on behalf of its nonwhite peoples. The Portuguese control of Angola could conceivably be relinquished as a result of political change in Portugal, or the supply of external aid to the rebels; if Angola falls, Mozambique will probably follow. White control over Rhodesia may collapse under some combination of internal unrest and external pressure. And Lesotho, Bechuanaland and Swaziland will soon become independent states under African control. Before long, therefore, South Africa will have common frontiers with several African-controlled states. Such a confrontation of antithetical systems will probably lead to local clashes, that in turn will evoke demands for United Nations' protection of the African states and for the implementation of the existing United Nations' resolutions for physical sanctions against the Republic.

Already the United States and its allies are confronted with a searching dilemma. On the one hand, white South Africans deserve sympathy and understanding. White communities have dominated other societies elsewhere, without opprobrium, until very recently. The resistance that many white Americans still offer to desegregation in the United States suggests that other white communities, placed as the white South Africans are placed, might have been just as uncompromising and no more capable of coming to terms with the modern world. Moreover, it is possible that the methods being used to maintain white supremacy in South Africa are so severe that many nonwhites have become alienated to the point where they, in turn, would be unwilling to cooperate with whites, even if they were in a position to do so. If this is so, we have the hallmarks of a classic revolutionary situation in South Africa; and the history of other revolutions suggests that once violence is unleashed on a scale sufficient to destroy the existing order, the ultimate shape of South African society will be unpredictable. These would seem to be potent reasons why the United States and its allies should refrain from becoming involved in the South African imbroglio.

But they are not the only relevant considerations. The African, the Asian and the Coloured peoples of South Africa also deserve sympathy and understanding. Until recently most of their leaders hoped that South African society would become more egalitarian by peaceful evolution from within; but that hope has been belied. The freedom of South African nonwhites has been curtailed and their human dignity has been outraged during the very period when their expectations have been enhanced by the passing of colonial systems elsewhere. It is now natural that they should regard the existing order as both evil and anachronistic, and that they should be highly suspicious of everyone who supports it, overtly or covertly. Moreover, the position of the United States and her Western European allies in the modern world is based not merely on material power, but also — and more fundamentally — on an identification with freedom and justice. Already the new Asian and African states are prone to regard the policy of the United States towards South Africa as the acid test of its good faith; prolonged evasion of the issue by the United States would create the risk that China or Russia may become the instrument of change in South Africa and, thereby, the ultimate beneficiary of the entire African revolution.

Enough has been said to show why, during the coming years, South Africa is likely to generate a series of crises, the outcome of which will not only determine the future of the local inhabitants, but also have profound repercussions on the main course of international relations and on the place of the United States and its allies in the world.

The purpose of this book is to explain the basic facts concerning the peoples and the economy of South Africa, to show how the South African political system has become what it is, and to analyze the system as it operates today. These data will assist the reader to comprehend the complexity of the situation and the problem, which is bound to be of concern to all.

CHAPTER II

The Context
of the Political System

To UNDERSTAND a political system, we must know something about the context in which it operates. In this chapter, the historical background and the demographic and economic conditions of South Africa are reviewed.

THE HISTORICAL BACKGROUND [1]

From time immemorial South Africa has been the scene of interactions between diverse peoples. Knowledge about most of these processes is still meager, but it is evident that by the 17th century there were three categories of human beings in South Africa: hunters, herders, and farmers. Bands of hunters, whom the whites were to call Bushmen, had become confined to the more arid and mountainous areas; communities of semi-nomadic herders of sheep and cattle, whom the whites were to call Hottentots, used the pastures in much of the western half of the country; and Bantu-speaking people (the ancestors of the present-day

[1] There is no good, modern, comprehensive history of South Africa. Cornelis W. de Kiewiet, *A History of South Africa: Social and Economic* (Oxford: Clarendon Press, 1941) is a brilliant introduction that has stood the test of time remarkably well; but, as its subtitle indicates, it does not deal with the political aspect. The standard works are still Eric A. Walker, *A History of Southern Africa* (3rd edn., London: Long-

Bantu or Africans), who owned cattle, raised grain, and utilized iron implements, occupied most of the better-watered eastern half.[2]

The position of the Bantu-speaking people of South Africa represents the southern limit of a prolonged and complex expansive movement that was probably initiated by negroes from the vicinity of the Cameroons early in the Christian era. By the 17th century, Bantu-speaking people were the most numerous and most powerful human element in South Africa, and if whites had not intervened it is probable that they would eventually have completed their occupation of South Africa and conquered and absorbed most of the other inhabitants, as they did north of the Limpopo River.

Before the 19th century the Bantu-speaking people of South Africa were organized in small units, varying from "clans" of a few hundred members who were (or were deemed to be) biologically related to one another, to "tribes" of up to several thousand members. Though the total population increased over the years, the units remained small because there was a tendency for new units to be formed by secession from old; the system as a whole was comparatively stable because wars were

mans, 1957) and Eric A. Walker, ed., *The Cambridge History of the British Empire,* Vol. VIII, *South Africa, Rhodesia and the High Commission Territories* (2nd edn., Cambridge: University Press, 1963); but these books were first published in the 1920's and 1930's, respectively, and they reflect the attitudes of the colonial epoch. The major Afrikaans history is A. J. H. van der Walt, J. A. Wiid and A. L. Geyer, eds., *Geskiedenis van Suid-Afrika* (2 vols., Cape Town: Nasionale Pers, 1951). The present state of historical writing on South Africa is discussed in a chapter by Leonard M. Thompson in Robin Winks, ed., *The Historiography of the British Empire and Commonwealth: Trends, Interpretations, and Resources* (Durham: Duke University Press, 1965).

2 The names "Bushmen," "Hottentots" and "Bantu" are unsatisfactory for various reasons: (a) "Hottentots" and "Bantu" have acquired perjorative connotations and are rejected by present-day nonwhite South Africans; (b) though "Bushmen" and "Hottentots" may be regarded as ethnic terms, "Bantu" is essentially a linguistic term; and (c) it is a serious oversimplification (written into virtually all the existing histories of South Africa) to regard the pre-colonial population as consisting of three clear-cut types, distinguished by ethnic, linguistic and economic factors. These three factors are independent variables. Clarification of these issues was furnished by Professor Monica Wilson of the University of Cape Town.

conducted within conventional limitations and because fresh land was available for occupation, either between existing settlements or beyond them, to the west and the southwest.

Each unit was ruled by a chief, who held office by virtue of some combination of hereditary and personal qualities. The powers of a chief were limited by well-established customs and by the fact that decisions could only be enforced if they had popular support. In fact, a chief made decisions in consultation with relatives — such as uncles, brothers and sons — and with commoners who held key offices; and there were usually some means for the rank and file to participate in the political process. These means differed. Among the Nguni people, who predominated on the coastal side of the mountain escarpment, decisions were generally announced once a year when the men were gathered together for the first fruits ceremony, and the popular element was comparatively feeble; but among the Sotho people, who predominated on the plateau to the northwest of the escarpment, public meetings were more frequent and at some such meetings a man was able to criticize a decision freely, and the men who made it. Thus, among the Nguni, the government was more autocratic than among the Sotho. This distinction may be carried further: the northern Nguni units (in modern Zululand) were more autocratic than the southern Nguni units (the Xhosa and their offshoots), and the western Sotho (the Tswana) were more "democratic" than the southern and the northern Sotho.[3]

The structure of society in southeastern Africa was transformed in the early 19th century. The transformation started among the northern Nguni. First, Dingiswayo organized the men of his tribe into regimental age sets. And then Shaka, who seized the chieftainship of the small Zulu clan from his half-brother in 1816, perfected the regimental system, introduced new weapons, and embarked upon unlimited wars of conquest.

Within a few years Shaka had created a large, despotic and militaristic "kingdom," stretching from the Pongola River in the north to the Tugela River in the south, and from the sea to the mountain escarpment. He disrupted numerous clans and

[3] Isaac Schapera, *Government and Politics in Tribal Societies* (London: Watts, 1956).

tribes, whose survivors were either absorbed into his kingdom or ejected as refugees. In a chain reaction, destruction and reorganization were carried throughout most of southeastern Africa. Between the Vaal and the Limpopo Rivers, Mzilikazi, starting as the leader of a small band of Nguni refugees from Shaka, created the Ndebele Kingdom on Zulu lines; elsewhere, local leaders amalgamated the survivors of other clans and tribes into defensive kingdoms, such as Moshweshwe's Sotho kingdom in the Caledon River valley. Therefore, the political system which had prevailed for several centuries in southeastern Africa was transformed by 1836, when the Afrikaner *Voortrekkers* began to penetrate north and east from the Cape Colony.

The white conquest of South Africa took place in two phases. In the first phase — roughly coterminous with the period of rule by the Dutch East India Company (1652-1795) — immigrants from the Netherlands, Germany, France and other parts of northwestern Europe established themselves in South Africa and became a distinct and fairly homogeneous community — the embryonic Afrikaner nation. They occupied the western half of South Africa, from the Cape northwards towards the Orange River and eastwards towards the Fish River; in the process they conquered the Bushmen and the Hottentots and contained the Bantu-speaking tribes along the line of the Fish.

Some of the Hottentots retreated north of the Orange, where they were conquered in the 19th century; others were killed in occasional fighting or died from the ravages of diseases they had not encountered before, especially smallpox. However, many remained within the expanding frontiers of white settlement, losing their land and their stock and their social cohesion and becoming shepherds and cattleherders for the white farmers. The Bushmen were less competent to come to terms with the whites. Most of them perished while attempting to contest the white advance, and the survivors retreated to the north where they, too, were conquered during the 19th century. The Dutch East India Company also imported several thousand slaves into the Cape Colony — from tropical Africa, from Madagascar and from Southeast Asia.

Miscegenation took place between members of the different

communities in the colony, but white fathers did not usually take responsibility for their children by slave and Hottentot women, so that the colonial society consisted of a more or less "white" landowning population and nonwhite landless communities of African and Asian slaves, Hottentots, and people of mixed descent. Later, after the slaves were emancipated (1834-1838), these nonwhite communities tended to merge with one another, and their descendants are known, comprehensively, as the Cape Coloured People.[4] Thus in South African terminology, unlike the American, the term "Coloured" is reserved for people of mixed descent.

During the second phase of white conquest, which roughly corresponds with the time of British ascendancy in South Africa (1795-1910), the Bantu-speaking tribes were conquered and white settlement was extended to its present limits.[5] In this period the white population was enlarged by further immigration, mainly from Britain, that began in 1820 and reached a considerable scale after the discovery of diamonds in Griqualand West (1867) and gold on the Witwatersrand (1885). Nevertheless, Afrikaners at all times outnumbered South Africans of British stock and they managed to preserve their identity, partly because

[4] J. S. Marais, *The Cape Coloured People* (London: Longmans, 1939); Isaac Schapera, *The Khoisan Peoples of South Africa* (London: Routledge, 1930).

[5] The first armed clash between whites and Bantu-speaking tribesmen took place in 1779; the first clear victory of whites over Africans was in 1812; the last Bantu-speaking tribes in South Africa were brought under white control in the 1890's; and the last flicker of resistance on a tribal basis to the imposition of white control was the Zulu rebellion of 1906. There is no adequate account of this process as a whole; but see Waldemar B. Campbell, "The South African Frontier, 1865-1885: A study in expansion," *Archives Year Book for South African History* (Pretoria: Government Printer, Vol. I, 1959); de Kiewiet, *op. cit.*, and "Social and Economic Developments in Native Tribal Life," in Walker, ed., *Cambridge History*, chapter XXX; John S. Galbraith, *Reluctant Empire: British Policy on the South African Frontier, 1834-1854* (Berkeley: University of California Press, 1963); William M. Macmillan, *Bantu, Boer and Briton: The Making of the South African Native Problem* (revised edn., Oxford: Clarendon Press, 1963); J. S. Marais, *Maynier and the First Boer Republic* (Cape Town: Maskew Miller, 1944); and Isaac Schapera, ed., *The Bantu-speaking Tribes of South Africa* (Cape Town: Maskew Miller, 1946).

some of them — the *Voortrekkers* — left the Cape Colony in and after 1836 and founded independent republics in the interior — the Orange Free State (1854-1900) and the South African Republic (1858-1877 and 1881-1900).[6]

The Bantu-speaking people were conquered piecemeal: some by peaceful penetration, others by force of arms; some by British troops and colonial levies, others by Afrikaner commandos. While the Hottentots lost their cultural cohesion more or less abruptly in the process of conquest, this rapid loss did not happen to the more numerous and formidable Bantu-speaking people. They retained some land for their exclusive use: all of modern Lesotho, most of modern Bechuanaland, and about half of modern Swaziland (territories remaining under British control when the Union of South Africa was founded in 1910); and the native reservations in the rest of South Africa. These reservations, now called "Bantu Areas," are the territorial bases of the Bantustan policy of the present South African government.

Thus, in the land that remained to them the Africans were left to their own devices to some extent, but subject to varying controls applied by the colonial and republican governments and to varying influences exerted by white settlers, traders and missionaries. In most areas their lands had been so reduced that by the beginning of the present century they were unable to maintain their self-sufficient tribal economies — and even less able to satisfy new needs which had been fostered by traders and missionaries, and to pay the taxes which were levied by the governments. However, white farmers allowed and encouraged some African families to stay on their farms in order to provide them with labor or to pay them rent, and when the mining industries developed they employed large numbers of Africans, who came from the reservations on short-term contracts and returned there when their contracts expired.[7] In addition, between 1860 and 1911, laborers were imported from India to the

[6] Eric A. Walker, *The Great Trek* (London: Black, 1938); F. A. van Jaarsveld, *The Awakening of Afrikaner Nationalism, 1868-1881* (Cape Town: Human and Rousseau, 1961).

[7] Sheila T. van der Horst, *Native Labour in South Africa* (London: Oxford University Press, 1942).

colony of Natal, mainly to work on the coastal sugar estates. When their contracts expired most of them stayed in South Africa, becoming the nucleus of the present Asian community.[8]

As a result of white settlement, the conquest of the Bushmen, the Hottentots and the Bantu-speaking peoples, and the importation of slaves and indentured Indians, a dual economy developed in South Africa: the economy of the "White Areas" and the economy of the African reservations (including the lands reserved for Africans in the High Commission Territories). The former was an expanding exchange economy, controlled by Afrikaners and British South Africans who produced agricultural, pastoral and mining commodities for consumption and for export with the use of Coloured, Asian and African labor. The latter was the remnant of the subsistence economy of the Bantu-speaking tribes. But the two systems were not mutually exclusive: the "White Areas" drew labor from the "surplus" which was available in the no longer self-sufficient reservations.

The Dutch Colonial Administration

During the Dutch period the Cape Colony was a minor dependency in a far-flung commercial empire, subordinate to the company directors in the Netherlands and the Council-of-the-Indies in Batavia, Java.[9] The company built forts and stationed garrisons in the Cape peninsula, which it valued as a stepping-stone on the sea route to Asia. From there, control over the entire colony was meant to be exercised by the governor and other senior officials, subject to instructions from Amsterdam and Batavia. The officials found it expedient to consult colonists when they were discussing colonial affairs, and in time it became accepted that colonists had the right to be consulted. Such consultation was achieved through "burgher councillors," who

---

[8] Mabel Palmer, *The History of Indians in Natal* (Cape Town: Oxford University Press, 1957); Leonard M. Thompson, "Indian Immigration into Natal, 1860-1872," *Archives Year Book for South African History* (Pretoria: Government Printer, Vol. II, 1952).

[9] On the administrative system in the Cape Colony during the Dutch period see G. W. Eybers, *Select Constitutional Documents Illustrating South African History, 1795-1910* (London: Routledge, 1918); M. Whiting Spilhaus, *The First South Africans* (Cape Town: Juta, 1949); and A. J. H. van der Walt, *et al., op. cit.*

were appointed by the government from names supplied by the existing burgher councillors.

Beyond the Cape peninsula the government did little to make its authority effective. It established district headquarters at Stellenbosch (1679), Swellendam (1746), and Graaff-Reinet (1786), and appointed to each district an official [*Landdrost*] who, aided by one or two clerks and perhaps a handful of soldiers, was expected to keep order throughout a vast district. This he could do only with the cooperation of the white farmers, some of whom [*Heemraden*] were appointed to assist him with advice and to sit with him in hearing petty civil disputes; but the only court with criminal jurisdiction in the entire colony was the Court of Justice in Cape Town, six hundred miles from the Fish River. Consequently, the farmers and, more particularly, the semi-nomadic pastoral farmers [*trekboers*] were very largely a law unto themselves. They improvised their own methods of defense against Bushmen, and later against Bantu-speaking tribes; in the 1790's and again in the 1800's they drove the *Landdrost* out of Graaff-Reinet when he tried to moderate the activities of the commandos against the Bushmen, to preserve the peace with the Xhosa tribes, and to take cognizance of the ill-treatment of Hottentot servants.[10]

The company built churches at Cape Town and elsewhere, appointed and paid their ministers [*predikants*], and exercised a veto over the appointments of deacons and elders as well as over the decisions of the church councils. Nearly all the white colonists were members of the Dutch Reformed Church. Most of them possessed Bibles, were married in church, and periodically travelled long distances where necessary to take communion [*nagmaal*]. There was no private printing press in the colony and no high school, but elementary schools of sorts were attached to the churches. Some of the farmers were close enough to send their children to the schools, while others improvised teaching programs as best they could to make their children literate.

Thus, in their formative days the embryonic Afrikaner peo-

10 On the *trekboers* see Marais, *Maynier;* and P. J. van der Merwe, *Die Trekboer in die Geskiedenis van die Kaapkolonie, 1657-1842* (Cape Town: Nasionale Pers, 1938).

ple spread out over a vast area and became a self-sufficient, individualistic community. Since there were no great opportunities for amassing riches, each man considered himself as good as his fellows, but local conditions, fortified by Calvinist theology, caused them to regard themselves as a race apart — a people chosen by God — innately superior to their slaves, their Hottentot servants, and their Bushmen and Bantu-speaking enemies.[11] While the Cape Colony was ruled by the Dutch East India Company in theory, in practice the company's writ was only effective over the Cape peninsula and some fifty miles inland, beyond which the vacuum was filled by the white farmers who, with their firearms, formed the dominant element in a loose-knit, pre-industrial, plural society.

British Colonies and Boer Republics

To prevent the sea route between Europe and Asia from becoming controlled by the French, the British conquered the Cape Colony in 1795 and again in 1806, and they retained it in the peace settlement of 1814-1815. British administrators gradually amplified and modified the institutions which the Dutch had created in the Cape Colony. They subdivided the districts into smaller units and applied the rule of law more effectively throughout the colony by sending judges on annual circuits to each district (1811ff.). They changed the high court into a Supreme Court consisting of qualified lawyers, applying English rules of procedure, including the jury system in criminal cases, while retaining Roman-Dutch Law as the common law of the colony (1827ff.). They freed the Hottentots from legal restrictions upon their movements (1828) and emancipated the slaves (1834-1838). They introduced a system of public education for white children and paid missionary societies small subsidies for educational work among the Coloured and African people. They freed the Dutch Reformed Church from state control, and while encouraging other Christian denominations to operate, they refrained from creating an established church. After a sharp dispute, they allowed freedom for the press, subject to the law of libel (1828).

Moreover, having introduced a representative element in lo-

[11] I. D. MacCrone, *Race Attitudes in South Africa: Historical, Experimental and Psychological Studies* (London: Oxford University Press, 1937).

cal government, in 1854 they created a colonial parliament, consisting of two Houses, both wholly elective by men who possessed a fairly low economic qualification, regardless of race or creed. In 1872, following the precedents set in Canada, Australia and New Zealand, the Parliament acquired control over the executive, subject to the overriding legal supremacy of the British Parliament. When, towards the end of the century, the Cape Colony incorporated the territories as far east as the Natal border at the Umzimvubu River, acquiring a large African population, the franchise qualifications remained color-blind, but the economic requirement was raised slightly and defined so that occupation of land on communal (i.e., tribal African) tenure did not suffice, and a simple writing test in the English language was introduced.[12]

In practice the political system in the Cape Colony was always dominated by the white inhabitants whose political groupings tended to correspond with the Afrikaner-British division. No Coloured or African man ever sat in the Cape Parliament, and in 1909, on the eve of the foundation of the Union, when the colony contained about 582,000 whites, 455,000 Coloured people, 8,000 Asians, and 1,520,000 Africans, 85 percent of the registered voters were white men, 10 percent were Coloured men, and fewer than 5 percent were African. Nevertheless, the nonwhite voters were numerous enough to determine election results in several constituencies and to act as a moderating influence over administration and legislation. Whether it was fully realized or not, the system pointed logically towards the progressive incorporation of members of the nonwhite communities into the political process.[13]

In the colony of Natal the position was similar in form but different in substance. The legal system and the institutions of government were modeled on those of the Cape Colony. A Parliament was created in 1856 and it was given control over the executive in 1893. The fundamental difference lay in the fact that, though the franchise was color-blind in theory, in practice Parliament legislated in 1864 to make it virtually impossible

---

[12] De Kiewiet, *History;* Eybers, *op. cit.;* William M. Macmillan, *The Cape Colour Question* (London: Faber, 1927); Marais, *Cape Coloured.*

[13] Leonard M. Thompson, *The Unification of South Africa, 1902-1910* (Oxford: Clarendon Press, 1960).

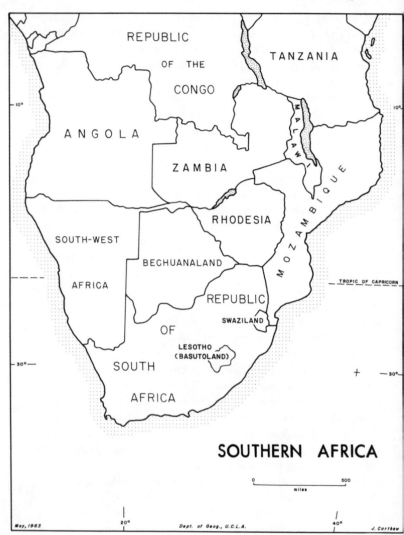

for all but a handful of Africans to become voters and in 1896 absolutely to prevent Asians from acquiring the vote, except the few who already possessed it. In 1909, when Natal contained about 98,000 white, 9,000 Coloured, 133,000 Asian and 953,000 African people, all the registered voters were white except 50 Coloured men, 150 Asians and 6 Africans. The consequence was that all branches of the Natal government tended to operate exclusively in the interests of the white community — and it was partisan tax laws coupled with partisan administration which led to a small but alarming African rebellion in 1906.[14]

The *Voortrekkers'* first constitutional improvisations were for the regulation of their own affairs as migrant communities, and when they developed those improvisations into territorial political systems, they ensured that they themselves should remain dominant by confining participation in the political process to white men and, when necessary, by limiting the political powers of white men who were not the product of their own communities. Of the two major Boer republics, one — the Orange Free State — developed stability, and the other — the South African Republic — was always chronically unstable. Initially this difference was caused by the fact that the tougher and more factious *Voortrekkers* went farthest north; it persisted because the Orange Free State remained a simple agrarian society of Afrikaners and their African farm laborers, devoid of the complications of extensive African tribal lands or major mining industries, whereas the South African Republic included large African tribal areas and also, ultimately, a great gold-mining industry, controlled by foreigners, and was the object of periodic British pressure.[15] The pressure came to a head in the war of 1899-1902, in which Britain conquered both the republics and incorporated them in the British Empire.[16]

14 *Ibid.*

15 On the constitutional history of the Boer republics see Eybers, *op. cit.*; Thompson, *Unification*, and "Constitutionalism in the South African Republics," *Butterworth's South African Law Review* (Durban: Butterworth, 1954) pp. 49–72; and van der Walt, *et al., op. cit.*

16 On the origins of the South African War of 1899-1902 see W. K. Hancock, *Smuts, the Sanguine Years, 1870-1919* (Cambridge: University Press, 1962); W. L. Langer, *The Diplomacy of Imperialism* (2 vols., New York: Knopf, 1935); R. I. Lovell, *The Struggle for South Africa: A study in economic imperialism* (New York: Macmillan, 1934); J. S. Marais, *The Fall*

Within six years from the end of the war the British Liberals, having won a landslide victory from the Conservatives at the polls, gave the Transvaal and the Orange River Colony responsible government, with constitutions which excluded all but whites from the franchise and enabled Afrikaner parties to come into power. Then in 1908-1909 a National Convention, attended by delegates from the Cape Colony, Natal, the Transvaal and the Orange River Colony [17] — all of them white men — unanimously adopted a constitution for a united South Africa. The constitution was endorsed by the four colonial Parliaments and enacted by the British Parliament, and the Union of South Africa came into being on May 30, 1910.[18] Since then, South African political history has been an evolutionary process, which is examined in the later chapters of this book.

Historical Mythologies

In order to understand a political system, historical background is important not merely in the direct sense that it explains the origins of the social structure and of the institutional framework within which the system operates, but also in the indirect sense that the views people have of their past are a determinant of their present political attitudes and conduct. This is particularly true of conservative people, and no people are

---

of Kruger's Republic (Oxford: Clarendon Press, 1961); Ronald Robinson and John Gallagher, with Alice Denny, *Africa and the Victorians: The official mind of imperialism* (London: Macmillan, 1961); G. D. Scholtz, *Die Oorsake van die Tweede Vryheidsoorlog, 1899-1902* (2 vols., Johannesburg: privately published, 1948–1949); Jean van der Poel, *The Jameson Raid* (London: Oxford University Press, 1951); and Richard H. Wilde, "Joseph Chamberlain and the South African Republic, 1895-1899," *Archives Year Book for South African History* (Pretoria: Government Printer, Vol. II, 1956).

[17] The Orange Free State Republic of 1854-1900 became the Orange River Colony of 1900-1910 and the Orange Free State Province of 1910ff.

[18] On the origins of the South African constitution see R. H. Brand, *The Union of South Africa* (Oxford: Clarendon Press, 1909); Hancock, *op. cit.;* Nicholas Mansergh, *South Africa 1906-1961: The Price of Magnanimity* (New York: Praeger, 1962); G. B. Pyrah, *Imperial Policy in South Africa* (Oxford: Clarendon Press, 1955); Thompson, *Unification;* Eric A. Walker, *Lord de Villiers and his Times: South Africa, 1842 to 1914* (London: Constable, 1925), and *W. P. Schreiner: A South African* (London: Oxford University Press, 1937).

more conservative than the Afrikaner Nationalists who rule South Africa.

The principal deduction they make from their history is that the rest of the world, so far as it has been concerned with them, has been hostile. They discern two sets of traditional enemies. One is composed of the British government and South Africans of British descent. The British government is seen as the oppressor of the Afrikaner people so long as it had power in South Africa, and the British settlers as its Trojan horse. British oppression reached its peak in the decade 1895-1905, when Joseph Chamberlain, Colonial Secretary, and Alfred Milner, High Commissioner in South Africa, exploited the presence of the Uitlander community on the Witwatersrand to provoke a war. The British military commanders resorted to inhumane methods to crush the resistance of the Boer guerrillas, and Milner tried to denationalize the Afrikaners by swamping them with British immigrants and educating them into a British mold.

The other set of traditional enemies comprises the nonwhite peoples of southern Africa. Bushmen and Bantu-speaking Africans are seen as bloodthirsty savages who blindly resisted the spread of white Christian civilization. In the Afrikaner view of history, the central saga is the Great Trek, when both sets of enemies acted in conjunction. The *Voortrekkers* left the Cape Colony because the government failed to control the Coloured people within the colony and the Africans on its eastern frontier; they had to endure attacks by barbarous hordes under Mzilikazi and Dingane, and pursuit by Britain, which annexed their first republic of Natal and their settlements between the Orange and the Vaal Rivers.

African nationalists, at the other end of the political spectrum, have a totally different view of South African history. To them, the central theme is white conquest and domination: the expropriation of African land, the perversion of traditional African political systems into subservient tools of white regimes, the reduction of all nonwhites to thinly disguised serfdom, and the exclusion of all nonwhites from any effective say in the government. All else is secondary. The quarrels between Afrikaners and the British government and South Africans of British descent are but the quarrels of robbers over the spoils.

As with other mythologies, both the Afrikaner and the African nationalist mythologies have germs of truth in them. However, each is so selective, each so continuously imputes pure motives to one group and impure motives to others, that both are grotesque distortions of the complex historical realities. The distortions are compounded because each mythology is projected from the past into the present, and used to inflame present passions and justify present policies. To some Afrikaner nationalists since Albion (England) was so perfidious throughout the 19th century, he cannot be trusted today, nor can other foreign powers with interests in South Africa; and since Africans were so savage, they must still be less than human beings.

To some African nationalists, on the other hand, since the essence of the white record in South Africa is nothing but invasion, oppression and exploitation, no white person has a just claim to an enduring place under the South African sun. The irreconcilability of these different historical interpretations is a measure of the schism that exists in modern South Africa.[19]

DEMOGRAPHIC CONDITIONS

South Africa has a racially stratified population, with a dominant white group and three nonwhite groups, which are officially designated Coloured, Asiatic, and Bantu. The growth of these groups between the census of May 7, 1911, and the census of September 6, 1960 is shown in the following table:

TABLE II.1   *Population of South Africa* [20]

| | 1911 | | 1960 | |
	Number	*Percentage*	*Number*	*Percentage*
White	1,276,319	21.4	3,088,492	19.3
Coloured	525,466	8.8	1,509,258	9.4
Asiatic	152,094	2.5	477,125	3.0
Bantu	4,018,878	67.3	10,927,922	68.3
	5,972,757	100.0	16,002,797	100.0

[19] Much of the ground of the last six paragraphs is covered in Leonard M. Thompson's chapter in Robin Winks, ed., *op. cit.*, and in Leonard M. Thompson, "Afrikaner Nationalist Historiography and the Policy of Apartheid," *Journal of African History*, III, No. 1 (1962) 125-41.

[20] Republic of South Africa, *Population Census, 6th September, 1960*, Vol. I, *Geographical Distribution of the Population* (Pretoria: Government Printer, R.P. No. 62/1963) p. 2.

The ethnic terminology used in South Africa has changed over the years and today it does not correspond with the terminology used elsewhere. Whites (formerly called Europeans in South Africa) are people who are accepted as being exclusively of European or Caucasoid descent, though in fact a considerable proportion of them have at least one nonwhite ancestor. Coloureds are people with a wide variety of ethnic origins. Their ancestors include the slaves who were imported from tropical Africa and Southeast Asia, local Hottentots and Bushmen, and white South Africans and white visitors to South Africa. The Asiatic group originated in immigration from India to Natal in the late 19th and early 20th centuries. The people labeled Bantu were formerly called Natives by white South Africans and are called Africans by themselves and by the rest of the world. In this book, except when official South African terminology is necessarily followed, the terms employed are those in general use elsewhere: whites, Coloureds, Asians, and Africans.

Notwithstanding the central place occupied by racial concepts in South African official thinking, the government has so far failed to devise and apply a single set of definitions.[21] Different laws include different definitions of the four groups, so that an individual may be white under one law, Coloured under another and Native or Bantu under a third. The government apparently intends [22] to achieve uniformity, as well as to block individual mobility from one group to another ("passing"), through the Population Registration Act, 1950, which provides for the compilation of a register of the entire population and for the issue to every South African aged sixteen years and over of an identity card, specifying his race. The registration is still incomplete, different definitions still exist in different laws, and

[21] For a discussion of the varieties of definitions of racial groups in South African laws see Arthur Suzman, "Race Classification and Definition in the Legislation of the Union of South Africa, 1910-1960," *Acta Juridica 1960* (Cape Town: A. A. Balkema, 1961) pp. 339-67; and Elizabeth S. Landis, "South African Apartheid Legislation: 1. Fundamental Structure," *Yale Law Journal*, LXXI, No. 1 (November 1961) 1-52.

[22] As stated by the Minister of the Interior, *House of Assembly Debates*, 1956, col. 7836, and 1959, col. 1123.

as recently as 1962 Parliament changed the definition of a white person in the Population Registration Act.[23]

The difficulties that the government has met in giving effect to this crucial part of its program flow from the facts that race itself is an unscientific concept and that, over the centuries, there has been a large but indefinite amount of miscegenation in South Africa. Under the current system, miscegenation between the white and the nonwhite groups, but not between the different nonwhite groups, is unlawful. The Immorality Act of 1957 (which replaced similar, earlier legislation) prohibits carnal intercourse between whites and nonwhites outside marriage and the Prohibition of Mixed Marriages Act of 1949 prohibits intermarriage between whites and nonwhites. Strenuous efforts are made to enforce these laws. For example, in the eleven years from 1950 through 1960, 3,890 people were convicted under the Immorality Act.[24] Consequently, so long as the present regime exists, white and nonwhite South Africans will be two virtually endogamous populations, except insofar as they are modified by migration.

The White Population

In a racially stratified society, demographic trends are of great importance since they affect the relative strengths of the different racial groups. In South Africa the proportions which the white group bears to the total population and which the Afrikaner community bears to the total white group are both crucial figures.

The white population increased two-and-a-half times between 1911 and 1960. This was partly due to immigration. From 1924 to 1963 inclusive, about 420,000 white people immigrated to South Africa, with a peak in 1948, under the United Party's immigration scheme which was then scrapped by the Nationalist government, and another steep rise in the economic boom of the 1960's. Before 1948 over half the white immigrants came from Britain; since then the British proportion has dropped to about a third. The balance has normally come from continental

[23] Population Registration Amendment Act, 1962.
[24] *Race Relations News,* April 1962, citing a statement by the Minister of Justice.

Europe, but in recent years there has been a large influx from tropical Africa as a result of the decolonization process. Although the department of immigration is now offering incentives to white people with industrial skills to come to South Africa from Europe, the immigration rate of recent years may not persist, because the contribution from tropical Africa will soon be exhausted.

There has always been a considerable emigration of whites from South Africa. About 260,000 left the country between 1924 and 1963, giving a net immigration of about 160,000 whites in those years. The exodus exceeded 10,000 a year for the first time in 1950, and did so again in 1951 and 1961, the basic cause in each case being political uncertainty. Among the emigrants were a high proportion of professional men, such as doctors and university teachers, and also considerable numbers of the most talented young South Africans.[25]

The primary cause of the increase in the white population is not immigration but a moderately high birth rate in conjunction with a very low death rate. The rate of natural increase is likely soon to decline because there has been an upward shift in the average age.[26] If, as seems likely, present trends continue, the white proportion of the total population, which has already been declining, will decline still further. The South African Bureau of Racial Affairs (SABRA) has predicted that it will fall below 15 percent by the end of the century.[27]

Within the white population there are still two fairly distinct major communities, identifiable by their different home languages — Afrikaans and English. The Afrikaners have always been the more numerous and their preponderance is increasing. In 1936, 55.9 percent of the total white population spoke Afri-

[25] For immigration and emigration statistics, 1924 to 1958, see Union of South Africa, *Union Statistics for Fifty Years* (Pretoria: Government Printer, 1960) section C; for 1959 to 1963 see *House of Assembly Debates*, 1963, cols. 194-95 and 385-86, and Republic of South Africa, *Monthly Bulletin of Statistics* (July 1964) pp. 12-13.

[26] *Union Statistics for Fifty Years*, section B; Republic of South Africa, *Monthly Bulletin of Statistics* (May 1963) p. 4; Republic of South Africa, *Population Census, 1960, Sample Tabulation No. 1*, p. 24.

[27] *Star*, weekly edition, April 13, 1963.

kaans at home and in 1960, an estimated 58.0 percent.[28] Immigration has strengthened the English-speaking community more than the Afrikaner, since many of the immigrants can speak English and others — some even among those from the Netherlands — have moved into the English-speaking community in South Africa.

On the other hand, emigration has been almost wholly to the detriment of the English-speaking community, as few Afrikaners have emigrated. Nevertheless, the major cause of the increase in the Afrikaner numerical superiority is that the Afrikaner birth rate has been higher, which is related to the fact that a much higher proportion of Afrikaners than of English-speaking whites are rural. Over the years intermarriages have taken place between members of the two communities, so that there are Afrikaans-speaking Smiths and English-speaking van Rynevelds. But intermarriages are frowned upon in some quarters on both sides and are not very frequent. The maintenance of the distinction between the two communities is promoted by the constitutional provision under which English and Afrikaans are both official languages of the Republic, and by the educational ordinances of the Transvaal, the Orange Free State and the Cape Province, which compulsorily divide most of the white children into two groups, to attend Afrikaans- or English-medium public schools.

By 1911 white farmers owned nearly all the usable land outside the African reserves. Afrikaners owned most of it, the only substantial pockets of farmland owned by English-speaking whites being in the southeastern Cape Province and in Natal. Even then, 52 percent of the white population — including the large majority of the English-speakers and a small minority of the Afrikaners — lived in towns and villages, but the Witwatersrand gold-mining industry was still the only major industry in the country.[29]

Today much the same area remains in white hands, but there has been some expansion of Afrikaner holdings at the expense of English-speakers. The number of white people living on the

---

[28] *Union Statistics for Fifty Years*, p. A-18; *Population Census, 1960, Sample Tabulation No. 1*, p. 24.

[29] *Union Statistics for Fifty Years*, p. A-10.

land has declined since 1936, so that the entire increase in the white population since 1911 — and more — has been absorbed in the towns.[30] In 1960, 84 percent of the white population was urban (93 percent of the English-speakers and 76 percent of the Afrikaners); and Afrikaners formed 56 percent of the white urban population and 74 per cent of the white rural population.[31] These trends are continuing. Thus the Afrikaners comprise a secure majority of the white population in every rural area except a portion of the southeastern Cape Province and central and southern Natal, and at least a substantial minority in every major industrial complex.

The Afrikaner community is extremely homogeneous. Descended very largely from about a thousand people who were "free burghers" in the Cape Colony in 1691, the Afrikaners have many of the characteristics of a family. Until recently they were united in a single economic interest, for the grandfathers of nearly every living Afrikaner were farmers; to this day nearly every Afrikaner is an active member of a Dutch Reformed Church congregation; and there are many powerful institutions and voluntary associations which are dedicated to the preservation of Afrikaner cohesion. On the other hand, the English-speaking white community is very heterogeneous. With South African ancestors dating back no further than 1820 — and rarely so far — the English-speakers are much more conscious of their external origins and links. Located in several separate pockets of settlement in South Africa, they have never had a sense of local solidarity. Their economic interests have always been diverse and often conflicting, and their religious beliefs vary widely. Moreover, though most of them are of British origin, about a tenth are Jews, who form a distinct sub-community.

The Coloured and Asian Populations

The Coloured group increased almost threefold between 1911 and 1960. This increase was not affected by migration, for practically all the Coloured people were born in South Africa

[30] The white rural population of South Africa was 696,471 in 1936, 571,014 in 1951, and 522,707 in 1960. *Population Census, 1960, Sample Tabulation No. 3*, p. 6.

[31] *Population Census, 1960, Sample Tabulation No. 1*, pp. 46-57.

and few have left it.[32] Nor has the increase been appreciably affected by "passing," although until recently passing did take place into the Coloured group from the Asian and the African, and out of the Coloured group into the white. The rate of increase is essentially the result of a remarkably high birth rate in conjunction with a moderately high death rate.[33] The Coloured group seems likely to continue to increase rapidly for some time to come, as their average age is still low, their birth rate remains high, and their death rate is dropping.[34] If the laws against miscegenation are repealed at some future date, ultimately the Coloured group would be likely to form a much higher proportion of the total population.

The Coloured people have virtually no ties with traditional nonwhite cultures, for the tribes of their Hottentot ancestors disintegrated long ago and their tropical African and Southeast Asian ancestors were removed from their traditional societies when they were brought to South Africa in the 17th and 18th centuries. Indeed, most of the traits of the Coloured people are those of the Afrikaners, with whom they have always been intimately associated. Most of them speak Afrikaans at home; the remainder speak English.[35] Nearly all of them are Christians, with a preference for the Dutch Reformed Churches, except for some 6 percent, known as the Cape Malays, who are Muslims and are treated in some respects as a separate subgroup.[36]

Ever since they began to emerge through the fusion of diverse stocks, the Coloured people have been part of a white-controlled society. Initially they were the slaves and the serfs of the Afrikaners in the pre-industrial Cape Colony. Today most of them are still dependent on white employers; and most of them still live in the western part of the Cape Province, where they form a majority of the total population and there are relatively few Africans. Two-thirds of the Coloured people now live

[32] *Union Statistics for Fifty Years*, p. A-23.

[33] *Ibid.*, pp. B-4, B-10.

[34] *Population Census, 1960, Sample Tabulation No. 2*, p. 18; *Monthly Bulletin of Statistics* (May 1963) p. 4.

[35] *Population Census, 1960, Sample Tabulation No. 2*, p. 33.

[36] *Union Statistics for Fifty Years*, p. A-27.

in towns.[37] Though most of them are very poor, there is a well-defined internal class system, with status dependent in part on educational and economic achievements and in part on skin color, with a light complexion carrying prestige. There is a considerable middle class, whose members have the tastes, the standards and the aspirations of the middle classes in modern Western societies in Europe and America.

Between 1911 and 1960 the Asian group multiplied more than threefold, the most rapid increase of any of the groups in South Africa. Like the Coloured population growth, the Asian was scarcely affected by migration in this period. The importation of indentured Indian laborers ceased in 1911 and, with very few exceptions, Asians have not been permitted to enter South Africa since 1913. Consequently, by 1951, 90 percent of the Asians were born in South Africa [38] and it will not be long before practically the entire group is South African born. In spite of the fact that until recently it was the policy of the South African government to treat Asians as temporary residents and to offer them inducements to return to India or Pakistan, few Asians ever made use of the opportunity; [39] and the government now acknowledges that the Asians form a permanent element in the South African population. The rapid increase in the Asian group is essentially the result of a birth rate that is very high, though not quite as high as the Coloured, in conjunction with a distinctly lower death rate than that of the Coloured people.[40] The Asians seem likely to continue to increase very rapidly for some time to come, as they are a young population, and their birth rate is increasing and their death rate is dropping.[41]

The internal structure of the Asian group is complex, with two superimposed types of differences. First, though most of their ancestors came as labor migrants from India, they came from different regions and different castes. There are still many

37 *Population Census, 1960, Sample Tabulation No. 3,* pp. 26-43.

38 *Union Statistics for Fifty Years,* p. A-24.

39 *Ibid.,* p. C-4.

40 *Ibid.,* pp. B-4, B-10.

41 *Population Census, 1960, Sample Tabulation No. 2,* p 52; *Monthly Bulletin of Statistics* (May 1963) p. 4.

linguistic, religious, and caste distinctions among South African Asians. Second, during the century since the Asian group took root in South Africa its members have been influenced in various ways through living as a minority and subordinate group in a plural society. For example, while most of them speak an Asian language at home, there are many such languages (with Tamil, Hindi, Gujarati, Telegu and Urdu, the most common); most of them understand English also, and about one in seven speaks English at home.[42] Again, while two-thirds call themselves Hindus and one-fifth Muslims, Hinduism and Islam bear many faces in South Africa, as elsewhere; 6 percent are Christians of one denomination or another.[43] Most Asians are extremely poor, but there are many small traders and clerks and a small peak of wealthy and sophisticated people, among whom the norms of the Western World tend to be dominant. Over four-fifths of the Asians live in Natal, and most of the balance in the Transvaal. Also, four-fifths of them now live in towns — half of them in Durban, where they are the most numerous of the four racial groups.[44]

The African Population

The African population enlarged by two-and-three-quarter times between 1911 and 1960. Other territories in southern Africa have contributed to this increase. Some of the immigrants entered South Africa under the auspices of the mining corporations' recruiting agencies, but others came independently and for the most part their entry has not been recorded, so that the total volume is not known. In 1951, 7 percent of the Africans in the Union were born outside it, and the government estimates that in 1961 there were 783,618 "foreign Bantu" in the Republic.[45]

Vital statistics are not available for the African population of the Republic as a whole because there is still a serious under-

[42] *Population Census, 1960, Sample Tabulation No. 2*, p. 62.

[43] *Union Statistics for Fifty Years*, p. A-28.

[44] *Population Census, 1960, Sample Tabulation No. 3*, pp. 44-56.

[45] *Union Statistics for Fifty Years*, p. A-24; Muriel Horrell, compiler, *A Survey of Race Relations in South Africa*, annual (Johannesburg: South African Institute of Race Relations, 1963) p. 144.

registration of births and deaths, but there is evidence of a remarkably high birth rate linked with a high death rate — including exceptional infant mortality, much malnutrition, and periodic local famine. However, in some areas at least, the death rate is now declining.[46] In Johannesburg, for example, the African infant mortality rate dropped by half, to 61 per thousand, between 1958 and 1962.[47] The African population is older than the Coloured and Asian, but considerably younger than the white; [48] as the diet and the medical facilities of Africans improve, a rapid increase in population may be expected. It certainly seems as though the Africans will continue to form over two-thirds of the total population of South Africa for the foreseeable future.

In South Africa, traditional differences, such as those between the Nguni and the Sotho peoples, and those between chiefs and commoners, are no longer the principal determinants of the structure of the African group. The reason for this is the Africans have experienced an exceptionally powerful alien impact, both in terms of duration and intensity. As early as the 1830's when, with a few exceptions, white activity in tropical Africa was still confined to the coastline, white missionaries in South Africa were working among all the major African kingdoms and tribes, and white settlers were moving into what became Natal, the Orange Free State and the Transvaal.

Fifty years later, when the scramble for tropical Africa was only just beginning, whites had firm control over all the traditional societies of South Africa. And later still, at a time when white governments were leaving most of the tropical African societies very much to their own devices, in South Africa white people were radically transforming African society. White South African governments were reducing the chiefs to petty local officials — appointing them, paying them, controlling their public conduct in detail, and dismissing them at will — and white South African farmers and industrialists were draw-

[46] Union of South Africa, *Summary of the Report of the Commission for the Socio-Economic Development of the Bantu Areas within the Union of South Africa: U.G. 61/1955* (Pretoria: Government Printer, 1955).

[47] *Survey of Race Relations,* 1963, p. 246.

[48] *Population Census, 1960, Sample Tabulation No. 5,* p. 28.

ing an ever-larger number of Africans into their service as laborers. Consequently, in tropical Africa most of the traditional societies remained more or less intact throughout the colonial epoch, and the post-colonial governments are experiencing great difficulties in welding the inhabitants of their states into nations. In South Africa the traditional societies have been more thoroughly disrupted; in their place, the primary regional division within the African group is between those who live in the "Bantu Areas," those who live in the "White Rural Areas," and those who live in the towns.

The Bantu Areas [49] are important in that they provide the territorial basis for the government's policy of apartheid. They include those parts of the Republic that are reserved exclusively for African occupation. These regions represent what is left to the Africans of their ancestral landholdings after the disturbances of the Shaka period and after white penetration, conquest and administration. In 1913, when about twenty-three million acres were occupied by Africans, the Natives Land Act gave Africans exclusive possession of those areas, prohibited Africans from acquiring possession of land outside them, and recommended that they should be enlarged. In 1936, by which time some three million acres had been added, the Native Trust and Land Act defined a number of "released areas" which were also to be added, but set no time limit for their transfer. Ultimately, if the 1936 Act is fully implemented, the Bantu Areas will be about forty-one million acres, or 13.7 percent of the land area of the Republic; in 1963 they were actually about thirty-six million acres, or 12 percent of its area.[50]

The Bantu Areas form not one block of territory, nor even a few large blocks, but several hundred separate units, varying in size from the Transkei, with over eight million acres, to holdings of a few hundred acres surrounded by farms owned by white men. Viewed together, they take the shape of a frag-

[49] See the map on page 42.

[50] *Survey of Race Relations,* 1963, pp. 111-13; Union of South Africa, *Social and Economic Planning Council Report No. 9: The Native Reserves and their place in the economy of the Union of South Africa: U.G. 32/1946* (Pretoria: Government Printer, 1946); *Summary of the Report, U.G. 61/1955.*

mented horseshoe, the southeastern arm lying on the seaward side of the mountains between the Fish River and the Mozambique border and the northwestern arm on the plateau from the northern Cape, across the northern Transvaal to the Kruger National Park. Lesotho and Swaziland are contiguous with parts of the southern arm — Bechuanaland with parts of the northern arm. Recently the government has been trying to consolidate the Bantu Areas by a compulsory removal of Africans from "black spots" and resettlement on land acquired contiguous to existing larger units; however, the position is still one of intense fragmentation.[51]

Currently, only approximately four million Africans are in the Bantu Areas at any given moment and some seven million are in the rest of the country, divided more or less equally between the rural areas, where most of them are farm laborers, and the towns, where most of them are industrial workers.[52] The farm laborers are the most static and depressed of the three subgroups. Scattered in tiny clusters over vast areas, they lack the facilities for corporate life that Africans have in the Bantu Areas and the opportunities for change that they have in the towns. The urban African population has been burgeoning throughout the 20th century, increasing sevenfold between 1911 and 1960. Many Africans, especially men of working age, still move at irregular intervals between the Bantu Areas and the towns, spending most of their working days in the towns, but maintaining a family in the Bantu Areas and keeping their rights to share in the use of tribal land, to which they retire when they are no longer employable. Perhaps half a million of the Africans who are in the towns fit in this category, and another one-third million are temporary immigrants from other territories;[53] but the number of Africans who have become essentially urbanized, having severed all connections elsewhere, has grown rapidly and now reaches about two and two-thirds millions.[54]

[51] *Ibid.*

[52] *Survey of Race Relations*, 1963, p. 75.

[53] *Ibid.*, p. 144.

[54] The concept of permanent urbanization is a difficult one to define and still more difficult to apply statistically in any country, especially to the Africans in the Republic of South Africa. The South African Council

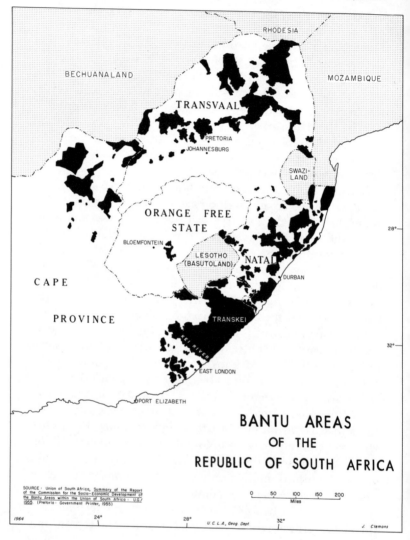

BANTU AREAS
OF THE
REPUBLIC OF SOUTH AFRICA

SOURCE : Union of South Africa, Summary of the Report
of the Commission for the Socio-Economic Development of
the Bantu Areas within the Union of South Africa : U.G./
1955. (Pretoria: Government Printer, 1955)

0   50   100   150   200
Miles

1964   24°   28°   U. C. L. A., Geog. Dept.   32°   J. Clemons

In their home environment, nearly all Africans speak one of nine related Southern Bantu languages. The languages in the Nguni group are close enough for easy communication, as are those in the Sotho group; but an Nguni-speaker cannot easily communicate with a Sotho-speaker. By 1951 about 30 percent of the Africans were able to speak English or Afrikaans and roughly the same number were able to read and write.[55] Since then both these proportions have been rising.

The achievements of Christian missionaries in South Africa are reflected in the religious statistics. By 1960 three-fifths of the Africans professed to be Christians: two-fifths were members of churches with international affiliations (the most popular being the Methodist, Catholic, Anglican, Dutch Reformed and Lutheran churches, in that order); and one-fifth were members of separatist churches, of which there are legion.[56]

As these statistics suggest, besides the division between the Bantu Areas, the white rural areas, and the towns, the other main cleavage that runs through the African population involves conservatives and modernists. The more conservative African is likely to be rural, illiterate, and pagan; the more modern African is apt to be urban, educated, and Christian. There are all sorts of permutations and combinations of these qualities, including urban clusters of Africans who remain illiterate and pagan, and rural clusters who are educated and Christian. The trend, however, seems to be away from traditionalism, since in all parts of the country, including the Bantu Areas, political autonomy and economic self-sufficiency, which were essential conditions of traditional African society, have completely disappeared. It is in the industrial centers, espe-

---

of Scientific and Industrial Research made a sample survey of more than a thousand mine laborers, employees of public authorities, and industrial workers in and around Johannesburg in 1961 and found that 70 percent could be counted as industrial workers who had never reverted to rural employment and 50 percent could be looked on as permanently urbanized in the sense that they had lived in town for at least five years, they had their families with them, they had no land rights in the Bantu Areas, and they never visited the rural areas. *Survey of Race Relations*, 1962, pp. 111-12.

55 *Union Statistics for Fifty Years*, pp. A-19, 21, 22.

56 *Ibid.*, p. A-29.

cially the Witwatersrand, where there are Africans from all parts of southern Africa, that a new urban culture is emerging: a culture shaped from the realities of modern industrial life. Within this urban subgroup there is a growing middle class, composed largely of teachers, nurses and businessmen of various sorts, who are comparable with their counterparts in other countries and to whom the Bantu Areas and their chiefs are relics of a bygone age.[57]

This review of the demography of South Africa concludes with a consideration of the ethnic structures of the populations of the three main types of areas — Bantu, White Rural, and Urban:

TABLE II.2   *Distribution of the South African Population in 1960* [58]

| | | *(Millions)* | | |
| | | *White Rural* | | |
	Bantu Areas	*Areas*	*Urban Areas*	*Total*
White		0.5	2.6	3.1
Coloured		0.5	1.0	1.5
Asian		0.1	0.4	0.5
African	4.0	3.4	3.5	10.9
Total	4.0	4.5	7.5	16.0

The Bantu Areas are overwhelmingly African. They do contain the homes of a few thousand whites and a few hundred Coloured and Asian people, as well as four million Africans,

[57] There is a dearth of systematic studies of African society in the major industrial centers of the Republic. Philip Mayer, ed., *Xhosa in Town: Studies of the Bantu-speaking Population of East London, Cape Province* (3 vols., Cape Town: Oxford University Press, 1961-1963) contains penetrating analyses of the Africans in a town with a total population (1960) of 116,056; and Monica Wilson and Archie Mafeje, *Langa: A study of social groups in an African township* (Cape Town: Oxford University Press, 1963) is a briefer but valuable analysis of a Cape Town African township. There is also much relevant information in the works of African authors such as Ezekiel Mphahlele, *The African Image* (New York: Praeger, 1962); of white journalists such as Anthony Sampson, *Drum: A venture into the new Africa* (London: Collins, 1956); and of white clergy such as Father Trevor Huddleston, C.R., *Naught for Your Comfort* (London: Collins, 1956).

[58] *Survey of Race Relations*, 1962, pp. 64-65, 1963, pp. 74-75.

plus perhaps another half million Africans who had homes in the Bantu Areas but were absent when the census was taken. Most of the migrants are young men, so that there are always many more women than men in the Bantu Areas. The distribution of the Xhosa-speaking people is an interesting example. It is estimated that in 1960 there were 3.4 million Xhosa-speaking people, of whom 1.4 million were in the Transkeian and half a million in the Ciskeian Bantu Areas, and 1.6 million were in the "white" parts of the Republic — some as farm laborers, others as industrial workers, some as temporary migrants, others as permanent residents of farms and towns.[59]

The White Rural Areas are white in the sense that most of the land is owned by whites, but not in the demographic sense. Indeed, the whites are only about one-ninth of the total population, and the overwhelming majority are nonwhite farm laborers — Africans in most parts of the country and Coloureds in the southwestern Cape Province.

In the towns, which are also regarded as white districts, the whites number only about one out of every three persons. The populations of the principal urban areas in 1960 were as follows:

TABLE II.3   *Urban Population Distribution* [60]

	White	Coloured	Asian	African	Total
Witwatersrand	766,379	78,134	39,915	1,296,486	2,180,914
Cape Peninsula	305,155	417,881	8,975	75,200	807,211
Durban	196,398	27,082	236,477	221,535	681,492
Pretoria	207,202	7,452	8,046	199,890	422,590
Port Elizabeth	94,931	68,332	4,247	123,183	290,693
Free State Gold Fields	47,589	511	——	121,677	169,777
Total	1,617,654	599,392	297,660	2,037,971	4,552,677

[59] *Ibid.*, 1962, pp. 85-86.

[60] *Population Census, 6th September, 1960*, Vol. I, pp. 66-67. The Witwatersrand includes the entire urban complex of Johannesburg, Benoni, Boksburg, Brakpan, Germiston, Kempton Park, Krugersdorp, Oberholzer, Randfontein, Roodepoort and Springs. The Cape Peninsula contains the magisterial districts of Cape Town, Wynberg, Simonstown and Bellville. Durban, Pretoria and Port Elizabeth include suburban areas adjacent to the towns.

The dynamic elements in South Africa are to be found in these towns. There most of the wealth of South Africa is produced. There, whatever the laws may be, complex and irreversible processes of cultural interaction are taking place. There the South African society of the future is being born. And there it is likely that the South African political struggle will be decided.

ECONOMIC CONDITIONS

Two facets of the South African economy [61] are of great political significance. The first is its strength: it is a strong economy by any standards and it is becoming stronger. The second is its inequality: there are exceptional inequalities of wealth in South Africa and the inequalities correspond closely with race.

The present South African economy is the cumulative product of four types of economic activity initiated at different times: subsistence farming, formerly practiced by the Hottentot and African tribes and by most of the white settlers; [62] farming to produce a significant surplus for local or overseas markets,

[61] The most useful general account of the South African economy is D. Hobart Houghton, *The South African Economy* (Cape Town: Oxford University Press, 1964). See also de Kiewiet, *op. cit.*; S. H. Frankel, *Capital Investment in Africa: Its course and effects* (London: Oxford University Press, 1938); Norton N. Franklin, *Economics in South Africa* (2nd edn., London: Oxford University Press, 1954); W. K. Hancock, *Survey of British Commonwealth Affairs*, Vol. II, *Problems of Economic Policy, 1918-1939* (London: Oxford University Press, 1942); A. J. Norval, *A Quarter of a Century of Industrial Progress in South Africa* (Cape Town: Juta, 1962); H. M. Robertson, *South Africa: Economic and political aspects* (Durham: Duke University Press, 1957); and C. G. W. Schumann, *Structural Changes and Business Cycles in South Africa, 1806-1936* (London: King and Staples, 1938). There are also several official periodicals, including the *Monthly Bulletin of Statistics*, the *Quarterly Bulletin of Statistics* of the South African Reserve Bank, and the *Official Year Book of the Republic of South Africa*, and a nonofficial periodical, *The South African Journal of Economics*.

[62] To describe a community as subsistence farmers is not to deny that it had some internal specialization, or that it bartered or sold some of its produce. The African tribes had specialist metal-workers and bartered from village to village; and the Afrikaner *trekboers* sold some of their stock on the hoof to travelling butchers' agents from Cape Town, thus acquiring the means to buy a few necessities, such as guns, ammunition, sugar, coffee and tea, from travelling traders.

which was first practiced by some of the early white settlers in the neighborhood of Cape Town but only became the practice of the majority of the white farmers during the 19th century; mining, which began on an extensive scale in the late 19th century and is still an expanding activity; and manufacturing, which received its first strong impetus when overseas supplies declined during World War I and has expanded greatly and more or less continuously since about 1935.

Today the Bantu Areas are a survival of the subsistence farming system of the African tribes, modified by a great increase in the density of population and by the existence of a large and growing market for African labor in the rest of the Republic. Nearly all the African inhabitants of the Bantu Areas are wholly, or partly, mixed farmers, holding their land under communal tenure, and producing very little for internal exchange and virtually nothing for sale outside the Bantu Areas. These areas are overstocked with poor quality cattle, sheep and goats; their crops — mainly corn and millet — are of low yield and poor quality; and soil erosion is widespread. Road and rail communications are poor.

Rehabilitation schemes are beginning to improve the agriculture, at the cost of depriving many of the people of their traditional rights to land. However, scarcely any industrial opportunities exist for the displaced Africans in the Bantu Areas, not only because their location is unfavorable, but also because the government prohibits private investment in the Bantu Areas by non-Africans and is itself making only a small contribution to their development. The only town in the entire Transkei with a population of more than 3,000 is Umtata, with about 12,000.[63] It is government policy to house many of the Africans who are removed from the land in new dormitory townships just inside the borders of the Bantu Areas and to employ them in new private manufacturing industries just outside their borders, but the new industries are slow to develop.

The Bantu Areas are therefore backward by any standards and seem doomed to remain so for the foreseeable future. In

---

[63] Umtata is the capital and principal trading center of the Transkei, with a population of 7,660 Africans, 3,449 whites and 1,112 Coloured people in 1960: *Population Census, 6th September, 1960*, Vol. I, p. 89.

the broader economic context they are reservoirs of labor for the expanding capitalist sector of the South African economy. In the broader political context, though the regions were originally proclaimed in part for the humanitarian purpose of saving for the Africans a portion of their ancestral land, they have for a long time provided white South Africans with a pretext for treating all Africans as temporary visitors elsewhere in the Republic.[64]

The White Rural Areas are divided into about a hundred thousand farms with an average area of about two thousand acres each. The farms are owned and managed by white people and operated by nonwhite laborers. Between 1911 and 1958-1959, when there was an agricultural census, the physical volume of their gross production increased about fourfold, largely as a result of technical improvements, and production has continued to increase in recent years. The principal field crops (in order of value) are corn (maize), fresh fruits, wheat, sugarcane, vegetables, tobacco, potatoes, vines, hay and groundnuts; the principal livestock products are wool, milk and other dairy products, beef, mutton, poultry and poultry products, and pork. South Africa is virtually self-sufficient in foodstuffs and has a considerable surplus for export.

The principal mining industries produce the following:

TABLE II.4   *Mining Products, 1963*[65]

	Quantity Sold	Value of Sales
Gold	27,421,000 fine ounces	$960,864,800
Coal	46,138,000 tons	94,796,800
Diamonds	4,272,000 carats	44,760,800
Asbestos	196,000 tons	31,329,200
Copper	59,400 tons	30,411,600
Manganese Ore	1,499,000 tons	18,270,000
Iron Ore	4,505,000 tons	16,702,000

[64] On the economy of the Bantu Areas see Edgar H. Brookes and Nathan Hurwitz, *The Native Reserves of Natal* (Cape Town: Oxford University Press, 1957); D. Hobart Houghton and Edith M. Walton, *The Economy of a Native Reserve* (Pietermaritzburg: Shuter and Shooter, 1952); *Social and Economic Planning Council Report No. 9, U.G. 32/1946;* and *Summary of the Report, U.G. 61/1955.*

[65] *Monthly Bulletin of Statistics* (July 1964) Section D.

The South African gold-mining industry has been the greatest in the world for three-quarters of a century. Since 1910 its production has multiplied fourfold, and is continuing to increase. In recent years the techniques for extracting gold at deep levels and from low-grade ores have improved and new mines have been brought into operation on the Far West Rand and in the Orange Free State. However, the future of the gold-mining industry is a matter of conjecture. The limit of profitable operations is determined by the world price for gold, which has remained unchanged at $35.00 an ounce for several years; and if no new reefs are discovered and the price continues to be static, it is predicted by some of those most competent to judge that South African gold production will reach its peak within a few years and then go downwards rather steeply as many of the old mines on the Witwatersrand cease production.[66]

South Africa's coal production has increased sevenfold since 1910 and there are still vast coal reserves. There are also considerable diamond reserves, but most South African diamonds are gems and their production and sale are geared to maintain prices and their value has not increased since 1910. Appreciable quantities of silver, platinum, antimony, nickel, tin, titanium and vanadium are also produced, as well as considerable quantities of atomic energy materials.

The manufacturing industry, like mining, is for the most part conducted by private enterprise; there are also several public corporations notably SASOL (South African Coal, Oil and Gas Corporation), which produces oil from coal, and ISCOR (Iron and Steel Corporation), which makes steel. The railways, harbors, telecommunications and much of the road transport are owned and operated by the public authorities.

Until 1961 the South African monetary system was the same as the British, and the South African £ was on a par with the British £. In 1961 a decimal system was introduced in South Africa, with one Rand (South African) = ten shillings (British), one shilling (South African) = $\frac{1}{10}$ Rand, and one cent (South African) = $\frac{1}{100}$ Rand. For the reader's convenience most monetary sums are given in dollars.

66 E.g., W. J. Busschau, Chairman, Goldfields of South Africa, reported in the *Star*, weekly edition, May 11, 1963.

When there was an industrial census in 1959-1960, the production of manufacturing industry, including the public corporations but not the public authorities, was rated as follows:

TABLE II.5   *Gross Value of Manufacturing Industry Output, 1959-1960*[67]

Food, drink & tobacco	$ 996,800,000
Textiles, clothing & footwear	470,400,000
Wood, cork & furniture	148,400,000
Paper, printing, publishing	238,000,000
Leather & rubber products	44,800,000
Chemicals & products of petrol & coal	450,800,000
Non-metallic minerals	187,600,000
Metal & metal products	610,400,000
Machinery & transport equipment	352,800,000
Miscellaneous manufactures	89,600,000
Total manufacturing industry	$3,589,600,000

Since this industrial census expansion has reached a very high rate, with the greatest increase in textiles, drink, paper and publishing, chemicals, petroleum and coal products, and metals. By the end of 1963 the volume of manufacturing production had increased over-all by another third.[68]

Nevertheless, South Africa is still basically an importer of manufactured goods, especially of machinery and transport equipment, and an exporter of raw materials, especially of gold. There is one striking exception to this general pattern: South Africa does not produce a drop of natural fuel oil. This is a grievous deficiency for an isolated state with an unpopular political system.

The government founded SASOL to convert coal to gasoline and diesel fuel, but the capital costs per unit are very high and the present output meets only a small porportion of the country's needs; [69] although extensive prospecting for natural oil is in progress, no substantial finds have yet been made. The fol-

[67] Economist Intelligence Unit, *Quarterly Economic Review, Annual Supplement: Republic of South Africa* (March 1964) p. 12.

[68] *Ibid.*, pp. 12-13.

[69] In 1962 SASOL produced 75 million gallons of gasoline and four million gallons of diesel fuel. *House of Assembly Debates,* 1963, col. 3256.

lowing table analyzes South Africa's foreign trade in terms of commodities:

TABLE II.6   *Foreign Trade: Commodity Groups, 1963 (Excluding gold bullion, atomic energy materials and ships' stores)* [70]

	Imports	Exports
Food & live animals	$ 84,000,000	$ 406,000,000
Inedible raw materials	151,200,000	425,600,000
Mineral fuel	106,400,000	22,400,000
Chemicals	120,400,000	42,000,000
Machinery & transport equipment	660,800,000	42,000,000
Other manufactured articles	529,200,000	302,400,000
Miscellaneous	44,800,000	28,000,000
	$1,696,800,000	$1,268,400,000

Britain is still South Africa's principal trading partner and the British stake in this economy continues to increase. However, the British proportion of South Africa's foreign trade is now declining as a result of increasing participation by the European common market countries (especially West Germany), the United States and Japan. South Africa's trade with tropical Africa north of the Zambezi, on the other hand, is negligible. The following table shows an analysis of South Africa's foreign trade in terms of direction:

TABLE II.7   *Foreign Trade: Direction of Trade, 1963 (Excluding gold bullion, atomic energy materials and ships' stores)* [71]

	Imports	Exports
Rhodesia & Nyasaland	$ 44,800,000	$ 106,400,000
Rest of Africa	67,200,000	44,800,000
United Kingdom	506,800,000	380,800,000
European common market area	333,200,000	271,600,000
Rest of Europe	106,400,000	50,400,000
U.S.A.	285,600,000	112,000,000
Rest of America	81,200,000	30,800,000
Japan	78,400,000	98,000,000
Rest of Asia	156,800,000	44,800,000
Oceania	19,600,000	19,600,000
Unspecified	16,800,000	109,200,000
	$1,696,800,000	$1,268,400,000

[70] *Monthly Bulletin of Statistics* (July 1964), Section G-1.
[71] *Ibid.*, Section G-2

South Africa has by far the strongest economy of any country in Africa south of Egypt and it stands comparison with the economies of other rapidly developing countries, like Canada and Australia. Its strength lies in considerable and varied natural resources, a reserve of incompletely-tapped potential manpower, and the capital investment and entrepreneurial experience that have accumulated during the century following the discovery of diamonds which triggered off the process of modernization. Thanks largely to the fact that South Africa is the source of over half the world's supply of gold, the country normally has a favorable balance of trade. The gross national product doubled between 1952 and 1962; [72] its real income per capita increased by an average of over 2 percent per annum between 1948 and 1960, and after a year of no change, by a still higher rate after 1961.[73]

A tradition of conservative financing has produced annual surpluses for the exchequer and the interest on the national debt consumes only about 5 percent of the revenue.[74] Though there was a crisis of confidence among foreign investors after the Sharpeville shootings in 1960, the foreign reserves soon recovered and the foreign capital required for continued development seems to be readily forthcoming from Britain, Western Europe and the United States. Industrial expansion continues to take place and there is a vast hydroelectric project along the Orange River.

Racial Inequality

Racial inequality pervades the entire South African economy. In 1961 the Minister of Finance estimated that in the country as a whole the average annual income of whites was $1148, of Asians $224, of Coloureds $162, and of Africans $129.[75] There is virtually full employment among whites, but nonwhites, especially Africans, experience serious unemploy-

[72] *Quarterly Economic Review* (March 1964) p. 6. This refers to GNP at market prices.

[73] Minister of Finance, *House of Assembly Debates*, 1963, cols. 3049, 3787.

[74] *Monthly Bulletin of Statistics* (July 1964) Section K.

[75] *House of Assembly Debates*, 1961, col. 1352.

ment. In 1960 about 41,000 whites, 90,000 Coloureds, 27,000 Asians, and 335,000 Africans were unemployed in the industrial areas, quite apart from those Africans in the Bantu Areas who were not seeking work.[76] The following table gives the average numbers of persons employed and their average wages in the mining industries, the manufacturing industries and the public services in 1962:

TABLE II.8   *Numbers Employed* [77]

	Mining	Manufacturing	Public Services*
Whites	64,932	213,300	373,580
Coloureds	3,850	129,400	59,769
Asians	470		9,691
Africans	538,581	359,300	386,629

Wages	Mining	Manufacturing	Public Services*
Whites	$3,428	$2,733	$2,293
Coloureds	574	843	798
Asians			1,025
Africans	207†	549	540

* Public Services include the public services of the Republic, the state railways and harbor service, the post office, and the provincial and local administrations. The average wage rates cited are those in the public service of the Republic.

† African mine workers are also provided with food, medical treatment, accommodation, clothing and other benefits.

The income tax returns are a good gauge of wealth in South Africa since, although Africans pay various types of special direct taxes, the income tax is common for all with a fairly high level of minimum liability. In the tax year 1961-1962, income taxes paid show a wide variation between the races.

[76] *Survey of Race Relations*, 1963, p. 210. These figures do include African migrants temporarily in the reserves, but, as stated in the text, they do not include Africans in the reserves who were not seeking work.
[77] *Ibid.*, pp. 199-205.

TABLE II.9   *Income Tax, 1961-1962* [78]

	Number of Persons Liable	Amounts Paid
Whites	887,150	$218,113,865
Coloureds	103,046	2,338,899
Asians	21,089	1,893,346
Africans	556	62,359

   Such inequalities exist partly because modern economic activities were pioneered in South Africa by white entrepreneurs and white skilled workers, and because a large number of Africans still do not participate effectively in the modern sector of the economy, or do so only intermittently. In time, however, the correspondence of race with economic status would have been expected to diminish, as nonwhites acquired industrial training and experience. There has, in fact, been a tendency in that direction, shown by the rise of middle classes among the African, as well as the Asian and Coloured groups; but the tendency has been checked by a vast volume of white-made laws and white-imposed customs, that have gone a long way towards perpetuating inequality on a racial basis. [79]

   There are laws that determine the ownership and occupation

---

[78] *Ibid.*, p. 209.

[79] On discriminatory legislation in South Africa see Edgar H. Brookes and J. B. Macaulay, *Civil Liberties in South Africa* (Cape Town: Oxford University Press, 1958); G. V. Doxey, *The Industrial Colour Bar in South Africa* (Cape Town: Oxford University Press, 1961); Economic Commission for Africa, *Economic and Social Consequences of Racial Discriminatory Practices* (New York: United Nations, 1963); S. H. Frankel, "The Tyranny of Economic Paternalism: A Study of Frontier Mentality," supplement to *Optima*, December 1960; B. A. Hepple, "Economic and Racial Legislation," in H. R. Hahlo, Ellison Kahn, *et al.*, *The Union of South Africa: The development of its laws and constitution* (London: Stevens, 1960); Muriel Horrell, *South African Trade Unionism* (Johannesburg: South African Institute of Race Relations, 1961), and *Legislation and Race Relations* (Johannesburg: South African Institute of Race Relations, 1963); International Commission of Jurists, *South Africa and the Rule of Law* (Geneva: International Commission of Jurists, 1960); Elizabeth S. Landis, "South African Apartheid Legislation," *Yale Law Journal*, LXXI, Nos. 1 & 3 (1961-1962) 1-52, 437-500; K. L. Roskam, *Apartheid and Discrimination* (Leyden: Sythoff, 1960); United Nations, *The Report of the Special Committee on the Policies of Apartheid of the Republic of South Africa* (New York: United Nations, 1963).

of land. Outside the Bantu Areas Africans may not own any land at all; in the White Rural Areas, African occupation of land as labor-tenants is restricted by registration and licensing; and for residence in the urban areas, Africans other than domestic servants are confined to compounds or locations where they cannot have freehold tenure. Asians may not possess or occupy land in the Orange Free State, and in Natal and the Transvaal they are restricted to what was in Asian hands in 1946. There are restrictions on Coloured ownership and occupation in the three northern provinces. Moreover, under the Group Areas Act, 1950, and its amendments, which are being applied piecemeal by proclamation, all urban areas are being divided into zones; in each zone, members of one race, and one only, may own real estate, reside, or conduct business.

Second, there are the laws that rèstrict the movements of Africans. Before 1964 no African had the right to be in an urban area unless he had resided there continuously since birth, or had worked there continuously for one employer for ten years, or had resided there for fifteen years, or was the wife, unmarried daughter or son under eighteen years of age of such a person, or had been given a permit to remain by the local authority. Permits were not valid for more than fourteen days, unless the African had obtained work. Furthermore, officials already had wide powers to banish Africans from towns, and such Africans had no right of appeal to the courts against a banishment order. Now, under the Bantu Laws Amendment Act, 1964, officials may remove any African from any town at any time. Coloured people have considerable freedom of movement throughout the White Areas, but Asians require special permission to move from one province to another. Whites, Asians and Coloureds may not enter African locations or Bantu Areas without a permit. In 1961, 375,417 Africans were convicted for breaches of restrictions upon their movements.[80]

Third, the apprenticeship system, in combination with the educational system, prevents Africans and most Coloureds and Asians from becoming trained as artisans. Fourth, employment in skilled work in the mining industries is reserved by law for whites and Coloureds; the government has the power to reserve particular types of work in other industries for particular

80 *House of Assembly Debates*, 1963, col. 984.

races, and it uses this power to protect whites from nonwhite competition. Fifth, the Industrial Conciliation legislation discourages African trade unions by failing to recognize them for purposes of industrial conciliation, and it also discourages the continued existence of mixed white, Coloured and Asian trade unions and prohibits the registration of new mixed unions. Sixth, breach of a labor contract is a criminal offense in South Africa (in practice prosecutions are limited to nonwhite offenders) and it is unlawful for Africans to strike.

These associated policies of an industrial color-bar and low wages for the unskilled have a wide range of retarding effects upon economic development. Human resources of South Africa are used irrationally: many whites are incompetent in the skilled employments in which they are placed by virtue of their color; and many nonwhites, with reasonable training, would be fully competent to perform skilled tasks that are denied to them. It is now widely recognized by South African economists, industrialists and financiers that the most serious limitation upon economic growth is the shortage of skilled workers; [81] this shortage is unlikely to disappear until the potential of the nonwhite inhabitants is released. Furthermore, the legal immobility and the insecurity of the African urban worker and the large surplus of African work-seekers result in a perpetuation of low wages and inefficiency; low wages in turn limit the local market for South African products. The economic growth that has taken place in South Africa has occurred in spite of, not because of, the color-bar and low wages.

The two facets of the South African economy — its strength and its inequality — closely relate to each other. Nonwhites as well as whites are benefiting from economic growth, so that the effects of economic inequality are to some extent offset by rising living standards and the expectation of further rises. The strength of the economy also enables the government to mobilize the resources required to suppress internal political opposition and to defy external opposition.[82]

[81] E.g., Dr. M. H. de Kock, Chairman, South African Reserve Bank, reported in the *Star*, weekly edition, March 2, 1963; Dr. D. J. Gouws, Director, National Institute for Personnel Research, reported *ibid.*, May 18, 1963; and A. B. Anderson, President, South African Institute of Mechanical Engineers, reported *ibid.*, June 29, 1963.

[82] See chapters 5 and 6.

CHAPTER III

The Framework of Political Life

THE CONSTITUTION of the Republic of South Africa was enacted by the Parliament of the Union of South Africa and
came into force on May 31, 1961.[1] But 1961 did not mark a
break in South African constitutional and political continuity. The new constitution was merely the South Africa
Act (which had been enacted by the British Parliament in
1909) as amended from time to time, and as revised at the
time South Africa ceased to be a kingdom and became a
Republic, when all extant South African legislation not
specifically repealed or amended by the new constitution
remained in force. Consequently South African politics are
affected by many surviving statutes of the Union Parliament and by the relevant decisions of the Supreme Court
of South Africa. Furthermore, in South Africa as in other
countries, the legal bases of politics are given life by the
conventions and practices that have developed over the
years.[2]

[1] Republic of South Africa Constitution Act, No. 32 of 1961. The
basic commentary on the South African constitution is H. R. Hahlo
and Ellison Kahn, *The Union of South Africa: The development of its
laws and constitution* (London: Stevens, 1960), supplemented by Ellison Kahn, *The New Constitution: Being a supplement to South Africa:
The development of its laws and constitution* (London: Stevens, 1962),
which includes a text of the constitution. See also Henry John May,
The South African Constitution (3rd edn., Cape Town: Juta, 1955).

[2] On the political and constitutional history of South Africa since
1910 see Gwendolen M. Carter, *The Politics of Inequality: South*

EXECUTIVE GOVERNMENT

The change to a Republic necessitated the creation of a new head of state. Formerly the South African monarch was also the monarch of the other kingdoms in the British Commonwealth and, as in all of them except the United Kingdom, he was normally represented in South Africa by a Governor-General. The monarch has been replaced by a "State President," who is elected by secret ballot by an electoral college consisting of the Senators and the members of the House of Assembly, at a meeting presided over by the Chief Justice or his deputy. The State President holds office for seven years, unless he resigns, or is removed for misconduct by resolution of both the Senate and the House of Assembly. The functions of the State President in South Africa remain similar to those of the King or Queen in Britain; where in Britain the duties are determined largely by convention, in South Africa many, though not all, of the British conventions are spelled out in the written constitution.

The State President is declared to be the Head of the Republic and the Commander-in-Chief of the Defence Force, and to have power to convene and prorogue Parliament, to dissolve either or both of its Houses, to make ministerial and other appointments, to confer honors, to pardon offenders, to appoint and receive ambassadors, to enter into and ratify treaties, to proclaim and terminate martial law, to declare peace and war, to perform the functions vested in him by other statutes, and to possess the prerogative powers formerly possessed by the

---

Africa since 1948 (London: Thames and Hudson, 1958); C. W. de Kiewiet, *The Anatomy of South African Misery* (London: Oxford University Press, 1956); W. K. Hancock, *Survey of British Commonwealth Affairs*, Vol. I, *Problems of Nationality, 1918-1936* (London: Oxford University Press, 1937) and *Smuts, The Sanguine Years, 1870-1919* (Cambridge: University Press, 1962); D. W. Krüger, *The Age of the Generals* (Johannesburg: Dagbreek, 1958); Nicholas Mansergh, *Survey of British Commonwealth Affairs* (2 vols., London: Oxford University Press, 1952-58) and *South Africa, 1906-1961: The Price of Magnanimity* (New York: Praeger, 1962); Michael Roberts and A. E. G. Trollip, *The South African Opposition, 1939-1945* (London: Longmans, 1947); and Eric A. Walker, *A History of Southern Africa* (3rd edn., London: Longmans, 1957).

Queen.[3] However, the constitution also ensures that in exercising every one of these powers the State President is normally the creature of the Executive Council. Every official instrument signed by the State President requires the countersignature of a Minister, and his every official action is required to be taken on the advice of the Executive Council, except only that he has discretion in appointing Ministers, convening and proroguing Parliament, and dissolving the House of Assembly. Even in these cases he is declared to be bound by the existing (but undefined) constitutional conventions, which means that he is to act on ministerial advice whenever possible, and only in exceptional circumstances would he have any real discretionary power.[4] Such circumstances might arise if a ruling party disintegrated. For example, if a Prime Minister lost the confidence of the House of Assembly and asked for a dissolution of the House, the President might have a real choice between agreeing to a dissolution and attempting to find someone else capable of forming a government. That is what happened in 1939 when the United Party Cabinet and Parliamentary Party disintegrated on the war issue and Governor-General Sir Patrick Duncan refused Prime Minister J. B. M. Hertzog's request for a dissolution, and J. C. Smuts, previously Deputy Prime Minister, formed a government.[5]

When the new constitution was being debated in Parliament, Prime Minister H. F. Verwoerd said it was the government's intention that the State President should be above politics — a symbol of national dignity and pride.[6] In a country that has cleavages as deep as those in South Africa this ideal is virtually unrealizable. Before the republican constitution came into force it was already an established custom that the Governor-General should be appointed on the advice of the South Afri-

[3] In fact, many of the prerogative powers are spelled out in the constitution (these are included in the list above) and in other South African statutes. Among those that are covered by the general grant in the constitution and not listed elsewhere are some of political significance, notably the granting and renewal of passports.

[4] Constitution, sections 7-23, 64.

[5] Mansergh, *Survey*, Vol. I, *Problems of External Policy, 1931-1939*, pp. 381-400.

[6] *Senate Debates*, 1961, col. 3157.

can Cabinet, and an ironical situation had developed: the last two representatives of the monarch in the Union were former members of an avowedly republican party — Dr. E. G. Jansen (1955-1960) and Charles Robberts Swart (1960-1961). The election of the first State President of the Republic of South Africa took place on May 10, 1961. Two persons were nominated — C. R. Swart and H. A. Fagan, a former Chief Justice of the Union; the vote followed party lines and Swart was elected by 139 votes to 71.[7]

The constitution vests the real executive power in an Executive Council of not more than eighteen Ministers, each of whom is head of one or more departments of state. It also allows for the appointment of not more than six Deputy Ministers, without seats in the Executive Council, and provides that the Ministers and Deputy Ministers shall not hold their appointments for more than three months without being members of the Senate or the House of Assembly, and that they shall be appointed by the State President.[8] Though the words "Responsible Government," "Prime Minister," "Cabinet," and "Party" have no place in the written constitution, this means a system of responsible government as practiced in the United Kingdom and most of the countries of the British Commonwealth — government by a Cabinet, consisting of a Prime Minister and other Ministers selected by him, and holding office by virtue of the Prime Minister's leadership of the party (or coalition of parties) having a majority of the seats in the dominant legislative chamber.

In South Africa the British doctrine of the collective responsibility of the Cabinet for every official action of every Minister does not possess the strength that it has in the United Kingdom. Indeed, there are several clearcut cases of independent action by Ministers, as in 1936 when J. H. Hofmeyr, though Minister of the Interior, spoke and voted against a government

[7] Kahn, *op. cit.*, pp. 5-6. Swart, an Afrikaner born in the Orange Free State in 1894, had played a major and often highly controversial role in politics: an organizer first of the Nationalist Party led by J. B. M. Hertzog and then of the Nationalist Party led by D. F. Malan; a member of Parliament (1923-1938, 1941-1959); and Minister of Justice (1948-1959), before he became successively Governor-General and State President.

[8] Constitution, sections 16-23.

bill to remove African voters from the common electoral roll in the Cape Province. However, if a Prime Minister decides to rid himself of a colleague he can easily do so (provided, as always, that he retains the confidence of a majority in the House of Assembly). Normally, the Prime Minister's request suffices, but if the colleague refuses to resign, the Prime Minister has only to tender his own resignation to the Head of State, who will then invite him to form a new Cabinet from which he will exclude the recalcitrant Minister, as Louis Botha did in 1912 when he excluded Hertzog.

At present there are only two politically significant parties in South Africa and both of them have clearly defined intra-party machinery for selecting leaders. Consequently the person who should be Prime Minister is readily identifiable and the State President has no option but to accept him and the colleagues he selects. This gives the Prime Minister immense strength in his relations with his own party, and the system has in fact produced an unbroken line of strong Prime Ministers in South Africa — Louis Botha (1910-1919), J. C. Smuts (1919-1924, 1939-1948), J. B. M. Hertzog (1924-1939), D. F. Malan (1948-1954), J. G. Strijdom (1954-1958), and H. F. Verwoerd (1958-   ).

PARLIAMENT

The legislative power is vested in a Parliament, consisting of the State President, a Senate, and a House of Assembly.[9] The State President's parliamentary functions are like those of the monarch in the United Kingdom. He formally opens each session of Parliament when he delivers a speech outlining the government's legislative program, but the speech is prepared by the Cabinet. He assents to bills which have been passed by the Senate and the House of Assembly, or withholds such assent, as advised by the Cabinet.[10]

[9] *Ibid.*, section 24.

[10] The constitutional provisions concerning assent to legislation are a good example of the way in which the President is deprived of effective discretion:

16. (2) Save where otherwise expressly stated or necessarily implied, any reference in this Act to the State President shall be deemed to be a reference to the State President acting on the advice of the Executive Council.

The constitution firmly subordinates the Senate to the House of Assembly, in much the same way as the British Parliament Act subordinates the House of Lords to the House of Commons. Money bills — "Bills appropriating revenue or moneys or imposing taxation" — may originate only in the House of Assembly; such bills are "taken to have been duly passed by the Senate" and are presented to the State President for his assent in the same session in which they were passed by the House of Assembly, even if they have not actually been passed by the Senate. Other types of bills may originate in either the Senate or the House of Assembly; these bills are presented to the State President for his approval if they have been passed by the House of Assembly in two successive sessions, even without actual Senate passage. The only exception is a bill affecting the official status of the English and the Afrikaans languages, which in order to pass requires a two-thirds vote of the total number of members of both Houses with the Senate and the House of Assembly sitting together at the third reading.[11] Therefore, the Senate is a weak Upper House in the British manner: it has no effective power over the raising and spending of money, and it has a delaying power of about one year over other types of legislation, with one exception.

The composition of the Senate has undergone many changes since 1910,[12] but one feature has been constant — only white people, who are qualified voters and at least thirty years of age, have been eligible. Formerly Senators also had a property qualification — now abolished.[13] Originally thirty-two Senators were indirectly elected, eight from each province, and eight Senators were nominated by the government. Between 1936 and 1960 there were also four Senators indirectly elected by Africans.[14] Since 1949 there have been four Senators from South-

---

64. (1) When a Bill is presented to the State President for his assent, he shall declare according to his discretion, but subject to the provisions of this Act, that he assents thereto or that he withholds assent.

[11] Constitution, sections 60-62, 118.

[12] B. Beinart, "The South African Senate," *Modern Law Review*, XX, No. 6 (November 1957) 549-65; Hahlo and Kahn, *op. cit.*, pp. 29-30.

[13] Senate Act, 1955.

[14] Representation of Natives Act, 1936; Promotion of Bantu Self-Government Act, 1959.

West Africa, two nominated and two indirectly elected.[15] In 1955 the main body of the Senate was enlarged and transformed to give the Nationalist Party seventy-seven members in a House of eighty-nine, needed to give effect to its policy of removing the Coloured voters from the common roll; in 1960, that purpose having been achieved, the Senate was again remodeled in a way that was continued under the 1961 constitution.[16]

There are now forty-three elected and eleven nominated Senators. Of the elected Senators, forty-one are divided between the provinces by a formula which gives each province at least eight Senators and the larger provinces a few more. In 1965 the Transvaal had fourteen elected Senators, the Cape Province eleven, and Natal and the Orange Free State eight each. They are elected by proportional representation, by electoral colleges consisting of the members of the Provincial Council and the members of the House of Assembly for the province. The other two elected Senators are elected by proportional representation by an electoral college consisting of the members of the South-West African Legislative Assembly and the members of the House of Assembly for South-West Africa. The government nominates two Senators for each province and for South-West Africa, one of whom in each pair is required to be "thoroughly acquainted . . . with the interests of the coloured population" (as distinct from the African or Asian population) in the province or territory; the remaining nominated Senator is appointed "on the ground of his thorough acquaintance . . . with the reasonable wants and wishes of the Coloured People of the Cape Province." [17] In practice these provisions have meant that since 1960 the Senate has contained thirty-nine members of the Nationalist Party and fifteen members of the United Party.

The composition of the House of Assembly has also changed over the years. Membership of the House has always been limited to white people who are qualified voters. The South Africa Act created a House of one hundred and twenty-one members — fifty-one from the Cape Province, thirty-six from

15 South-West Africa Affairs Amendment Act, 1949.

16 Senate Act, 1955; Senate Act, 1960.

17 Constitution, sections 28-30, 33-34; South-West Africa Affairs Amendment Act, 1949; Separate Representation of Voters Act, 1951.

the Transvaal, and seventeen from the Orange Free State and from Natal — and provided a formula for the gradual increase in the size of the House to one hundred and fifty, and for the division of the one hundred and fifty seats between the provinces thereafter in proportion to their numbers of white men. The House reached its total of a hundred and fifty members in 1936. In the 1950's the basis of the division of the seats between the provinces was changed twice, and the division is now made in proportion to their numbers of registered white voters.[18] In practice, under these provisions there has been a continuous increase in the number of seats allotted to the Transvaal.

The South Africa Act also laid down a system for the periodic redelimitation of each province into electoral divisions. This, too, has been continued under the republican constitution. New delimitations are made at intervals of between five and ten years by commissions of Supreme Court Judges. The commissions are required to divide each province into its correct number of single-member electoral divisions, each containing approximately the same number of voters; but the commissions are entitled to allow a latitude of up to 15 percent either way from a provincial norm, and in so doing to give "due consideration" to five factors, including "sparsity or density of population."[19] In practice, delimitation commissions have always tended to give considerable emphasis to this factor and to apply it in favor of rural areas, which have had between three and six more seats than they would on a basis of strict equality. Though the maximum latitude thus permitted is small by American standards, its political effects have been appreciable since the party supported by the Afrikaner voters has always been overwhelmingly stronger in the rural areas.

Nevertheless, what has given Afrikaner parties their greatest advantage is the single-member constituency system itself, rather than the details of its application. This is due to the fact that their own strength has been efficiently spread throughout the rural constituencies and some urban ones, whereas a wastefully high proportion of their opponents' strength has always

18 Hahlo and Kahn, *op. cit.*, pp. 163-66.
19 Constitution, sections 42-45.

been concentrated in a few urban constituencies, which they win by vast margins. The Nationalist Party was able to come into power in 1948 primarily because of this, and to retain power in 1953, though on both occasions it was supported by fewer voters than the United Party.[20] Only a system of proportional representation would have prevented the return of minority governments; such a system was in fact provided in the first report of the National Convention, before being abandoned in the final report of May 1909.[21]

The parliamentary franchise has always been the most contentious political issue in South Africa.[22] The initial compromise, under which the franchise laws of the four colonies remained in force in the respective provinces of the Union, survived for two decades, during which there was a slight increase in the number and the proportion of the nonwhite voters in the Cape Province. In 1929 there were 167,184 whites, 25,618 Coloureds, and 15,780 Africans registered as voters in the Cape Province, by virtue of their capacity to sign their names and write their addresses and occupations, and of their earning £50 a year or occupying a house and land together worth £75 (exclusive of the value of any land occupied under African tribal tenure).

Then in 1930 and 1931 the number of white voters was more than doubled by the enfranchisement of white (but not nonwhite) women and the elimination of the educational and economic qualifications for white (but not nonwhite) men in the Cape Province; at the same time the qualifications became applied more stringently to nonwhite applicants.[23] The result was that in 1935 there were 382,103 whites, 24,793 Coloureds, and 10,628 Africans registered as voters in the Cape Province. In 1936 the African voters were removed from the ordinary

20 Carter, *op. cit.,* pp. 158-60.

21 Leonard M. Thompson, *The Unification of South Africa, 1902-1910* (Oxford: Clarendon Press, 1960) pp. 133-34, 236-42, 369-74.

22 Hahlo and Kahn, *op. cit.,* pp. 164-66; Leonard M. Thompson, "The Non-European Franchise in the Union of South Africa," in Sydney D. Bailey, ed., *Parliamentary Government in the Commonwealth* (London: Hansard Society, 1951) pp. 166-77.

23 Women's Enfranchisement Act, 1930; Franchise Laws Amendment Act, 1931.

voters' rolls in the Cape Province and given the right to elect
three whites to represent them in the House of Assembly; this
representation was abolished in 1960.[24]

The number of Coloured voters reached a peak of 54,134 in
1946 and then declined under stricter scrutiny of applicants,
until the Separate Representation of Voters Act, 1951, which
was validated and enforced in 1956, removed them from the
common roll and gave them the right to elect four whites to
represent them in the House of Assembly. Since then the number of Coloured voters has declined further, to 24,306 in 1959.
Meanwhile, in 1949 the white voters of South-West Africa were
given six seats in the House, delimited on the same principle
that applied in the Union proper, though they have about half
as many voters per member. In 1958 the voting age for whites
was reduced from twenty-one to eighteen.[25]

The republican constitution of 1961 made no substantial
changes in the franchise and electoral arrangements.[26] The
House of Assembly elected in October 1961 contains a hundred
and sixty members. All of them are whites. A hundred and fifty-
six are elected by white voters, four by Coloured voters, none
by Asians or Africans.

The constitution provides that there shall be a session of
Parliament each year and that the maximum duration of both
the Senate and the House of Assembly shall be five years. It
also empowers the State President to dissolve the House of
Assembly, or both the House of Assembly and the Senate, at
any time.[27] Most South African Parliaments have lasted nearly
the full five years, but the Parliament elected in 1958 was dissolved in 1961 to enable the government to take advantage of
the favorable electoral climate following the peaceful change
from a monarchy to a republic. There are also provisions to
help an incoming government obtain a majority in the Senate.
The eleven nominated Senators vacate their seats when the gov-

[24] Representation of Natives Act, 1936; Promotion of Bantu Self-Government Act, 1959.

[25] South-West Africa Affairs Amendment Act, 1949; Electoral Laws
Amendment Act, 1958.

[26] Constitution, sections 40-47.

[27] *Ibid.*, sections 26, 29-30, 47, 53.

ernment changes (including a change of Prime Minister within the same ruling party), and the Senate may be dissolved within a hundred and twenty days of the dissolution of the House of Assembly or the expiration of a Provincial Council.[28]

The quorum for the Senate is fifteen and for the House of Assembly thirty.[29] Each House elects from among its members a presiding officer, known as the President of the Senate or the Speaker of the House of Assembly, who has a casting vote but no deliberative vote.[30] A Minister or Deputy Minister may sit and speak, but not vote, in the House of which he is not a member.[31] In practice this last provision further accentuates the inferiority of the Senate. In the ministry formed after the general election in 1961, for example, there are sixteen members of the House of Assembly and only two of the Senate.

The standing rules of both Houses were originally derived from those of the British House of Commons, and in form it is British parliamentary procedure that still prevails. There is the same distinction between public, private, and hybrid bills. A bill goes through the same stages. It is introduced into either House first (normally the House of Assembly) and read a first time, when there is rarely any discussion. The second reading is the occasion for debate on the principle of the bill. That is followed by the committee stage, when the House resolves itself into a committee and goes through the bill clause by clause and considers amendments. Finally there is the third reading, when the bill as amended in committee is approved. It is then introduced into the other House, where it goes through the same stages.

Apart from legislation, the most important business of the House of Assembly takes place when the House, in Committee of Supply, considers the budgetary proposals of the Minister of Finance and scrutinizes the conduct of every department when its appropriation is reviewed. As in the United Kingdom, question time is an important chance for the opposition party: it occurs twice a week, when Ministers reply to questions, notice

28 *Ibid.*, section 33.
29 *Ibid.*, sections 38, 50.
30 *Ibid.*, sections 35-36, 39, 48-49, 51.
31 *Ibid.*, section 54 (4).

of which has been given in advance. There are strict time limits on nearly all speeches, so there is no chance of a filibuster in either House. When the majority party desires it may, by majority vote, accelerate decision on a motion in various ways: by continuing a debate throughout the night until the opposition has exhausted its members' time limits; by applying the closure to the debate; or by imposing in advance specific time limits for each stage of a bill's progress. These expedients have all been used with increasing frequency in recent years when the government has often proposed a vast legislative program and has been able to have most of it enacted.

The debating chambers are arranged on the British pattern, with "Government" and "Opposition" benches facing each other; unlike the British Parliament, each member has a seat for his exclusive use. Although standing committees and *ad hoc* committees of various sorts do exist, they do not perform the vital functions of committees in the U.S. Congress. Most important official business is conducted in open Parliament. Nevertheless, party discipline is even more strict in South Africa than in Britain, with the result that it is not in open Parliament, but in the closed party caucus that individual opinion is freely expressed. Once a caucus — consisting of the members of both Houses of a party — has decided what line to take on a particular issue, its members will rarely disagree in Parliament, because to do so would incur the grave risk of expulsion from the party, with the almost certain sequel of defeat in the next election.

The typical parliamentary debate is on a motion moved by a Minister, with the Government benches supporting it and the Opposition benches opposing; the objective is not so much to clarify the issues and come to a demonstrably wise decision, but rather to publicize and justify the decision that the caucus has already adopted. Debate is therefore often repetitious (in spite of rules against repetition) and replete with arguments *ad causam* and *ad hominem;* and the quality of South African parliamentary humor, unlike the quality of Shakespeare's mercy, is very strained. The acrimony of debate often gives the uninitiated the impression that the differences between the two parties are fundamental, which is not the case. In the House of Assembly elected in 1961 the only fundamental opposition to the Government benches came from the solitary member of the Progressive Party, Mrs. Helen Suzman, and the most revealing dialogue was that between her and the ministry.

THE SUPREME COURT

Judicial authority in South Africa is vested in a single superior court, known as the Supreme Court of South Africa, which consists of the Appellate Division, presided over by the Chief Justice, Provincial Divisions, presided over by Judge Presidents, and Local Divisions. The Appellate Division has appellate jurisdiction only; while the Provincial and Local Divisions are courts both of first instance and of appeal from inferior courts. The administration of the department of justice is under the control of a Cabinet Minister. Appointments to the bench are made by the State President on the recommendation of the Cabinet, as advised by the Minister of Justice. Originally, the number of judges was fixed by statute, but since 1949 the government has had complete discretion, and there are now about sixty judges and a number of acting judges. Appointments to the Local and Provincial Divisions are usually made from among the senior practicing advocates, but a few have been made from the public service. Nearly every appointment to the Appellate Division has been by promotion from another Division.

Once appointed a judge has effective security of tenure until he reaches the retiring age of seventy. He is removable by the State President only on receipt of an address from the Senate and the House of Assembly praying for the removal for misbehavior or incapacity; in actuality, no such address has been made and no removal has taken place in the Union or Republic. Though advocates who have been active in politics have often been appointed to the bench, the judiciary has a reputation for integrity and ability; the roll of Chief Justices, at any rate from Lord de Villiers (1910-1914) to Albert van de Sandt Centlivres (1950-1957), is distinguished. The judges have always tended to construe somewhat narrowly the powers that statutes have delegated to Ministers and, where possible, they have applied the equitable principles of the Roman-Dutch Law regardless of persons, though the scope for such action has been narrowed to a remarkable extent in recent years.[32]

The inferior courts are in lesser repute. They have very considerable powers and are staffed by magistrates and Bantu Commissioners who are invariably white men, who are appointed from the public service, who for the most part possess no legal training beyond the modest requirements for a public service examination, and who have administrative as well as judicial functions.[33]

A curious legacy of the colonial rivalries of 1908-1909 is that the Republic still has no single Capital. Pretoria is the basic seat of government and administration, but Parliament still meets a thousand miles away in Cape Town, which means that Ministers and many public servants spend several months each year in each place. The Appellate Division of the Supreme Court sits in Bloemfontein.[34]

POWERS OF PARLIAMENT

The most important section of the constitution concerns the powers of Parliament. It reads as follows:

> 59.   (1) Parliament shall be the sovereign legislative authority in and over the Republic, and shall have full power to make laws for the peace, order and good government of the Republic.
>
>   (2) No court of law shall be competent to enquire into or to pronounce upon the validity of any Act passed by Parliament, other than an Act which repeals or amends or purports to repeal or amend the. provisions of section *one hundred and eight* or *one hundred and eighteen.*

This section of the constitution is the outcome of a series of disputes extending over half a century. During most of that time controversy centered on the question of national status and the basic process was the elimination of British power from South Africa. Initially, South Africa marched in step with the other Dominions, especially Canada. South Africa was separately represented at the Versailles Peace Conference and in the League of Nations. In the report of the Imperial Conference of

32 *Ibid.*, sections 94-95; Hahlo and Kahn, *op. cit.*, pp. 249-67.
33 Hahlo and Kahn, *op. cit.*, pp. 270-75.
34 Constitution, sections 23, 27, 94 (3).

1926 the Dominions obtained a formal statement of their equality with the United Kingdom, and in the Statute of Westminster of 1931 some aspects of that statement were translated into British law.

Thereafter, however, South Africa took separate initiatives. In 1934 the Status of the Union Act provided that Acts of the British Parliament were not valid unless they had been enacted by the South African Parliament, and that the Governor-General must act on the advice of his South African Ministers. In 1950 the Privy Council Appeals Act removed the right, which was already obsolescent, of appeal from the Supreme Court to the British Privy Council. Finally, in 1961 the Republic of South Africa Constitution Act eliminated the British monarchy from the South African legal system. Some people had hoped that South Africa would remain a member of the Commonwealth; but in the face of sharp attacks upon her racial policies at a Commonwealth Prime Ministers' Conference in March 1961, Prime Minister Verwoerd withdrew his request for continued membership, so South Africa ceased to be a member of the Commonwealth when the Republic was inaugurated on May 31, 1961.

In eliminating the last legal vestiges of South Africa's colonial origins, the Afrikaner Nationalists displayed a combination of radicalism and legalism that is the distinctive mark of their performance in all controversies. During the 1950's there was a great struggle concerning the structure of the South African Parliament and the powers of the Supreme Court over South African legislation. This struggle, discussed in the succeeding pages, is a most instructive example of the South African political process.

From the first, the greater part of the South African constitution was fully flexible. Most of its sections could be amended by the ordinary legislative process of bare majorities in the House of Assembly and the Senate and the assent of the Governor-General. There was nothing in it analogous to a Bill of Rights restraining the legislature from infringing the liberties of the individual.

Initially there were three types of exceptions to this general flexibility. Two of these — the complex of imperial controls and a few provisions that were specially safeguarded for the limited period of time in which they were to operate — had lapsed by the end of 1931. There remained the third type of exception: safeguards for section 35 of the constitution, which entitled qualified nonwhites as well as whites to vote in parliamentary and Provincial Council elections in the Cape Province, section 137, which placed English and Dutch on the same footing as the official languages of the Union, and section 152, the amending section itself. These three sections could only be amended by an act passed in a joint sitting of both Houses of Parliament and, at the third reading, agreed to by two-thirds of the total membership of both Houses.

Before 1948 South African governments complied with these provisions when necessary. For example, when section 137 was amended in 1925, to make Afrikaans an official language in place of Dutch, and when section 35 was amended in 1936, to remove the Cape Province African voters from the common roll, the unicameral, two-thirds majority procedure was used.[35] The Nationalist government which came into power in 1948 wished to remove the Cape Coloured voters from the common roll, although it did not possess a two-thirds majority. It found that the balance of legal opinion, in Britain as well as South Africa, held that since the enactment of the Statute of Westminster the safeguards had lost their legal efficacy and the South African Parliament, like the British Parliament, was competent to adopt any procedure it thought fit to pass valid legislation on any topic. Indeed, in *Ndlwana* v. *Hofmeyr N.O.,* 1937, Acting Chief Justice Stratford had declared that "the procedure expressed or implied in the South Africa Act is . . . at the mercy of Parliament like anything else." [36]

Consequently in 1951 a Separate Representation of Voters Act removing the Cape Coloured voters from the common roll was passed through both Houses of Parliament by the ordinary bicameral procedure. But when this Act was challenged in the Supreme Court, the Appellate Division, in *Harris* v. *Minister of the Interior,* 1952 (the *Vote* case), decided that to legislate with

[35] Official Languages of the Union Act, 1925; Representation of Natives Act, 1936.

[36] 1937 A.D. 229, p. 238.

effect in the fields covered by the entrenched sections the South African Parliament was bound to comply with the requirements laid down in them. The Appellate Division therefore struck down the Separate Representation of Voters Act as invalid because it had not been enacted in the prescribed manner.[37]

Parliament then passed another act by the ordinary bicameral procedure, setting up a High Court consisting of the members of Parliament, and empowering it by a bare majority to review any judgments of the Appellate Division of the Supreme Court that invalidated acts of Parliament.[38] The High Court of Parliament then met and reversed the recent judgment of the Appellate Division. However, the act creating it was in turn declared invalid by the Appellate Division in *Minister of the Interior* v. *Harris,* 1952 (the *High Court* case) for the reason that the High Court was Parliament in disguise, and not the protection implicit in the constitution.[39]

After some delay, during which the government twice tried and failed to get a two-thirds majority in a joint sitting, in 1955 Parliament by the ordinary bicameral procedure passed an act requiring a quorum of eleven judges in the Appellate Division when the validity of an act of Parliament was in question, and another act reconstituting the Senate in such a way as to give the government a two-thirds majority in a joint sitting.[40] The government then made the necessary additions to the Appellate Division, which had previously consisted of only six judges, and dissolved the Senate creating a new one in terms of the Senate Act. In 1956 an act amending the South Africa Act was passed by the unicameral, two-thirds majority procedure, revalidating the 1951 Separate Representation of Voters Act, disentrenching section 35 of the South Africa Act, and denying the courts the power to inquire into the validity of any act of Parliament, save only an act affecting the equal status of the two official languages.

This South Africa Act Amendment Act was then challenged

37 1952 (2) S.A. 429 (A.D.).
38 High Court of Parliament Act, 1952.
39 1952 (4) S.A. 769 (A.D.).
40 Appellate Division Quorum Act, 1955; Senate Act, 1955.

in the Supreme Court, in *Collins* v. *Minister of the Interior,* 1957, but the Appellate Division declared it valid by a ten-to-one majority. The majority held that though the purpose of the Senate Act was to provide the government with its two-thirds majority, it was valid because it did not tamper with the entrenched sections, while the South Africa Act Amendment Act was valid because it was passed by a two-thirds majority in a joint sitting.[41] Thus, after a struggle lasting nearly six years, the government had successfully circumvented the safeguard provided for the Cape Coloured people.[42]

The position established by the 1956 legislation is maintained in the 1961 constitution. The surviving entrenched sections of the South Africa Act appear in the new constitution as section 108, which makes English and Afrikaans the official languages of the Republic, and section 118, which empowers Parliament to repeal or alter any of the provisions of the constitution, provided that no repeal or alteration of sections 108 or 118 shall be valid unless passed by the Senate and the House of Assembly sitting together, and at the third reading agreed to by two-thirds of the total membership of the Senate and the House of Assembly.[43] The substance of the South Africa Act Amendment Act, 1956, is taken over into section 59, quoted on page 70. Even the safeguard for the official languages can now have little practical value, except that of causing a slight delay, for what has been done once could be done again.

The outcome of the elimination of imperial controls, the re-

[41] 1957 (1) S.A. 552 (A.D.).

[42] For reviews of this legal struggle see B. Beinart, "Parliament and the Courts," *Butterworth's South African Law Review* (1954) pp. 134-81; D. V. Cowen, *Parliamentary Sovereignty and the Entrenched Sections of the South Africa Act* (Cape Town: Juta, 1951), and "Legislature and Judiciary," *Modern Law Review* (July 1952) pp. 277-96, and (July 1953) pp. 273-98; Hahlo and Kahn, *op. cit.,* pp. 146-63; and Geoffrey Marshall, *Parliamentary Sovereignty and the Commonwealth* (Oxford: Clarendon Press, 1957) chapter xi.

[43] Since the Republic of South Africa Constitution Act, 1961, was enacted by the ordinary bicameral procedure, it is arguable that sections 137 and 152 of the South Africa Act, 1909, which were only repealable by the joint sitting procedure, have not been repealed. Even if this is so, the political realities are no different. See Kahn, *op. cit.,* p. 31.

duction of the powers of the Senate and the constitutional struggle of 1951-1957 is that the party with a majority in the House of Assembly has virtually the same plenary powers in South Africa as the party with a majority in the House of Commons has in Britain. Either body has the legal power to transform any or every institution in the state, brushing aside any opposition in the Upper House after an interval of one year. Neither the "unwritten" constitution of the United Kingdom nor the "written" constitution of South Africa provides effective legal impediments to such action.

Nevertheless, the extralegal differences between the two cases are substantial. The House of Commons is elected by the mass of the British adult population, regardless of race; the House of Assembly is elected by a racial oligarchy comprising one-fifth of the total population of South Africa. Moreover, though political passions often run high in Great Britain, the party with a majority in the House of Commons continues to recognize the principal conventions that have developed over the years, if only because it would suffer politically if it ignored them. On the other hand, the party having a majority in the House of Assembly since 1948 has been able with impunity to ignore convention on several occasions, largely because the conventions themselves are not a local product, but an importation from Britain. In British practice the doctrine of parliamentary supremacy masks limitations upon the powers of the government of the day which are scarcely less effective for being extralegal; in South African practice the doctrine has made Parliament little more than a convenient mechanism for giving legislative effect to the will of the caucus of the ruling party. The British system has been perverted in South Africa, and what remains is the empty shell of responsible parliamentary government.

LOCAL GOVERNMENT

South Africa is a unitary state — that is to say, the central government is supreme over all the regional and local authorities. Of these the most important have hitherto been the provinces, which coincide with the pre-Union colonies. Their system of government, which has not altered greatly since 1910, is set out in Part VI of the 1961 constitution.[44] It includes several original features that are of some interest to the student of government, but can only be dealt with summarily here.

The chief executive officer of a province is an Administrator, appointed by the central government. He is chairman, with both a deliberative and a casting vote, of an Executive Committee, the other four members of which are elected by the Provincial Council. Formerly the election was by proportional representation, the National Convention having assumed that party politics would not enter into provincial government. In fact, the national parties became involved in provincial elections from the very beginning, with the result that in the Transvaal and the Cape Province the Executive Committees always included members of more than one party, and the same was often the case in Natal and the Orange Free State. This awkward situation was terminated in 1962; since then a party with a majority in a Provincial Council has been able to elect all four of the elected members on the Executive Committee.[45] Both the Administrator and the Executive Committee hold office for a fixed term of five years. Since the Administrator is appointed by the central government and neither he nor the elected members of the Executive Committee are dismissable by the Provincial Council, the system of responsible government does not exist in the provinces.

A Provincial Council contains as many members as the province has in the House of Assembly, with a minimum of twenty-five. They are elected in single-member electoral divisions by the voters who possess the parliamentary franchise, for a fixed period of five years. The provincial electoral divisions correspond with the parliamentary ones in the Transvaal and the Cape Province, but in Natal and the Orange Free State, which have always had fewer than twenty-five members in the House of Assembly, the delimitation commissioners make separate delimitations for provincial purposes. When the African voters were removed from the common roll in 1936, they were given the right to elect two white provincial councillors in the Cape

[44] Sections 66-93. Hahlo and Kahn, *op. cit.*, pp. 175-82.
[45] Provincial Executive Committees Act, 1962.

Province, but those seats were abolished in 1960.[46] When the Coloured voters were removed from the common roll in 1956, they too were given the right to elect two white provincial councillors in the Cape Province, and these seats still exist.[47] So long as there were African or Coloured voters on the common roll, nonwhites were eligible for election to the Cape Provincial Council, and one African and two Coloured men were, in fact, elected. Neither the provincial councillors who represented Africans, nor those representing Coloured voters have had the right to take part in the election of Senators — the one function of the Provincial Councils that affects the composition of Parliament.

Provincial Councils have the power to make ordinances in a number of fields specified in the constitution. The most significant fields are direct taxation, hospitals, municipal and other local institutions, local (as distinct from national) roads and other local public works, and the school education of whites (as distinct from the education of nonwhites and as distinct from university, technical, and adult education). Within these fields provincial legislation is subject to the approval of the central government. Moreover, Parliament may freely legislate, expressly or implicitly, in any of these fields, and in the event of a conflict, acts of Parliament always prevail over provincial ordinances. Parliament may at any time restrict the competence of the Provincial Councils or change the system of provincial government.[48] In fact, the powers of the provinces have diminished over the years. The central government has narrowed their taxing powers,[49] it has taken from them the control of African and

[46] Representation of Natives Act, 1936; Promotion of Bantu Self-Government Act, 1959 (effective on June 30, 1960).

[47] South Africa Act Amendment Act, 1956, and Separate Representation of Voters Amendment Act, 1956, validating and amending the Separate Representation of Voters Act, 1951.

[48] The constitution still includes a provision that Parliament shall not alter the boundaries of a province, nor abolish any Provincial Council, nor abridge its legislative powers, except upon petition from the Provincial Council concerned (section 114); but this provision has no legal efficacy.

[49] E.g., by the Financial Relations Act, 1913; the Financial Relations Consolidation and Amendment Act, 1945; and the Financial Relations Amendment Act, 1957.

Coloured school education,[50] and it has established the basic legal patterns of urban life.[51] In addition, the provinces have always been handicapped by an insufficiency of revenue for the performance of their obligations and they are now heavily dependent on subsidies from the central government.

At this stage the *de facto* status of South-West Africa, with its *de jure* status in the eyes of the South African government, approximates that of a province, with similar institutions. South-West Africa, conquered in World War I by South African forces which defeated the German, became a C Class Mandate under the League of Nations, which meant that South Africa was entitled to administer the territory as an integral part of the Union, and undertook to "promote to the utmost the material and moral well-being and the social progress of the inhabitants of the Territory," to make annual reports to the Council of the League of Nations, and to accept the jurisdiction of the Permanent Court of International Justice in the event of any dispute concerning the interpretation of the mandate.

Since World War II the South African government has contended that following the dissolution of the League of Nations in 1946 there have been no legal limitations upon the competence of the government of South Africa over South-West Africa.[52] The Territory has an Administrator and an Executive Committee like a province, and a Legislative Assembly elected by the white inhabitants. The South-West African voters have also been represented in the South African Parliament since 1949. In 1960 the white population numbered 73,464, of whom about two-thirds speak Afrikaans, one-quarter German, and the rest English. The 452,540 nonwhite inhabitants have no political representation.[53]

---

[50] Bantu Education Act, 1953; Coloured Persons Education Act, 1963. The education of Asians was still in the hands of the provinces in 1965, but was expected soon to be taken over by the central government.

[51] E.g., Group Areas Act, 1950, and its many amendments.

[52] The issue was before the International Court of Justice in 1965.

[53] The principal South African laws concerning South-West Africa are the South-West Africa Affairs Act, 1922, and its amendments of 1925 and 1949. For South African plans for South-West Africa see the *Report*

The Nationalist Party now has majorities in the Provincial Councils of the Transvaal, the Cape Province and the Orange Free State, and in the Legislative Assembly of South-West Africa, and consequently all the members of their Executive Committees are Nationalists. In Natal, on the other hand, the Administrator is a Nationalist nominee and the other members of the Executive Committee are members of the United Party. This creates some minor embarrassment to the Nationalist government. In particular it means that the educational system for white children in Natal is out of step with the system in the other provinces. Even in this field the central government is successfully working towards uniformity.[54] The impotence of the Natal electorate significantly to affect the main trends in national life has been demonstrated time after time — most recently in 1960, when the Natal Provincial Council passed a resolution calling for the entrenchment of a Bill of Rights in a rigid constitution at the time of the change to a republic, and the resolution was ignored by the central government.[55]

BANTU AUTHORITIES

Another system of local government, which may develop into something more far-reaching, has emerged alongside the provincial system. The South Africa Act vested the control and administration of "native affairs" in the Governor-General-in-Council and gave him the wide powers over Africans that were previously possessed by the colonial governors. These powers were defined and enlarged by the Union Parliament and carried over into the republican constitution, with the result that the President of the Republic is the "Supreme Chief" over all the African inhabitants, and has unfettered powers to legislate by proclamation and government notice for the Africans in the Bantu Areas, and wide powers of summary arrest and detention of Africans without judicial intervention.[56] In practice these

---

of the Commission of Enquiry into South-West Africa (3 vols., Pretoria: Government Printer, 1964).

54 See chapter 4, p. 101.

55 Kahn, *op. cit.*, p. 2.

56 Native Administration Act, 1927; Republic of South Africa Constitution Act, 1961, section 111. Under the 1927 Act proclamations must be

powers are exercised by the Minister and the Department of Bantu Administration and Development, by white Bantu Affairs Commissioners, and by "Bantu Authorities."

The predecessors of the Bantu Authorities were councils containing both tribal and western ingredients, which originated and took deepest root in the African reserves of the Cape Province.[57] Since 1948 the councils have been superseded by Bantu Authorities, which approximate the tribal system more closely, but with profound modifications created by the omnipresence of governmental controls.[58] The Bantu Authorities form hierarchies, from Tribal Authorities, through District (in the Transkei only) and Regional Authorities, to Territorial Authorities.

At every level the head of an Authority is a chief, and all chiefs are appointed according to local African custom, subject to a veto by the government and deposition by the government. In the years 1955 to 1958 inclusive, thirty-four chiefs and headmen were deposed.[59] The government also pays the chiefs — partly in proportion to the numbers of their taxpaying followers and partly in the form of bonuses dependent upon favorable reports from the white Commissioners.[60] The other members of Bantu Authorities are chiefs, or tribal councillors appointed by chiefs, or government nominees, except in the Transkei where a minority of the members of the Tribal and District Authorities are elected directly or indirectly by taxpayers, subject to a government veto. Bantu Authorities are responsible for law and order in their areas and have varying powers of local taxation and legislation, subject always to government approval.

This system is now nearing completion. By late 1963 there were 432 Tribal Authorities, 26 District Authorities, 60 Regional Authorities, and 6 Territorial Authorities. The latter were for the Xhosa of the Transkei, the Xhosa of the Ciskei,

---

tabled in the Senate and the House of Assembly, which may compel their repeal or amendment, but they have never done so.

[57] Their origin lay in the Cape Colony Glen Grey Act, 1894.

[58] Bantu Authorities Act, 1951; Promotion of Bantu Self-Government Act, 1959. On the Bantu Authorities system see Hahlo and Kahn, *op. cit.*, pp. 798-802, and *Survey of Race Relations*, 1951ff. See the map on p. 42 for the location of the Bantu Areas.

[59] *House of Assembly Debates*, 1959, col. 324.

[60] *Ibid.*, 1963, cols. 3870-73; *Survey of Race Relations*, 1959-60, p. 109.

the Tswana of the Western Transvaal and northeastern Cape Province, the Northern Sotho of the Northern Transvaal, the Tsonga of the Northern Transvaal, and the Venda of the Northern Transvaal.[61] It is the government's aim soon to create one or more Territorial Authorities for the Zulu of Natal, and perhaps others for the Southern Sotho of the Orange Free State and the Swazi of the Transvaal and Natal. These tribal communities are officially regarded as separate African "national units" and there is no intention to create a linking Authority at the apex.[62] The government has appointed Commissioners-General to supervise these "emergent national communities."

As mentioned earlier, the Bantu Areas in which this administrative system has been established are scattered lands which, viewed in isolation, are economic backwaters but, viewed in the broader context, are reservoirs of labor for the white farmers and industrialists of South Africa and a pretext for discriminating against Africans.[63] At the present time fewer than 40 percent of the African inhabitants of the Republic are physically present in the Bantu Areas and many of those who are absent have no connection with the Bantu Areas at all. Moreover, even in the Bantu Areas tribal and linguistic affiliations do not correspond precisely with geographical boundaries,[64] while the Southern Sotho, the Tswana and the Swazi are scattered around the peripheries of Lesotho, Bechuanaland and Swaziland, respectively, which are outside the control of the Republic.

THE TRANSKEI

The Transkei is the nearest approach to a homogeneous Bantu Area and it is there that the Bantu Authorities system was most rapidly developed, because it was built upon the foundation of a council system dating back to the 19th century.

[61] *Survey of Race Relations,* 1963, pp. 107-10; *House of Assembly Debates,* 1963, cols. 1584-86.

[62] At the apex of the previous system there was a Natives Representative Council, which was created by the Representation of Natives Act, 1936, and abolished by the Bantu Authorities Act, 1951.

[63] See pp. 40-41, 47-48.

[64] Among each of the "emergent national communities" there are large minorities who speak other African languages.

Nevertheless, the imposition of the Bantu Authorities met with serious opposition in the eastern part of the Transkei, where a revolt broke out in 1959.[65] Chiefs and councillors were killed and their huts were burned; meetings convened by the government were boycotted; taxes were not paid. Late in 1960 the government issued a proclamation for the entire Transkei — imposing severe restrictions on entry, prohibiting meetings of more than ten Africans without the consent of a Bantu Affairs Commissioner, and giving the police and the chiefs extraordinary powers of arrest and banishment.[66] By the end of 1961 the revolt had been suppressed by the police, assisted by chiefs' "home guards," by detachments of the South African army, and by aircraft and helicopters. Unrest continued and the restrictive proclamation remained in force in the Transkei throughout 1963, 1964 and 1965.

This is the Bantu Area in which the government decided to make an ambitious experiment. In December 1961 after consulting the Prime Minister and the Department of Bantu Administration and Development in Pretoria, a committee of the Transkei Territorial Authority, under the chairmanship of Kaiser Matanzima, chief of the Emigrant Tembu tribe, drafted a constitution for the Transkei and had it approved by the Transkeian Territorial Authority in the face of opposition from Sabata Dalindyebo, paramount chief of the Tembu, who wanted the Transkei to become a multi-racial state with equal rights for all its inhabitants and with a wholly elective lower House in a bicameral legislature, and Victor Poto, paramount chief of the West Pondo, who wanted the Transkei to have greater autonomy. Their opposition was hampered by the ban on public meetings and by the astute conduct of the chairman of the Territorial Authority.[67] In 1963 the constitution was enacted by Parliament in much the same form as it had been approved by the Territorial Authority.[68]

65 *Survey of Race Relations*, 1959-60, pp. 39-48, 1961, pp. 42-52, and 1962, pp. 11-19.

66 Proclamation R400, dated November 30, 1960, amended by Proclamation R413, dated December 14, 1960.

67 *Survey of Race Relations*, 1962, pp. 77-88.

68 Transkei Constitution Act, 1963. In the parliamentary debates on the bill, see especially the second reading speeches by the Minister of Bantu

The Transkei constitution embodies the language and the symbolism of democracy and self-government. The Transkei is a "self-governing territory within the Republic of South Africa," with its own flag, its own official language,[69] its own anthem, its own "Cabinet" and "Legislative Assembly," and with adult suffrage. It includes the previously existing Bantu Areas of the Eastern Cape Province, between the Kei River and the Natal border, but no white-owned farms (e.g., in East Griqualand), nor the several townships other than Umtata, nor the harbor of Port St. Johns. The Legislative Assembly consists of the four paramount chiefs and sixty chiefs of the Transkei, among whom vacancies are filled by the Regional Authorities subject to the confirmation of the State President,[70] and forty-five adult citizens of the Transkei elected by the adult citizens. Citizens are defined as all Africans born or domiciled in the Transkei and all Xhosa-speaking Africans, wherever they may live in the Republic, who are not domiciled in other Bantu Areas. Non-Africans may not become citizens. The Cabinet consists of a Chief Minister and five other Ministers, elected by the Legislative Assembly.

All existing laws remain in force in the Transkei except insofar as they are repugnant to the Transkei constitution.[71] Bills

---

Administration and Development and by Helen Suzman: *House of Assembly Debates,* 1963, cols. 2226-47 and 2379-90.

[69] The language is Xhosa, but Afrikaans and English are also official languages in the Transkei. This provision, being an amendment to section 108 of the 1961 constitution, was authorized by a special act passed by a two-thirds majority in a joint sitting of the Senate and the House of Assembly — the Constitution Amendment Act, 1963.

[70] Stated thus in section 45. Presumably the republican government retains its power of dismissing chiefs under section 73(v) — " 'Chief' means a person duly appointed or recognized as a chief in terms of . . . the Native Administration Act, 1927. . . ."—and section 65 (see fn. 71).

[71] This is an important provision, especially since the President has the power to determine all cases of ambiguity:

65. (1) Subject to the provisions of this Act, all laws which immediately prior to the commencement of this Act were in force in . . . [the Transkei] . . . shall continue in force until repealed or amended by the competent authority.

(2) If any provision of this Act or any other law is found to be ambiguous . . . the State President may, by Proclamation in the *Gazette,* determine the extent to which . . . such other law shall

passed by the Transkei Legislative Assembly are submitted through the office of the Commissioner-General and the Minister of Bantu Administration and Development to the State President, who may give his assent or refer them back for further consideration. The Legislative Assembly may pass bills on specified subjects, of which the most important are the direct taxation of Transkei citizens, African education, land and agriculture, and local institutions and public works. The list may be extended by the State President by proclamation, with the approval of the Senate and the House of Assembly, but (unless the Transkei constitution is amended by the republican parliament) the Legislative Assembly may at no time pass bills dealing with a long list of subjects, including: the establishment or control of military or quasi-military forces; the manufacture of arms or ammunition; postal, telegraph, telephone, television or radio services; railways, harbors, national roads or civil aviation; currency, public loans or banking; foreign relations; and the amendment of the Transkei constitution.

Beneath the liberal phraseology of this document, the Transkei acquires a status similar to that of a province of the Republic; and the structure of the Transkei institutions seems to be designed to maintain the ascendancy of the chiefs while admitting a minority elective element and, above all, to give a new plausibility to the old pretext for discriminating against Africans in the "White Areas" of the Republic by the expedients of denying the four hundred white inhabitants of the Transkei a say in local government,[72] and attaching most of the Xhosa-speaking Africans of the Republic to a territory that many of them have never seen.

The constitution in no way detracts from the sovereignty of the Parliament over the Transkei, nor (apparently) from the capacity of the State President to legislate by proclamation for

apply . . . in any manner he may deem necessary to remove the ambiguity. . . .

72. All laws which in their application to the Transkei may be repugnant to or inconsistent with the provisions of this Act are hereby repealed to the extent of such repugnancy or inconsistency.

[72] The white inhabitants of the Bantu Areas of the Transkei will continue to participate in the political life of the Cape Province.

the Transkei Africans. Indeed, the proclamation banning public meetings remained in force while the first elections were held late in 1963. Additionally, since the Transkei has no more than a backward rural economy, and all investment in the Transkei by non-Africans has to be channelled through a public corporation established and controlled by the government of the Republic,[73] the Transkei continues to be utterly dependent upon that government for subsidies for economic development.

Towards the end of 1963 the Transkei constitution came into force. The Legislative Assembly elected Chief Kaiser Matanzima Prime Minister by 54 votes (including a majority of the chiefs) to 49 votes (including a majority of the elected members) for Paramount Chief Victor Poto. During 1964 Matanzima founded the National Independence Party, which supported the republican government's policy of separate development, and Poto founded the Democratic Party, with a policy of democracy and multi-racialism throughout South Africa. The senior officials in the Transkei Civil Service, including the administrative heads of the six departments, are whites, who are seconded by the government of the Republic.[74]

The Transkei constitution may be compared with the constitution for a colony under a system of dyarchy, in which the metropolitan power retains control over everything that is vital, while allowing the indigenous people the qualified management of a limited range of local affairs, mainly through the medium of chiefs, whom the metropolitan power can influence in many overt and covert ways.

COLOURED AND ASIAN COUNCILS

The government is creating another system of local administration for the Coloured and Asian inhabitants of the Republic. The Asians own no large blocks of land. Though some Coloured people have exclusive occupation of several reserves, with a total area of about four million acres, most of this land is in the extremely arid northwestern part of the Cape Province and these reserves are occupied by only 2 percent of the Col-

[73] Bantu Investment Corporation Act, 1959.
[74] *Survey of Race Relations*, 1964, pp. 140-53.

oured population of South Africa.[75] Consequently, there are no territorial bases, like the Transkei, Zululand and some of the other Bantu Areas, where a significant proportion of the Coloured and Asian peoples can administer their own local affairs, so that the government finds it even more difficult to discover methods of applying apartheid or separate development to the Coloured and Asian peoples than to the Africans. Nevertheless, the government has been establishing separate institutions for both these groups.

The process is further advanced for the Coloured people than for the Asians. For some years there has been a Department of Coloured Affairs, which now administers many of the public services for the Coloured people including the educational and welfare services, though this group remains subject to other departments of the central government and to the provincial and municipal authorities regarding many important aspects of their lives. In 1959 the government established a Council for Coloured Affairs — an advisory body of fifteen Coloured men nominated by the government and twelve Coloured men elected by the Coloured parliamentary voters in the Cape Province. When the elections to this Council took place they were boycotted by most Coloured organizations and the twelve elected seats were obtained by conservatives who were returned unopposed.[76]

In 1964 Parliament passed a new law on the subject.[77] Its application means the replacement of the Council for Coloured Affairs by a Coloured Representative Council, with sixteen nominated members and thirty members elected by the Coloured men and women twenty-one years of age, voting in single-member constituencies. This Representative Council is to form a link between the government and the Coloured people, and to give advice to the government when asked to do so. The law authorizes the President at a later stage to delegate to the Coloured Representative Council legislative powers in fields such as local government, education, welfare and pensions; however, before the Council may discuss any proposal it must

75 *Ibid.*, 1961, pp. 138-41, 1962, pp. 126-28, and 1963, pp. 152-53.
76 *Ibid.*, 1958-59, p. 153, 1959-60, p. 132.
77 Coloured Persons' Representative Council Act, 1964.

have been approved by the Minister of Coloured Affairs and the Minister of Finance, and before a proposal becomes law it will also require the assent of the President. There will also be an Executive Committee, consisting of four members chosen by the Council and a fifth, nominated by the government, who will be chairman.

Similar arrangements are foreshadowed for the Asian people. A Department of Indian Affairs was created in 1961, and by 1964 it was responsible for Indian higher education and for Indian welfare and pension services. During 1964 the Minister of Indian Affairs appointed a consultative Indian Council and in time it is expected that this body, too, will be replaced by an Indian Representative Council, similar to the Coloured Representative Council provided for in the 1964 law. The government does not intend to give the Indians any representation in Parliament.[78]

Other laws passed in 1962 and 1963 have empowered the government to establish Bantu urban councils in some urban locations, consisting of elected majorities and minorities composed of representatives of tribal chiefs, with advisory powers; and also consultative or management committees of Coloured people and Indians in Coloured and Indian reserves and group areas. By 1965 several of these bodies had come into being.[79]

One effect of these changes in the administration of nonwhites is that the powers of the old hierarchy of provincial and municipal authorities are being undermined. Originally the provincial and municipal authorities were responsible for the conduct of specified local affairs of all the inhabitants of defined localities. Now they have been stripped of many of their powers over nonwhites, some of which have been allocated to departments of the central government and others of which have been delegated to new subordinate authorities, manned by nonwhites. Ultimately, if the logic of present policy is fulfilled, below the central government there will be a series of

[78] *Survey of Race Relations,* 1961, pp. 141-42, 1962, pp. 120-22, 1963, pp. 159-62, 1964, pp. 201-204.

[79] *Ibid.,* 1962, pp. 122-25, 1963, pp. 155-57, 1964, pp. 188, 204-208; Group Areas Amendment Act, 1962; Rural Coloured Areas Act, 1963; Bantu Laws Amendment Act, 1964.

separate structures, each consisting of members of one racial group elected by the adult members of that group and possessing some responsibilities for the affairs of that group. They would include white provincial and municipal councils,[80] African Bantustans and urban councils, and Coloured and Asian representative councils and consultative and management committees.

There are still many problems to be solved before such a system can be perfected. For example, it is not yet clear to what extent the provincial authorities will continue to exercise power over nonwhites. The Prime Minister has also hinted that eventually there may be some sort of body in which representatives of the white, the Coloured, the Asian, and the several African authorities would consult with one another, but these hints have been extremely vague.[81]

In whatever ways these problems are resolved and these hints are translated into reality, one point cannot be emphasized too strongly: unless there is a fundamental change of policy, absolute legal power over the entire Republic will continue to be exercised by the central government of South Africa. Parliament retains sovereign legal power to legislate as it wishes on any topic over any area and for any community in the country, and it is accustomed to using its power with the utmost vigor. This means that notwithstanding the proliferation of subordinate authorities, including the Transkei "Bantustan," there is in all South Africa only one political process of vital significance: the process that determines the composition of Parlia-

[80] The municipal councils in the Transvaal and the Orange Free State have always been composed exclusively of whites, elected exclusively by whites. In Natal perhaps five thousand Coloured and Asian people are entitled to vote in municipal elections. Nonwhites are no longer being added to these electoral rolls, so that when the present Coloured and Asian voters have died only whites will remain. In the Cape Province, Coloured owners and occupiers of urban property, equally with whites, still possess the municipal franchise and the right to be elected to municipal councils, and in the 1963 municipal elections seven Coloured people were elected to the Cape Town City Council. But these vestiges of Cape liberalism are likely to be eliminated by Parliament in the near future. *Survey of Race Relations,* 1961, pp. 125-28, 1962, pp. 122-26, and 1963, pp. 157-58.

[81] *Star,* weekly edition, January 25, 1964.

ment — a process from which all nonwhites are wholly excluded, the only exception being that some Coloured people elect four whites to the House of Assembly.

POLITICAL PARTIES

Since the parliamentary electorate has always been overwhelmingly white, South African political divisions have been divisions within the white community, its basic historic and cultural cleavage being between the Afrikaners and the South Africans of British descent. There have been three main types of political parties: parties led by Afrikaners, consisting almost exclusively of Afrikaners, and dedicated to the promotion of the interests of Afrikaners; parties led by British South Africans, consisting almost wholly of British South Africans, and dedicated to the promotion of their interests; and middle parties, comprising both Afrikaners and British South Africans and dedicated to the reduction of the historic tensions between the two groups and the creation of a united white South African nation.

Because the British South Africans have always been a minority within the white South African population and have been hampered by an unfavorable demographic distribution and by unfavorable delimitations, no British party has ever looked as though it would obtain a parliamentary majority. The main struggle has, therefore, been between Afrikaner parties and middle parties. British voters have often had no effective alternative to supporting a middle party, whereas Afrikaners have normally had an effective choice between a middle party and an Afrikaner party. Politics have thus been determined primarily by the conduct of the Afrikaner voters. In effect an Afrikaner party has been able to prevail when it has been supported by about two-thirds of the Afrikaner voters, while a middle party has required the support of at least a third of the Afrikaners as well as virtually all the British voters.

The political history of South Africa since 1910 falls into two periods, each of which started with middle party government and developed into Afrikaner government. The first was terminated by the great depression and the second is still in progress. From 1910 to 1924 the dominant party was the South African Party (SAP) — a middle party led by Louis Botha (died 1919) and J. C. Smuts, Afrikaners whose policy was to create a united white South African nation through the gradual fusion of the two stocks, to develop South Africa's material resources within the capitalist framework, to advance South Africa's autonomy within the evolving British Commonwealth, and to cooperate with Britain in international affairs. Initially the official opposition was the Unionist Party — a British party led by L. S. Jameson; in 1913 the first Afrikaner party was founded by J. B. M. Hertzog, who feared that the policy of the Botha government (of which he had formerly been a member) would result in the virtual absorption of the Afrikaners by the British, and the subordination of the interests of the white urban workers to the capitalists, and of South Africa to Britain.

Assisted by the Afrikaner reaction against South Africa's participation in World War I (which included a small-scale rebellion), Hertzog's Nationalist Party (NP) whittled more and more Afrikaners away from the SAP in successive elections. The SAP became increasingly dependent on British support, so that it formed a coalition with the Unionist Party in 1915 and absorbed it in 1921. By that time the basic Afrikaner party–middle party alignment was being distorted by the existence of a white Labour Party, consisting largely of urban workers of British descent who were concerned about obtaining protection both from management and from nonwhite competition. The SAP government supported management in industrial disturbances on the Witwatersrand, so that the NP was able to obtain the cooperation of the Labour Party and form with it a coalition government in 1924. In 1929, however, the NP won a clear majority of the seats in the House of Assembly and if the depression had not followed, the NP might have maintained its control indefinitely.

As it was, the depression threw South African politics — like the politics of many other countries — into a state of confusion. The government lost support largely because of factors beyond its control, but also because of its doctrinaire and inexpedient decision to remain on the gold standard after Britain had left it. In the 1933 election the NP lost seats for the first time since its foundation, though it remained the strongest party in the House of Assembly. By that time, however, Hertzog had reached the conclusion that the *raison d'être* for an exclusive Afrikaner party had disappeared. He believed that the protective legislation his government had sponsored had ensured that the Afrikaner people could cooperate with the British South Africans without endangering their cultural identity, and that it was desirable that the two streams of the white South African nation should cooperate to protect themselves against the Africans. Accordingly, in 1933 the SAP and the first NP formed a coalition government and in 1934 they fused, to found the United Party (UP), with Hertzog as Prime Minister and Smuts as Deputy Prime Minister.

At its birth the UP had a large majority in Parliament. However, a small British group, led by Colonel C. F. Stallard, refused to follow Smuts and formed the Dominion Party, while a somewhat larger number of Afrikaners, under D. F. Malan, rejected following Hertzog and became a second Nationalist Party (NP). Malan aimed at preserving the identity of the Afrikaner people, pure and unsullied by British influences, and by constitutional means to achieve an Afrikaner domination of South Africa, thus completing the work that, however well he had begun it, Hertzog was deemed to have compromised by the fusion.

World War II had effects similar to World War I. After the war debate in the House of Assembly, Smuts formed a coalition government of the diminished UP and the Labour and Dominion Parties, all of which increased their strength in the 1943 election. For a time the Afrikaners who were opposed to South Africa's participation in the war were fragmented between the NP, which pursued a constitutional course, and several lesser organizations such as the *Ossewa Brandwag* and the New Order, which prepared for the expected Nazi victory. Malan applied himself doggedly to the task of uniting the fragments and winning Afrikaners away from the UP, while the UP absorbed the Dominion Party as the SAP had previously absorbed the Unionist Party.

The 1948 election was decisive. It enabled the NP to form a government in alliance with the small Afrikaner Party. In that election the last Independent members disappeared from the House of Assembly, and soon afterward third parties were virtually eliminated, as the NP absorbed the Afrikaner Party and the UP extinguished what remained of the Labour Party. The Nationalist government improved its position by granting parliamentary representation to the white voters of South-West Africa, by placing the Coloured voters on a separate roll, by removing the African representatives from Parliament, by reducing the minimum voting age for whites from twenty-one to eighteen, and by securing skillful delimitations. It also won an ever higher proportion of the Afrikaner votes, so that it increased its strength in the House of Assembly in every election — from seventy-three seats in 1948 to ninety-four in 1953, a hundred and three in 1958, and a hundred and five in 1961, while the UP declined from sixty-five in 1948 to forty-nine in 1961.

Before World War II the color question was never a major determinant of South African party allegiance. All the main parties were agreed on the maintenance of white supremacy, all of them, when in power, sponsored legislation for this purpose, and there was no serious challenge to the dominant position of the whites from inside or outside South Africa. Even so, one of the factors in the rise of the first NP was its success in presenting itself to the electorate as the party which was best able to maintain white supremacy. It was Hertzog who labeled his policy towards the Africans a policy of Segregation; one of the conditions of the fusion of 1934 was that the UP should promote this policy by removing the Cape African voters from the common roll.

After World War II, white supremacy became more difficult to maintain in the face of the involvement of vast numbers of Africans in the urban economy and demands for radical concessions, at a time when tropical Africa was being decolonized, and the new Asian and African states were using the United Nations as a forum for criticism of South Africa. The second NP came into power in 1948 largely because it insisted that Segregation, as applied by the UP, was no longer enough, and a more far-reaching policy, labeled "apartheid," was needed if white supremacy was to be maintained in South Africa in the postwar world. Since then apartheid has been the major substance of political controversy in South Africa and a major cause of the successive triumphs of the NP under the leadership of D. F. Malan, J. G. Strijdom and H. F. Verwoerd. The UP, led first by J. G. N. Strauss and then by Sir D. P. de Villiers Graaff since the death of Smuts in 1950, has been continuously on the defensive, on the assumption that to oppose white supremacy would be politically disastrous. It has tried to find points of difference from the NP within the framework of white supremacy, and over the years it has moved closer and closer to the Nationalist position.

Between elections the UP has lost several of its parliamentary members — some hiving off towards the NP and eventually joining it, others moving in the other direction, only to be eliminated from Parliament in the next election. The most notable secession was of eleven members who broke with the UP and founded the Progressive Party in 1959, with a policy of repealing discriminatory laws, gradually incorporating non-whites in the common roll electorate subject to educational and economic qualifications, and providing protection for all in a rigid constitution with a Bill of Rights. But in the 1961 election all of them except Mrs. Suzman were defeated by UP candidates. The NP has suffered fewer parliamentary defections; after J. D. du P. Basson left it and founded a National Union Party, he could return to Parliament in 1961 only by grace of the UP, which allowed him a safe urban seat, and soon afterwards he joined the UP.

The present distribution of seats in the House of Assembly represents the logical working out of South Africa's political arithmetic. The ruling NP has consistently applied the only formula for success under the South African political system: an appeal to the Afrikaner voters as Afrikaners, combined with an appeal to the British voters as whites. By the middle of the 1960's the Party had consolidated its position to the extent that it could only be dislodged by some major catastrophe. It is supported by an overwhelming majority of the Afrikaner voters. It is also making a serious bid for the support of British voters, with some success. In 1961, for the first time since 1948, two English-speaking South Africans — men of ultra-conservative views — were included in the Cabinet.[82] Whereas in the 1948 and 1953 elections, and possibly also in the 1958 election, the NP won a majority of the seats though supported by a minority of the electorate, the 1960 referendum produced a clear majority for a republic. In the 1961 election the NP was indubitably supported by a majority of the electorate.[83]

The NP currently holds all the House of Assembly seats for the Orange Free State and South-West Africa, all of the Cape Province seats except ten in the Cape peninsula and eight in the 1820 settler country of the southeast, all of the Transvaal seats except sixteen on the Witwatersrand and one in Pretoria, and two seats in northern Natal; most of these seats are held securely. The UP is therefore confined to four separate and predominantly urban pockets of British settlement, centered in Cape Town, Port Elizabeth, Johannesburg and Durban, and the NP has footholds in all of these areas except the last.[84] Moreover, in several of these areas the UP faced a challenge from the other side in 1961 when, although the Progressive Party won only the Witwatersrand seat of Houghton, it came within a thousand votes of the UP in seven other urban divisions. The short-lived National Union Party, which fought the election in alliance with the UP, fared less well and subse-

[82] They are: A. E. Trollip, UP Member of Parliament, 1938-1958; Administrator of Natal, 1958-1961; Minister of Immigration and of Labour, and nominated Senator, 1961-   ; and F. W. Waring, UP Member of Parliament, 1943-1953; re-elected as a UP candidate in 1953 but then left the party; National Conservative Party Member of Parliament, 1953-1957; Independent Member of Parliament, 1957-1958; Minister of Information 1961-   and NP Member of Parliament 1962-   . Both Trollip and Waring joined the NP before being appointed to the Cabinet.

[83] Precision is not possible because of the large number of unopposed seats in recent South African elections. In constituencies where NP candidates opposed UP candidates in both 1958 and 1961, the NP percentage of the total vote increased from 58.9 in 1958 to 64.3 in 1961. Newell M. Stultz and Jeffrey Butler, "The South African General Election of 1961," *Political Science Quarterly*, LXXVIII, No. 1 (March 1963) 86-110.

[84] The NP holds Bellville, Parow and Vasco in the Cape Peninsula, Port Elizabeth North, Queenstown and Uitenhage in the 1820 settler country, and many seats on the Witwatersrand. It has also wiped out UP parliamentary representation in Kimberley and (except for one seat) in Pretoria.

quently disintegrated. The 1961 election results are summarized in the following table:

TABLE III.1   *1961 General Election* [85]

| | Seats Won | | | Contests | |
	Unopposed	Opposed	Total	Seats Contested	Votes Polled
Nationalist Party	50	55	105	60	370,431
United Party	20	29	49	67	289,233
National Union Party	0	1	1	13	47,220
Progressive Party	0	1	1	23	69,042
Liberal Party	0	0	0	2	2,461
Conservative Workers' Party	0	0	0	4	8,554
Independents	0	0	0	9	10,704
Total	70	86	156		797,645

[85] Compiled from data in *Survey of Race Relations*, 1961, pp. 18-21 and the *Cape Times*, October 20, 1961. See also Stultz and Butler, *op. cit.* J. D. du P. Basson, who left the NP in 1959, was a founder of the National Union Party in 1960 and joined the UP in 1962. The Liberal Party and the Progressive Party had an understanding not to put up candidates in the same constituency. The Conservative Workers' Party was founded in 1961 to promote the interests of the white workers on the Witwatersrand.

The election of the four Coloured representatives is not included in the table. That election was boycotted by many Coloured people; and the Progressive and Liberal Parties did not put up candidates, nor did the NP. Two candidates were returned unopposed—one UP and one Independent; the winners of the other two seats were both Independents; the poll was only about 40 percent. *Survey of Race Relations*, 1961, pp. 21-26.

The tide continued to flow in favor of the NP in the Provincial Council elections of March 1965. The NP increased its majority in the Transvaal Provincial Council by six and in the Cape Provincial Council by four, and doubled its representation from four to eight in Natal. The Progressive Party fared badly, winning no seat at all from white voters; but it contested and won both Coloured seats in the Cape Provincial Council. *Africa Digest*, XII, No. 6 (London: June 1965) 160-61.

CHAPTER IV

How the System Works

REDUCED TO the simplest meaningful terms, South African society may be represented thus:

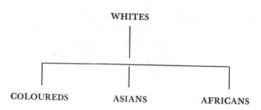

This shows graphically that the primary ingredients of South African society are a dominant white group and three subordinate nonwhite groups. Since the white group is wholly endogamous by law and the nonwhite groups are almost wholly endogamous by custom, we shall call the South African a *caste society,* and the whites, the Coloureds, the Asians, and the Africans the four South African *castes,* even though not all the ingredients of the classic Indian caste system are present in South Africa.

Each South African caste contains two or more distinguishable *communities.* In the white caste there are Afrikaner and English-speaking communities; in the Coloured caste, Christian and Muslim communities; in the Asian caste, Hindu and Muslim communities; and in the African caste, the traditional Xhosa, Zulu, Sotho and other tribal communities are still discernible. While the caste lines are extremely rigid, the community lines within each caste are flexible. There is individual mobility from one community to another and a tendency for class stratifications, based upon individual attainment, to supersede the old community divisions within each caste.

In a modern society a man has numerous loyalties — sub-national, national and even supra-national — and no one loyalty absolutely subsumes all the others. Loyalty to the nation, comprising all the citizens of the territorial state, transcends and moderates, without destroying, loyalties to sub-national communities, institutions and associations; and supra-national loyalties in turn transcend and moderate nationalism. In a caste society, too, a man may have many loyalties, but loyalty to caste tends to dominate and subsume all others. The ruling caste equates itself with the "nation"; the symbols of the ruling caste become the authorized "national" symbols; and caste loyalty is the overriding loyalty that members of the ruling caste, and their educational and even religious institutions, transmit to their children, by example and by manifest indoctrination. When we analyze the political socialization process in such a society, we are studying the social techniques by which a ruling caste seeks to preserve its power. The principal technique is the avoidance or even the prevention of inter-caste contacts, except between master and servant, ruler and ruled. Therefore, in the model caste society the ruling caste coexists with others in the same social, political and economic system, but without mutual understanding or a sense of shared humanity.

The South African case approximates rather closely to this model. Few members of the ruling caste dream of egalitarian association with members of other castes, and fewer still practice it. But in South Africa there is the further complication that the ruling caste itself contains two ethno-cultural communities between which there is a long tradition of competition and hostility. Moreover, within the ruling caste there are still two rival policies concerning the relations between the two communities: the policy of the United Party which says they should fuse into a single white "nation"; and the Nationalist Party policy which states the integrity of the *Afrikaner* "nation" must be preserved and any fusing that takes place must be on Afrikaner terms, and amount to the enlargement of the Afrikaner nation through its absorption of the English-speaking white community.

THE POLITICAL SOCIALIZATION PROCESS

In this section we shall consider the socializing experiences of members of the different South African castes and communities in the family and in educational and religious institutions. The contributions that voluntary associations, communications media, and political parties make to the political socialization process will be dealt with later.

Afrikaans- and English-speaking Whites

The nuclear white South African family has two special characteristics. The first is that it almost invariably employs one or more nonwhite domestic servants. In his earliest years a white child will often be left in the charge of a nonwhite servant; if he is a farm child he may have playmates among the children of the nonwhite farm laborers. As his social awareness develops the white child perceives that the nonwhite is treated by his parents and his older brothers and sisters as an inferior, attached to but not of the family. Thus family life inculcates an early familiarity with individual nonwhites, which is soon overlaid with a consciousness of difference and superiority.

The second special characteristic of the white South African family is that its members are usually drawn exclusively from either the Afrikaner or the English-speaking community, and the other community is simply not encountered in the family situation. If by chance some relative has married outside his community, the fact will certainly be a matter of comment, and probably adverse comment. In this or some other way the child will at an early age become aware of the existence of the other community as an object of rivalry and hostility.

The white child is by law required to attend school and in most cases he goes to a public school, where education is free. There his experiences confirm and strengthen the attitudes he has acquired in his home. His school environment is as exclusive as his home environment. His teachers and fellow pupils are drawn almost entirely from his own community; the only nonwhites to be found on the school premises are servants; and the major loyalty inculcated by the school is to the community, or, at most, to the white caste.

Formerly there were a number of schools which catered for both communities, partly as a matter of convenience in areas where they lived intermingled, and partly because it was United Party policy to encourage such schools as a means of reducing community exclusiveness.[1] This policy was opposed by the Nationalist Party, which feared that Afrikaner children would become denationalized in such schools. In 1948 the *Instituut vir Christelik–Nasionale Onderwys* [Institute for Christian National Education] of the *Federasie van Afrikaanse Kultuurverenigings* [Federation of Afrikaner Cultural Associations] produced a tract called *C.N.O.–Beleid* [Christian National Education Policy].[2] Its basic thesis was that each of the white communities should provide children with an education preserving and perpetuating its own peculiar heritage, and that the Afrikaner schools should "be imbued with the Christian–national spiritual and cultural material of our nation. . . . We wish to have no mixing of languages, no mixing of cultures, no mixing of religions and no mixing of races."[3]

In such schools religion should be the key subject and all secular subjects should be taught in a "Christian" spirit: history as the revelation of the purpose of God, who has "willed separate nations and peoples," and the natural sciences so that "There shall be no attempt to reconcile or abolish the fundamental oppositions."[4] The parents should have the decisive

---

[1] A useful work on education is A. P. Hunter, *The Reorientation of Educational Policy in South Africa* (D.Ed. dissertation, University of California, Los Angeles, 1962); also Gwendolen M. Carter, *The Politics of Inequality: South Africa since 1948* (London: Thames and Hudson, 1958) pp. 261-66, and Leo Marquard, *The Peoples and Policies of South Africa* (3rd edn., London: Oxford University Press, 1962) chapter 8.

[2] *C.N.O.–Beleid* was published in Johannesburg in 1948. It is a pamphlet of 31 pages, containing a foreword by J. C. van Rooy, chairman of the F.A.K., and fifteen Articles.

[3] J. C. van Rooy, *ibid.*, p. 6.

[4] *Ibid.*, Articles 2, 6 and 11.

say in the appointment and control of teachers, and the Church in supervising the youngsters' faith. This document was approved by the synods of the Dutch Reformed Churches, and although it has never been officially adopted by the Nationalist Party, its principles have been applied in varying degrees in the different provinces.

Christian National Education is the dominant educational philosophy in the Transvaal, where it is compulsory for the white child to be educated in his home language, as determined by a school principal (with the provincial Director of Education as the final arbiter). The child's parents are not even permitted to pay for his education in the other language at a private school in the province. The Transvaal administration has the power to divide any existing mixed government schools into separate Afrikaans- and English-medium schools, and it has used this power in several cases, even in the teeth of the opposition of a large majority of the parents at a former mixed school in Vanderbijlpark. F. H. Odendaal, the Administrator of the Transvaal, has publicly exhorted school principals to imbue their pupils with a spirit of mastery over nonwhites: "We must strive to win the fight against the nonwhite in the classroom instead of losing it on the battlefield." [5]

A new subject, Race Studies, has been added to the curriculum, with a syllabus and textbooks that ensure it will amount to indoctrination for apartheid:

> Our forefathers believed, and we still believe today, that God himself made the diversity of peoples on earth. . . . Inter-racial residence and inter-marriage are not only a disgrace, but are also forbidden by law.
>
> It is, however, not only the skin of the white South African that differs from that of the nonwhite. The white stands on a much higher plane of civilization and is more developed. Whites must so live, learn and work that we shall not sink to the cultural level of the nonwhites. Only thus can the government of our country remain in the hands of the whites.[6]

[5] The *Transvaler*, March 6, 1961, cited in Hunter, *op. cit.*, p. 54.

[6] L. C. Bekker and G. J. Potgieter, *Voorligting vir Standard VI* (Johannesburg, 1960) pp. 30-31, cited in Hunter, *op. cit.*, pp. 52-53.

No books other than officially approved books may be placed in school libraries or even introduced onto school premises. No private school, and no private school teacher, may operate in the Transvaal without being registered and accepting provincial control over the curriculum and attendance.[7] Within this legal framework the English-medium government and even private schools of the Transvaal are hard-pressed to pursue universal standards — even where (as is still often the case) the teachers would like to do so — while there is nothing to prevent and much to encourage the Afrikaans-medium schools to propagate the extravagances of *Christelik–Nasionale Onderwys*.

In the Orange Free State and the Cape Province the trend is in the same direction, but is not so far advanced. In Natal, on the other hand, the United Party, with a secure majority in the Provincial Council, was able to resist the application of Nationalist educational policies for a long while, but this resistance is being broken. In 1959 the government used its overriding powers to appoint as Director of Education in Natal J. H. Stander, a sympathizer with *Christelik–Nasionale Onderwys*, against opposition from the Administrator, the Executive Committee and the Provincial Council.[8] In 1962 Parliament passed a law creating a National Education Advisory Council, consisting of persons appointed by the Minister of Education, to advise him on a national education policy.[9] The Council has been set up, with an Executive Committee of one English-speaking and four Afrikaans-speaking members, and it is expected to pave the way for further uniformity in the field of white school education.[10]

On leaving school a white student who has passed the matriculation (twelfth grade) examination may, if he wishes, proceed to a university. There are nine universities for white students in South Africa, all of them semi-autonomous institutions. They charge low fees because they receive heavy state

[7] Transvaal Education Ordinances of 1949, 1953, 1955, 1957 and 1960, summarized in Hunter, *op. cit.*, chapter 5.

[8] Hunter, *op. cit.*, pp. 61-63.

[9] National Education Advisory Council Act, 1962.

[10] *House of Assembly Debates*, 1963, col. 978.

support, based on their enrollment, with the result that a high proportion of white South Africans receive a university education. In the Universities of Cape Town, the Witwatersrand, Natal, and Rhodes University, the medium of instruction is English; in the Universities of Stellenbosch, Pretoria and the Orange Free State, and Potchefstroom University for Christian Higher Education, the medium is Afrikaans. The University of Port Elizabeth, founded in 1965, is dual-medium. There is no legal compulsion on the white student to enroll in a university where his home language is the medium of instruction, but the number who do not do so is small and is probably decreasing. The Afrikaner youth who attends an English-medium university defies strong social pressures and weakens his prospects of joining the administrative and political establishment.

The tone of the English-medium universities is cosmopolitan. Their faculties are recruited from outside as well as inside South Africa and they strive for universal standards of teaching and research. However, their circumstances are increasingly adverse. The Afrikaans-medium universities are staffed almost entirely by Afrikaners and their teaching and research in the social sciences are usually limited by myopia, if not marred by serious bias.[11] Thus, the limitations of the family as an agent of socialization in a plural society are shared by the school and the university.

For many white South Africans another major socializing agent is a church or synagogue.[12] Nearly all Afrikaners are members of one of three Dutch Reformed Churches — the *Nederduitse Gereformeerde Kerk* (N.G.K.), which is the strongest in all parts of South Africa, the *Nederduitsch Hervormde Kerk* (N.H.K.), whose main strength is in the Transvaal, and the *Gereformeerde Kerk van Suid Afrika* (G.K.S.A.), the smallest but most fundamentalist of the three and the one which

[11] See, e.g., Leonard M. Thompson, "Afrikaner Nationalist Historiography and the Policy of Apartheid," *Journal of African History*, III, No. 1 (1962) 125-41.

[12] On religion in South Africa see Marquard, *op. cit.*, chapter 9; also Edwin S. Munger, *African Field Reports, 1952-1961* (Cape Town: Struik, 1961) pp. 733-94.

controls the Potchefstroom University for Christian Higher Education.[13] All three churches are derived from the same Dutch colonial institution and each is today a completely autonomous body. Membership of the Dutch Reformed Churches is limited to whites, but nonwhites are admitted to separate mission churches. The Dutch Reformed Churches have been intimately associated with the rise and triumph of Afrikaner Nationalism. Many *predikants* [clergy] were staunch opponents of Milner's anglicization policy and have always propagated the ideal of an exclusive Afrikaner nation with a divine mission. Consequently, the typical Dutch Reformed Church congregation is as much a racial corporation as the Afrikaner family or school: a racial corporation with the special function of invoking the awe-inspiring rituals and sanctions of fundamental Calvinism in support of the separation of South African society into racial units.

Most English-speaking white South Africans profess to be members of Protestant Churches (notably Anglican, Methodist and Presbyterian), and there are sizeable minorities of Catholics and Jews.[14] Unlike the Dutch Reformed Churches the English-speaking religious organizations are branches of, or closely associated with, international bodies. In a series of pronouncements all of them have condemned apartheid. Nevertheless, all of them practice racial separation to some extent. Most English-speaking white church-goers are members of all-white congregations; or, if the congregation is mixed, there are different services for whites and nonwhites; or, if the services are mixed, the nonwhites sit together at the back of the church. Leaders such as Catholic and Anglican archbishops have tried to eliminate these practices and promote genuinely multi-racial Christian congregations, but in so doing they have risked the loss of white lay support.

13 At the time of the 1960 census, 42.9 percent of the white population of the Republic belonged to the N.G.K., 6.2 percent to the N.H.K., and 3.3 percent to the G.K.S.A. Muriel Horrell, compiler, *A Survey of Race Relations in South Africa,* annual (Johannesburg: South African Institute of Race Relations, 1964) pp. 17-18.

14 At the time of the 1951 census the Anglican Church had 416,472 white adherents, the Methodist Church 219,021, the Presbyterian Church 100,739, and there were 141,330 Roman Catholics and 108,497 Jews: *ibid.*

The socialization experiences of the Afrikaner are all of one piece — in family, school and university, and church the same values are cherished, and these are the values that preserve the domination of the white caste and the autonomy of the Afrikaner community. On the other hand, the socialization experiences of English-speaking white South Africans reveal a dichotomy between ideal and actuality. The Afrikaner, therefore, tends to possess a singular sense of moral and intellectual rectitude, even when his conduct is abhorrent to the rest of mankind, whereas the English-speaking white South African is prone to cynicism.

Africans, Coloureds, Asians

A major problem for a ruling caste is how to reconcile the members of the subordinate castes to their place in the social order. In this process, education has a key role.[15] In South Africa, as elsewhere in the continent, Christian missionaries took the initiative in introducing Western education to African peoples. By 1948 there were over five thousand mission schools in South Africa and they received considerable subsidies from the state. Most of the missionaries were of European rather than South African origin, affiliation and outlook, and they regarded it as their purpose as educators to transmit modern knowledge rather than to attempt to adapt it to the peculiar circumstances of subject peoples. From the Nationalist Party's point of view this was dangerous, for while the party leaders realized that the economic system demanded that some modern education should be provided for the subordinate castes, they wished to prevent it from making them dissatisfied with their subordinate roles. As H. F. Verwoerd saw it:

> . . . good racial relations are spoilt when the correct education is not given. Above all, good racial relations cannot exist when the education is given under the control of people who create wrong expectations on the part of the Native himself. . . . It is therefore necessary that Native education should be controlled in such a way that it should be in accord with the policy of the State.[16]

[15] Hunter, *op. cit.*
[16] *House of Assembly Debates*, 1953, col. 3576.

Accordingly, following the report of a commission under the chairmanship of Dr. W. W. M. Eiselen, then secretary for Native Affairs,[17] Parliament in 1953 passed the Bantu Education Act, which started a radical transformation of African school education.

The transformation is now almost complete.[18] African education is dealt with and, for the most part, controlled by a central government department of Bantu Education. No private college for training African teachers is allowed to exist, so that the training of African teachers is now conducted exclusively in government colleges. No private school for Africans may exist without an annual license from the government. In several cases the government has refused to grant licenses — for example, to the school of Christ the King in Sophiatown, Johannesburg, which was formerly controlled by the Anglican Community of the Resurrection, and to Adams College in Natal, a distinguished high school, founded by American missionaries in 1853.

In most cases it has not been necessary to refuse licenses, because the private schools no longer receive state subsidies. Their withdrawal was a lethal blow to missionary education. Most of the missionary schools have now been transferred to the government. By 1962 fewer than seven hundred schools, with an enrollment of about 120,000 pupils, remained under private control. Most of these were Roman Catholic schools. The Catholic Church made a successful appeal for funds to continue its educational work after the withdrawal of the subsidies. Now the government is exerting further pressure by prohibiting Catholic schools from admitting non-Catholic pupils, so the number of private schools is dwindling still further.

The Bantu Education Department provides some elementary education for most African children and secondary education

---

17 Union of South Africa, *Report of the Commission on Native Education, 1949-51: U.G. 53/1951* (Pretoria: Government Printer, 1951).

18 Muriel Horrell, *A Decade of Bantu Education* (Johannesburg: South African Institute of Race Relations, 1964); Nathan Hurwitz, *The Economics of Bantu Education in South Africa* (Johannesburg: South African Institute of Race Relations, 1964); I. B. Tabata, *Education for Barbarism in South Africa* (London: Pall Mall Press, 1960).

for a few, and it controls the content of the education at all levels. Its resources amount to about $33.6 million a year — $18.2 million as a fixed subsidy from the general revenue of the Republic and the balance comprising the proceeds of the African general tax and miscellaneous receipts, such as boarding fees. The Department has managed to increase the total number of African pupils by increasing the ratio of pupils to teachers and restricting the advancement of pupils to the high school grades, so that the cost per pupil has dropped from $23.94 per pupil in 1954 to $17.22 in 1962.[19] In 1962 a total of 1,562,843 Africans were enrolled in all types of schools in the Republic, but only 51,794 passed the eighth grade, 5,660 the tenth grade, and 362 the twelfth grade examinations.[20] The government schools are known as Community Schools. Committees of Africans — some of whom are nominated by the government and others by the Bantu Authorities (subject to government approval) — have a say in their management; still the influence of the government is pervasive through its control over syllabuses, books and examinations, and its power to withhold the salaries of teachers it disapproves of.

The most conspicuous pedagogical changes that have taken place concern languages. Most of the mission schools used English as the medium of instruction after the first year or two, so that English was the main literary language of the African population, and seemed likely to become the lingua franca. Today the Bantu language of an area is the sole medium of instruction in public schools through the eighth grade and the sole medium of examination in all grades except the twelfth, and as much time is given to the teaching of Afrikaans as of English. As a result there has been a marked decline in the transmission

[19] *House of Assembly Debates,* 1963, col. 2129. The cost to the province for the education of a white pupil in 1961 was $126 (Transvaal), $168 (Cape Province), $185 (Natal), and $190 (Orange Free State): *Survey of Race Relations,* 1961, p. 247.

[20] *House of Assembly Debates,* 1963, cols. 2129, 3867. The American grade equivalents are used: in South Africa the eighth grade is called standard six, the tenth grade standard eight, and the twelfth grade standard ten. The failure rate in the high school examinations is high. In 1962 the 5,660 passes in grade ten were from 9,933 candidates, and the 362 passes in grade twelve were from 911 candidates: *ibid.,* col. 3867.

of English — the one South African language that is a universal language — and an erection of further barriers between Africans.[21]

Before 1963 the education of Coloured and Asian children was a provincial matter, conducted for the most part in state-aided schools run by missionary and other private organizations, and to a lesser but increasing extent in government schools. Asians had themselves subscribed large sums of money for building schools, which they had handed over to the provinces for administration. Most Coloured and Asian children received at least an elementary education. It was compulsory for Coloured children in Natal, and the Cape Provincial Council had accepted the principle of compulsion for both Coloured and Asian children and was applying it where practicable.[22] In 1963, however, Parliament passed a law transferring Coloured school education to the central government's Department of Coloured Affairs and the transfer will probably be followed by the same sort of process that has been applied to African schools — the elimination of the private schools and the tightening of controls over teachers and syllabuses.[23] The Minister of Indian Affairs has announced that control of Indian education, likewise, will be transferred to his department as soon as it seems politically practicable to do so.[24]

Apartheid is now applied in a far-reaching way at the university level. Until recently the South African universities were free to determine whom to admit as students: the Universities of Cape Town and the Witwatersrand had admitted nonwhites equally with whites and taught them in mixed classes; the University of Natal had admitted nonwhites equally with whites to its Durban (but not its Pietermaritzburg) campus and taught them in separate classes; the other five universities enrolled

---

21 This process is, however, being reversed in the Transkei. In 1964 the Transkei Legislative Assembly decided that in Standard III (fifth grade) English or Afrikaans, as selected by parents, should gradually be substituted for the mother tongue as the medium of instruction. *Survey of Race Relations*, 1964, p. 147.

22 For summaries of the state of Coloured and Indian education see *ibid.*, 1961, pp. 241-47, 1962, pp. 188-94, and 1963, pp. 229-35.

23 Coloured Persons Education Act, 1963.

24 *House of Assembly Debates*, 1963, cols. 6391-93.

white students only; and the University College of Fort Hare, a former mission institution affiliated to Rhodes University, was attended by Coloured, Asian and African students and seemed to be on the verge of acquiring full university status.[25] In 1959 the composition of the student bodies was as follows:

TABLE IV.1   *Racial Proportions in Universities* [26]

	White	Coloured	Asian	African	Total
Closed Universities	16,025				16,025
University of Cape Town	4,471	461	133	39	5,104
University of the Witwatersrand	4,813	30	193	74	5,110
University of Natal	2,679	50	489	187	3,405
University College of Fort Hare		70	100	319	489
	27,988	611	915	619	30,133

Legislation was passed in 1959 making it unlawful for non-whites who were not previously registered as students in the established universities, to register there in the future without special permission from the government, empowering the government to create new "University Colleges" for nonwhite students, and transferring Fort Hare to the government as such a college.[27] Since then the number of nonwhite students at the established universities has declined, admission to Fort Hare has been limited to Xhosa-speaking Africans, and separate col-

[25] Conference of Representatives of the University of Cape Town and the University of the Witwatersrand, Johannesburg, *The Open Universities in South Africa* (Johannesburg: Witwatersrand University Press, 1957). There is also the University of South Africa, which teaches by correspondence only.

[26] *Survey of Race Relations*, 1961, p. 252. In 1959 the University of South Africa provided correspondence courses for 7,107 white, 211 Coloured, 601 Asian and 1,252 African students.

[27] Extension of University Education Act, 1959; University College of Fort Hare Transfer Act, 1959. Nonwhites may continue to register in the nonwhite medical school which remains attached to the University of Natal, and in the University of South Africa which continues to teach by correspondence.

leges have been founded for Zulu-speaking Africans, Sotho-speaking Africans, Asians and Coloured people. The nonwhite colleges are subject to stringent controls: for example, no student organization may exist without the permission of the Rector, no meeting may be held without his permission, no publication may be prepared or circulated without his permission, no student may leave the campus without his permission, and he may dismiss any student who infringes any regulation. The faculties of the colleges include a few nonwhite members, who are paid less than their white colleagues of equal status and segregated from them to the extent that the white members serve on the college senates and the nonwhite members on separate "advisory" senates. In 1963 the three African colleges had a total enrollment of 402 students in degree courses and 222 in diploma courses, and a total faculty of 134 (113 whites and 21 nonwhites); the Indian college had 547 degree and 90 diploma students; and the Coloured college had 219 degree and 131 diploma students.[28]

It is difficult to assess the full psychological and political consequences of the present educational arrangements for South African nonwhites. There have been numerous disturbances in the South African schools and colleges under the new regime. For example, in March 1963 all the pupils at Lovedale High School refused to attend classes and four-fifths of them left the school.[29] The government presumably hopes that opposition will diminish in the course of time — with the increase in the proportion of teachers and pupils who have never experienced the previous system and the elimination of obstructive teachers — and that eventually the schools and colleges will effectively mold the minds of the members of the subordinate castes to accept apartheid between white and nonwhite, between Coloured and Asian and African, and between Xhosa and Zulu and Sotho, as a natural and beneficial phenomenon. But this outcome is by no means certain.

For one thing, in colonial situations Western education has

[28] *Survey of Race Relations,* 1959-60, pp. 231-32; *House of Assembly Debates,* 1963, cols. 1147, 6579.

[29] *Ibid.,* col. 2987; *Survey of Race Relations,* 1963, p. 229.

always tended to corrode traditional particularism, however carefully it may have been controlled by the colonial power. This is also the case in South Africa. Among the host of impediments to the indoctrination of nonwhite youth in South African schools is the fact that nearly all the teachers are necessarily nonwhites, who are themselves very conscious of the differences between their own conditions of employment and the conditions of employment of white teachers in South Africa, and who cannot easily be perverted into reliable propagators of the ruling philosophy.

Moreover, the government cannot control the other socializing experiences of nonwhites to the same extent that it controls their education. Among rural Africans, and even among Africans who have spent most of their lives in towns, there are still many conservatives who reject Western cultural influences. In contrast, there are also many who have turned their backs upon the past and think and act essentially (though not necessarily exclusively) as members of a contemporary proletariat.[30] The former, in rejecting modernity, go a long way toward meeting the requirements of the ruling caste; the latter, in accepting modernity, do not. Continually confronted with the contrast between their own poverty, insecurity and powerlessness, and the wealth, the freedom and the power of the whites, they are bound to conclude that social morality and South African law are irreconcilable and that their own hardships are due to the political system, and to transmit these conclusions to the next generation.[31] The same is true of many Coloureds and Asians.[32]

Some Christian churches in South Africa, especially the Dutch Reformed Churches, reflect the structure of South African so-

---

[30] Philip Mayer, *Townsmen or Tribesmen: Conservatism and the process of urbanization in a South African city* (Cape Town: Oxford University Press, 1961); Monica Wilson and Archie Mafeje, *Langa: A study of social groups in an African township* (Cape Town: Oxford University Press, 1963).

[31] E.g., Albert Luthuli, *Let My People Go: An autobiography* (London: Collins, 1962); Z. K. Matthews, *Social Relations in a Common South African Society* (Johannesburg: South African Institute of Race Relations, 1961); Bloke Modisane, *Blame Me on History* (New York: Dutton, 1963); Ezekiel Mphahlele, *The African Image* (New York: Praeger, 1962).

[32] E.g., Peter Abrahams, *Tell Freedom* (New York: Knopf, 1954).

ciety and encourage their nonwhite members to accept their subordinate lot. Others, however, do not conceal from their nonwhite members their rejection of the caste principle and their abhorrence of its practical effects, while the separatist, African-controlled churches have a wide range of attitudes towards the state and society, including, in some cases, radical opposition.[33]

The struggle that is taking place for the minds of the nonwhite peoples of South Africa is not, of course, a simple struggle between "traditionalism" and "modernity." The essence of traditional societies cannot be recreated in South Africa, for the conditions in which traditional societies flourished — political, economic and psychological self-sufficiency — no longer exist anywhere in the Republic.[34] Nor is the government trying to recreate traditional societies in their original form. What it is attempting is a form of neo-traditionalism, by cementing alliances with the most conservative elements in each of the subordinate castes and communities. Of these, the African chiefs are the most important. The chief who cooperates with the government at Pretoria may obtain material comforts, the satisfaction of exercising power at the local level and the illusion of autonomy. On the other hand, conformist chiefs are under strong pressures from below and are liable either to throw in their lot with a group of modernists, or to try to translate the illusion of power into reality. The Transkei is the test case of this policy of neo-traditionalism.

Furthermore, in South Africa as in other countries modernity takes many different forms. First, there are great variations in the extent to which nonwhite South Africans have experienced alien influences. Most of the Coloured people and Asians have had a long, intense and continuous exposure. Africans whose ancestors lived near the eastern frontier of the old Cape Colony — such as the Xhosa and the Fingo — have had a more protracted exposure, and in general a more concentrated one, than those of Zulu or Sotho origin. Also, nonwhites who have always

[33] Bengt G. M. Sundkler, *Bantu Prophets in South Africa* (2nd edn., London: Oxford University Press, 1961).

[34] See pp. 38-44.

lived and worked in towns have experienced a more intense exposure to alien influences than Coloured and African labor-
tenants on white farms and Africans who migrate periodically
between the Bantu Areas and the towns. Second, nonwhites
have gained very different impressions from their contacts with
members of the ruling caste. To some, the dominant impression has been the paternalism of a responsible employer; to
others, the seemingly capricious conduct of a policeman. Third,
nonwhite South Africans make many different types of selec-
tions from the modern elements around them. Some try to create stable, middle-class homes; others turn to criminality. Some
become liberals or nationalists; others, Communists or racialists.

The Effects of Political Socialization

The new generation of South African whites absorbs the
mystique of a dominant caste, but in varying degrees. The
main internal cleavage within the dominant caste corresponds
with its ethno-cultural division into an Afrikaans- and an English-speaking community. In the Afrikaner community the mystique is effectively transmitted because family, school, university
and church combine to promote it, with comparatively few exceptions. In the English-speaking community the mystique is
less effectively transmitted because the churches, the universities, some of the schools and even a sizeable minority of the
families do not accept the validity of the caste principle, even
though they may tend to conform in practice. At present, however, the superior numbers, cohesion and political power of the
Afrikaners, and the growing challenge of the nonwhites and
the external world to the existing political system are weakening the anti-caste influences on the English-speaking white community. White South Africans are becoming increasingly united
in defense of their privileges.

If South Africa had a backward preindustrial economy, the
government might manage to reconcile the subordinate castes
to their status, as was done in the past. The country, however,
is irrevocably committed to economic modernity, and economic
modernity is incompatible with a caste system. White South
Africans are not able to control the socialization experiences of
the nonwhites. Although the scope of law has been extended to
make egalitarian contacts between members of the white and

the nonwhite castes extremely difficult, and although the educational system has been remodeled with the purpose of reconciling nonwhites to subordination, the continuous absorption of more and more nonwhites into the modern sector of the economy produces rising expectations that are only partly satisfied by minor advances in material prosperity. The anti-racial climate of world opinion strengthens South African nonwhite resentments against the effects of apartheid. These expectations and resentments are transmitted in nonwhite families, in nonwhite churches and even, *sub rosa,* in the government-controlled nonwhite schools and colleges.

A balance sheet cannot be drawn up contrasting the forces making for acceptance and the forces making for rejection of the caste system; the dominant trend at this stage of its history seems to be towards some form of modernity and universalism among nonwhite South Africans in opposition to white reaction and particularism. If the ruling caste is becoming increasingly united, so are the subject castes. The primary social process in South Africa is a process of polarization: white versus nonwhite. But it may not remain so. The longer the present political system endures, the greater the prospect that the government may succeed in creating enduring divisions between caste and caste, and community and community.

RECRUITMENT TO POLITICAL ROLES

In South Africa all powerful executive, legislative, judicial, administrative and military roles are limited by law to members of the white caste, and the overwhelming majority of the members of the Cabinet, of the majority side in the legislature, of the judiciary, and of the senior echelons in the bureaucracy and the armed forces are drawn in practice from the Afrikaner community. That is to say, ascriptive criteria set out in law define an outer oligarchy from which recruitment to authoritative governmental roles may take place; and further ascriptive criteria of an extralegal character determine an inner oligarchy from which most of the decisive roles are filled. Within the inner oligarchy — the Afrikaner community — on the other hand, individuals are recruited and promoted by criteria of achievement. Thus, nearly all the key political positions in

South Africa are filled by well-educated Afrikaners who have given long and efficient service to the Afrikaner community.

The Afrikaner Leadership

Only Afrikaners were members of the Cabinets of D. F. Malan, J. G. Strijdom and H. F. Verwoerd before 1961, when Verwoerd appointed two conservative white South Africans of British descent to junior ministries as a step towards the consolidation of the white caste under Afrikaner leadership.[35] In 1963 the State President was an Afrikaner; sixteen of the eighteen Cabinet Ministers were Afrikaners; and the four Deputy Ministers were Afrikaners:

TABLE IV.2   *The State President, Afrikaner Ministers and Deputy Ministers in order of status (1963)*

C. R. Swart	State President
H. F. Verwoerd	Prime Minister
P. O. Sauer	Minister of Lands, of Forestry and of Public Works
E. H. Louw	Minister of Foreign Affairs
T. E. Dönges	Minister of Finance
B. J. Schoeman	Minister of Transport
J. J. Serfontein	Minister of Social Welfare and Pensions
J. de Klerk	Minister of the Interior and of Education, Arts and Science
M. D. C. de Wet Nel	Minister of Bantu Administration and Development
P. M. K. Le Roux	Minister of Agricultural Technical Services and of Water Affairs
W. A. Maree	Minister of Bantu Education and of Indian Affairs
N. Diederichs	Minister of Economic Affairs and of Mines
A. Hertzog	Minister of Posts and Telegraphs and of Health
D. C. H. Uys	Minister of Agricultural Economics and of Marketing
J. J. Fouché	Minister of Defence
P. W. Botha	Minister of Coloured Affairs, of Community Development and of Housing
B. J. Vorster	Minister of Justice

[35] The South African Cabinet Ministers of British descent are A. E. Trollip, Minister of Labour and of Immigration, and F. W. Waring, Minister of Information and of Tourism, who rank after J. J. Fouché and B. J. Vorster, respectively; see chapter 3, footnote 82.

M. Viljoen	Deputy Minister of the Interior, of Education, Arts and Science, of Labour and of Immigration
M. C. Botha	Deputy Minister of Bantu Administration and Development
J. F. W. Haak	Deputy Minister of Planning, of Economic Affairs and of Mines
J. G. H. van der Wath	Deputy Minister for South West Africa Affairs

As these twenty-one men are representative of the ruling Afrikaner elite, an analysis of their backgrounds provides insight toward understanding their motives and actions.[36] All but one of them were born into the Afrikaner community. The exception is Prime Minister H. F. Verwoerd, whose birthplace was the Netherlands and who migrated to South Africa with his Dutch parents when he was a child. After vicissitudes in the Cape peninsula and Southern Rhodesia, the family settled in Brandfort, Orange Free State, when he was seventeen, and thereafter he moved exclusively in Afrikaner circles.

All but three of these men were born on South African farms or in South African country towns, the exceptions being Sauer (in the Cape Peninsula), Schoeman (on the Witwatersrand), and Verwoerd. The leadership is therefore overwhelmingly of rural origin.

The Afrikaner leaders are the product of an internally egalitarian community. Insofar as there was an Afrikaner elite half a century ago, it was already an elite of achievement, consisting of *predikants,* politicians and war heroes. The fathers of at least five of the twenty-one were in that group. Dönges is the son of a *predikant* of the N.G.K., de Klerk of a *predikant* of the G.K.S.A., Sauer of a Cabinet Minister of the Cape Colony and the Union, Hertzog of a Prime Minister of South Africa, and Serfontein of a Free State general and Union Senator. The other sixteen fathers were not particularly conspicuous. Most of them were landowners, and at least ten were farmers, pure and

36 The analysis that follows is based on the biographical files in the library of the *Cape Times,* Cape Town, which were studied for the author by Miss Clodagh O'Dowd of the University of Cape Town. During 1963 and 1964, Louw and Sauer retired, H. Muller joined the Cabinet as Minister of Foreign Affairs, Haak was promoted to full ministerial status, H. E. Martins became a Deputy Minister, and there was some shuffling of portfolios.

simple. There also were a country attorney, a small town merchant, a small town bookshop owner, and a railway employee. Notably absent from the list are industrial occupations, on both the management and the labor sides. Half a century ago the Afrikaner had scarcely begun to move to town and nearly all the successful entrepreneurs and the skilled artisans of South Africa were members of the English-speaking white community, with the result that the Afrikaner leaders of the 1960's grew up in an anti-capitalist, but not a socialist, environment.

Born between 1890 (Louw) and 1920 (Maree), these men became associated in their youth with the struggle for the protection of the Afrikaner community from the forces of anglicization. Anglophobia was then a more dominant emotion than negrophobia, because Britain and British South Africans seemed to be challenging their group integrity, whereas nonwhite South Africans still seemed to pose no serious threat to white supremacy.

The Afrikaner leaders are well educated. All twenty-one graduated from high school and all except Schoeman attended a university. Thirteen obtained at least one degree; nine, more than one; and Verwoerd, Dönges, Diederichs and Hertzog earned doctorates. Nineteen attended Afrikaans-medium universities. Stellenbosch was the most popular — indeed, every South African Prime Minister except Louis Botha (who was innocent of formal education) was a student at Stellenbosch. Three attended an English-medium South African university as well as an Afrikaner university. Six studied abroad after graduating from Afrikaner universities: Swart took a diploma in journalism at Columbia University; Verwoerd studied psychology at the universities of Hamburg, Leipzig and Berlin in 1926-1927; Dönges took an LL.B. degree at London University and was called to the Bar of the Middle Temple; Diederichs studied philosophy in Munich, Cologne and Leiden in 1926-1929; Hertzog took the B.A., B.C.L. degrees at Oxford and the LL.D. at Leiden; and van der Wath studied agriculture at the University of Halle in 1936. On the other hand, perhaps seven of the twenty-one had never travelled outside South Africa as of 1963, and several others had not done so before they became members of the government.

Prior to entering politics, five of the twenty-one were farmers

(Sauer, Le Roux, Maree, Uys, Fouché), and several others combined farming with a profession. Six were initially educators — university professors (Verwoerd, Diederichs) and school teachers (Serfontein, de Klerk, M. C. Botha and van der Wath). Seven were lawyers (Swart, Louw, Dönges, Nel, Hertzog, Vorster, Haak). Two were public servants — a railwayman (Schoeman) and a postal clerk (Viljoen); one has apparently had no employer other than the Nationalist Party (P. W. Botha).[37] It is a striking fact that none of them has ever worked in a mining or manufacturing industry; Louw, who managed his father's business in Beaufort West for some years, is the only one with commercial experience. He is also the sole Minister with diplomatic experience, having held foreign service appointments in the United States, Canada, Britain, Italy, France and Portugal between 1925 and 1937.

These men are second, not first, generation Nationalists. All of them have been politically active for many years, the older ones supporting J. B. M. Hertzog's Nationalist Party until 1934 and then more or less immediately following D. F. Malan into the second Nationalist Party, suspecting Hertzog of being too tender towards the British South Africans (except for Schoeman, who was a member of the United Party until 1939). Some, like Sauer, Serfontein, Le Roux, Uys and Fouché, took the traditional South African route to political leadership, starting with service on local party committees and graduating to a provincial committee and parliamentary candidature. Others first became politically prominent through paid or unpaid service in organizations connected with the party.

As students, Vorster, Viljoen and Haak were active in the *Jeugbond* [Youth League]. Dönges, while practicing as an advocate in Cape Town from 1927 onwards, became active in the

---

[37] Each individual has been included in one category only — the one that was his first full-time occupation. In fact, several of them have worked at a variety of occupations besides politics. For example, President Swart, who has been classified as a lawyer, practiced intermittently as an advocate from 1918 onwards, but also played some minor roles in Hollywood films (1921-1922), lectured at Grey College, Bloemfontein (1917-1918) and the agricultural college, Glen, O.F.S. (1920), and acquired a farm at Brandfort, O.F.S. Schoeman, classified as a railwayman, left the South African Railways in 1938 and subsequently became a farmer, estate agent, building contractor and company director.

Reddingsdaadbond [Savings Association], the *Federasie van Afrikaanse Kultuurverenigings* [Federation of Afrikaner Cultural Unions] and the *Broederbond* [Brothers' League]. Verwoerd first became known in political circles as the organizer of a conference on the poor white problem, and in 1937 he resigned his Stellenbosch chair to become founder–editor of the *Transvaler*. De Klerk was a paid organizer of the *Blankewerkersbeskermingsbond* [White Workers' Protection Association], Diederichs of the *Reddingsdaadbond,* Hertzog of the *Mynewerkersbond* [Mine Workers' Association], M. C. Botha of the *Afrikaanse Taal en Kultuur Vereniging* [Afrikaans Language and Culture Union], and Vorster of the *Ossewa Brandwag* [Ox-wagon Guard: a wartime pro-Nazi sabotage organization]. Complete political professionalism is shown in the careers of Nel, who became a party organizer in 1936 at the age of thirty-five, and, above all, of P. W. Botha, who left the Orange Free State university in 1936 at the age of twenty to become a party organizer and has never held any non-political position. This type of politician is increasing in number. Many of the new Nationalist Party members of the Parliament elected in 1961 were former party employees.

Seven of the twenty-one men have held high office in local government: Fouché as Administrator of the Orange Free State, de Klerk, Nel and Viljoen as members of the Transvaal Provincial Council, van der Wath as a member of the South-West African Legislative Assembly, Hertzog as a Pretoria City Councillor, and Haak as mayor of Bellville in the Cape peninsula.

Twelve of them, including Prime Minister Verwoerd, were not in Parliament before 1948 and have therefore never had the salutory experience of membership of a parliamentary opposition. In the time of D. F. Malan, a majority of the members of the Cabinet were Cape men; by 1963 nine of the twenty-one leaders were Transvalers and only seven were from the Cape.[38] Furthermore, by 1963 only six of the members of the Cabinet were given ministerial appointments by Verwoerd's predeces-

[38] In terms of place of birth, nine are from the O.F.S., eight from the Cape, three from the Transvaal and one (Verwoerd) from Holland; but in terms of residence and political base, nine are from the Transvaal, seven from the Cape, three from the O.F.S., one from Natal and one from South-West Africa.

sors, which means that most of the present leaders owe their elevation to office to H. F. Verwoerd.

There has been one outstanding addition to the material interests of many of the leaders since they entered politics. In spite of the fact that none of them came into politics from mining, manufacturing or commercial backgrounds, many have now been drawn into the business world as directors of companies.[39] This growing personal involvement of the political leadership in capitalist enterprises is a factor of political significance. Formerly, the Nationalist Party represented the white rural interest and the white urban workers' interest, and was distinctly suspicious of big business. That is no longer the case. As the Afrikaner share of industrial, commercial and financial management has increased, the leaders of the Nationalist Party, notwithstanding their rural origins and their anti-capitalist traditions, have become personally involved in the capitalist interest.

South African public servants are protected by statute against arbitrary dismissal, but appointments and promotions are vested in Cabinet Ministers, provided they consider the recommendations of the Public Service Commission and similar bodies.[40] In the early years of the Union, most senior posts were held by English-speaking white South Africans, but the Hertzog government aimed at establishing equality between the two white communities and the governments of Malan, Strijdom and Verwoerd have almost invariably appointed Afrikaners to senior posts. The transformation is now virtually complete. Indeed, the Afrikaans language prevails in the Union Buildings to such an extent that it is surprising to hear English being spoken.

[39] It is the policy of the government to allow Ministers to be directors of mutual companies and of publishing companies, but not of other public companies. Thus Prime Minister Verwoerd is chairman of Voortrekker Pers, a large publishing and printing company, and of the Dagbreek group of companies, which has several subsidiaries. It is possible that some Ministers are in fact directors of other types of companies. *House of Assembly Debates*, 1962, cols. 3081-3119.

[40] B. Beinart, "The Legal Relationship between the Government and its Employees," *Butterworth's South African Law Review* (1955) pp. 21-72; H. R. Hahlo and Ellison Kahn, *The Union of South Africa: The development of its laws and constitution* (London: Stevens, 1960) pp. 185-86.

In 1963 the Commandant General of the South African Defence Force, General Pieter Hendrik Grobbelaar, and the
Army, Air and Naval Chiefs of Staff were all Afrikaners, who
started their military careers between 1922 and 1938 and par-
ticipated in World War II, and three of the four have attended
British staff courses at Camberley or Greenwich. Most of the
officers at intermediate levels of command are also Afrikaners,
but the government has experienced some difficulty in finding
men of military experience as well as political reliability to
appoint to key posts, since the officers most narrowly loyal to
the Nationalist Party did not volunteer for service outside
South Africa in World War II. Nearly all the senior police
officers also are Afrikaners from wholly Afrikaner environments; somewhat surprisingly the Commissioner of Police,
Lieutenant-General Johannes Marthinus Keevy, took a B.A.
degree at the English-medium Rhodes University College back
in 1928.[41]

The present intake into all branches of the public service is
overwhelmingly Afrikaner. A young English-speaking white
South African comes from a community with a strong industrial and commercial tradition and he knows he can easily be
absorbed into the private sector of the economy, with good
prospects for promotion and material success, while he also
suspects that if he were to join the public service his prospects
of promotion would be poor. A young Afrikaner, on the other
hand, assumes that he will find the atmosphere in the public
service congenial and his prospects good. Consequently, the
Afrikaner community has as complete control over the bureaucracy, the police and the armed forces as it has over the
Parliament and Cabinet.

The Nonwhite Leadership

The leaders of nonwhite political organizations have always
been drawn from the modern elements in the nonwhite groups.
In recent years the leadership of such organizations as the
African National Congress, the Pan-Africanist Congress, the
South African Indian Congress and the South African Coloured
People's Organization has been in the hands of people with a
good modern education. For example, of twenty-two Bantu-

---

[41] *Cape Times* biographical files.

speaking South Africans listed in a recent survey of politicians in Africa, at least eighteen had a high school education. At least twelve of the latter had some further education, and eight of these have a university degree.[42] Beyond that, it is difficult to generalize. The leaders have come from the most varied origins. A few are of chiefly lineages, such as A. J. Luthuli and Nelson Mandela, but most are commoners by traditional standards. Ten originated in the Cape Province, five in the Transvaal, four in Natal and three in the Orange Free State; they originated in all three categories of land — Bantu Areas, white rural areas and towns — though nearly all of them have lived more or less for long periods in the towns. A few, like J. G. Matthews and Tennyson Makiwane, are second or third generation political activists.

The major cleavages between nonwhite political organizations, notably the cleavage between the A.N.C. and the P.A.C., is primarily a generational shift. The older leaders have tended to remain with the A.N.C., and the younger leaders to switch to the P.A.C.

Courage has always been a prerequisite for political activity among nonwhite South Africans. Since 1960, with overt activity banned or harrassed, this is truer than ever. It is an open question how long nonwhites will engage in any political activities which are in opposition to the South African political system.[43]

THE COMMUNICATIONS SYSTEM

The first modern political communications in South Africa were created by whites for whites, and from an early stage two parallel sets of publications developed: books and papers in the English-medium designed for the English-speaking white community, and an Afrikaans-medium set for the Afrikaners.[44] In time the caste line became more and more remote from the line dividing South Africans who use modern communications media from those who do not. It is true that there are still South Africans in rural areas for whom political communica-

[42] Ronald Segal, *Political Africa: A Who's Who of Personalities and Parties* (London: Stevens, 1961).

[43] On political activity in opposition to the caste system, see chapter 5.

[44] Theo. E. G. Cutten, *A History of the Press in South Africa* (Cape Town: National Union of South African Students, 1935).

tion is still exclusively a matter of face-to-face confrontation, and that most of them are Africans. However, the continuous expansion of modern primary education and the continuous growth of the modern sector of the economy have for years been reducing the number who rely entirely upon this traditional means of communication. Today a high proportion of the African population have at one time or another worked in town, where they have been exposed in some measure to modern communications; the proportion of Asians and Coloured people who have been exposed is far higher.

The modern communications network is necessarily fragmented in South Africa; some of this is due to geographical factors. People live at different distances from the major population centers where modern communications are most readily available and therefore experience different intensities of exposure; and the great distances between the main population centers create regional variations. But the importance of geographical differentials is diminishing, for radio reception now extends to every part of the country and the English language daily newspapers are very much the same in all the main centers, relying on the same news services and expressing similar political views, and the Afrikaans dailies are also similar to one another. Fragmentation is mainly due to differences of interest and, above all, of language.

With the growth in the number and the variety of the users of modern communications, there has been an increase in the range of services available. Newspapers are now produced in many languages for the different nonwhite communities. But since the newspapers designed primarily for whites have by far the best news coverage, they are read by the more sophisticated nonwhites; and because the English language papers are at least to some extent critical of the government, nonwhites prefer the English to the Afrikaans press.

Therefore, the section of the press which caters primarily to the opposition section of the ruling caste is read by increasing numbers of members of the subordinate castes. Furthermore, since English is a universal language and Afrikaans is exclusive to South Africa, foreign correspondents and diplomats take their South African news mainly from the English press. For these reasons the government is anxious to de-emphasize the teaching of English in nonwhite schools, to censor the English press, to make the radio an instrument of propaganda, and to disseminate large quantities of printed propaganda among the nonwhite communities of South Africa and in foreign countries. Thus the initial fragmentation of the modern communications system in South Africa was beginning to be overcome by the ascendency of the English-medium press; but the government is now trying to check this process by state control and forced re-fragmentation.[45]

The oldest newspapers in South Africa are English language papers which were founded in the 19th century. The Argus Printing and Publishing Company has control of six dailies — the *Cape Argus* (founded 1857), the Johannesburg *Star*, the Durban *Natal Daily News*, the *Pretoria News*, the Bloemfontein *Friend*, and the Kimberley *Diamond Fields Advertiser* — and also one weekend paper, the Durban *Sunday Tribune*. The South African Associated Newspapers Group includes three dailies — the Johannesburg *Rand Daily Mail*, the Port Elizabeth *Eastern Province Herald* and the Port Elizabeth *Evening Post* — and two weekend papers — the *Sunday Times* and the *Sunday Express*, both of Johannesburg. The *Cape Times* and the *Natal Mercury*, dailies, are loosely linked with Associated Newspapers. There are also two independent English dailies — the Pietermaritzburg *Natal Witness* and the East London *Daily Dispatch*. The Argus and the Associated Newspapers groups are both related to mining and industrial interests, while the others are under local control.

In 1959 these papers had a total daily circulation of about 680,000, and a weekend circulation of about 860,000.[46] The core of the circulation consists of English-speaking white South Africans, but since they numbered fewer than 1,200,000 men, women and children, it is evident that the English press was read by many Afrikaners and nonwhites. None of these papers

---

[45] On the South African press generally see Morris Broughton, *Press and Politics of South Africa* (Cape Town: Purnell, 1961); Carter, *op. cit.*, pp. 38-47, 457-61; Alex. Hepple, *Censorship and Press Control in South Africa* (Johannesburg: The author, 1960); Anon., "La Presse en Afrique au Sud du Sahara," part 2, *Afrique* (Paris: July 1963) pp. 40-44.

[46] Circulation figures in Broughton, *op. cit.*, pp. 304-306; Carter, *op. cit.*, pp. 457-61; and Hepple, *op. cit.*, pp. 71-73.

is directly linked with a political party. Nevertheless, they all oppose the Nationalist Party, with degrees of vehemence ranging from the generally mild criticisms of the Argus newspapers to the more fundamental opposition of the *Rand Daily Mail* and the *Cape Times.* Some contend that the Argus papers are excessively mild because they are the creatures of their major shareholders, who are willing to acquiesce to any policy that promotes economic expansion, regardless of the cost in human welfare. Others contend that papers like the *Cape Times* are essentially negative and unconstructive, being actuated by jealousy of Afrikaner achievements.

The Afrikaans dailies are the Cape Town *Burger* (founded 1915), the Johannesburg *Transvaler,* a morning paper, the Johannesburg *Vaderland,* an evening paper, and the Bloemfontein *Volksblad.* The Port Elizabeth *Oosterlig* is bi-weekly. All these papers have senior Nationalist politicians on their boards and give enthusiastic support to the Nationalist Party. The *Burger,* the *Volksblad,* and the *Oosterlig* are in one group, the Nasionale Pers. Prime Minister Verwoerd, who was editor of the *Transvaler* from its foundation in 1937 till 1948, is now chairman of the board of Voortrekker Pers, which publishes the *Transvaler,* and three other Cabinet Ministers are members of the board. Verwoerd is also chairman of Afrikaanse Pers, which publishes the *Vaderland* and also a weekly, *Dagbreek.* In 1959 the combined circulation of the Afrikaans dailies was 168,000, and the weekend circulation was 184,000.[47] Since the

[47] *Ibid.* In the first half of 1964 the newspapers with the largest circulation per issue (reported in *Survey of Race Relations,* 1964, p. 47) were:

English		Afrikaans	
	Dailies		
Star	163,000	*Vaderland*	50,000
Rand Daily Mail	109,000	*Burger*	48,000
Cape Argus	101,000	*Transvaler*	37,000
Natal Daily News	75,000		
Cape Times	67,000		
Natal Mercury	61,000		
	Weeklies		
Sunday Times	394,000	*Landstem*	156,000
Cape Argus	152,000	*Dagbreek*	154,000
Star	131,000		

Afrikaner population was nearly 1,800,000 men, women and children, this means that many Afrikaners were still not buying Afrikaans papers and that very few nonwhites or English-speaking whites bought them.

In most parts of the country there is competition between English and Afrikaans newspapers. Very little rivalry exists between newspapers in the same language, for in no center is there more than one morning or one evening daily paper in English or in Afrikaans. The effects of the greater circulation of the English press on intra-white politics are negligible, for most Afrikaners who read English papers have an engrained resistance to alien political views. In addition, the proportionate circulation of the English press among white South Africans may be expected to decline as a result of the increase in the Afrikaner proportion of the white population, the rise of Afrikaner industrial and financial power, and the further consolidation of Afrikaner political control.

African readers are catered to not only by the English dailies which have been mentioned, but also by periodical publications produced specially for them. Formerly, several papers were under African control, but they have all either ceased publication or been acquired by white companies. The Bantu Press, which was absorbed by the Argus Printing and Publishing Company in 1963, publishes the Johannesburg *World* daily, in English; the Durban *Ilange Lase Natal* weekly in English and Zulu; and three weeklies, partly in English and partly in Sotho, Tswana and Zulu, for Lesotho, Bechuanaland and Swaziland, respectively. Drum Publications, under the control of J. R. A. Bailey, who is the son of a gold-mining magnate and a member of the board of South African Associated Newspapers, issues *Post,* a weekly newspaper in English. Another publication controlled by English-speaking white South Africans is the monthly pictorial, *Zonk.* Protea Press, a subsidiary of Afrikaanse Pers, publishes *Bona,* an illustrated monthly, in Zulu, Xhosa and Sotho editions, and *Imvo Zabantsundu,* which was previously a Bantu Press publication and originally an independent Xhosa newspaper, founded in 1884. Nasionale Tydskrifte, also under Afrikaner Nationalist control, produces monthly magazines in four Bantu languages and another recent Afrikaner Nationalist venture is *Elethu Mirror,* a weekly newspaper in English, founded in 1962.

With the continuous growth in the African market as a result of industrial expansion and urbanization, there is the keenest competition for this readership. In 1964 the *World* (daily) had a circulation of 69,000 and *Post* (weekly) of 90,000.[48] Most of these papers have African reporters and staffs; because all are subject to white boards, their political tones reflect the divisions within the white community. *Post* is a vigorous proletarian journal, which gives prominence to sex and crime stories, but also exposes specific scandals in white and African society and opposes racialism, both Afrikaner and African. At the other extreme *Bona* and the other Nationalist-controlled publications emphasize African traditional culture and either overtly support apartheid or, at least, refrain from criticizing it. All these publications are financed largely by advertisements and the advertisement rates are higher than in newspapers with similar circulations catering to white readers, mainly because one copy sold to an African is read by many more people than one copy sold to a white.

There are also a number of small weekly and fortnightly newspapers owned by Indian and Coloured people. The Indian papers are all published in Natal. They are moderate in tone compared with two left-wing Cape Town Coloured publications — *Torch,* the mouthpiece of the Non-European Unity Movement, and the *Citizen,* a "pure" Trotskyite journal.

More effective as a radical critic of white supremacy was a paper which has had many names during its career. The *Guardian* was founded in Cape Town in 1937 by members of the Communist Party of South Africa. It survived a series of bannings by adopting a succession of new names — *Clarion, Advance, New Age* and finally *Spark,* which ceased publication in 1963.[49]

The Nationalist Party regards the English South African press as one of its most dangerous opponents and it has taken a

[48] *Survey of Race Relations,* 1964, p. 47.

[49] Brian Bunting, *The Story behind the Non-White Press* (Cape Town: New Age, 1960); *Survey of Race Relations,* 1963, pp. 65-66.

series of steps to restrict its operations by legislation, intimidation and prohibition. The onslaught started with the Suppression of Communism Act, 1950, which, as amended, empowers the State President to prohibit the publication of any journal if he "is satisfied" that it "serves 'inter alia' as a means for expressing views or conveying information, the publication of which is calculated to further the achievement of any of the objects of communism" and then Communism itself is defined in extremely loose terms in the Act. Under the Public Safety Act, 1953, the State President may declare a state of emergency in any or all of the districts of the Republic, and rule by proclamation. It was in terms of this law that *Torch* and *New Age* were banned during the state of emergency after the Sharpeville shootings in 1960. Under the Criminal Law Amendment Act of 1953 tough penalties are prescribed for "Any person who . . . uses any language or does any act or thing calculated to cause any person or persons in general to commit an offence by way of protest against a law or in support of any campaign against any law or in support of any campaign for the repeal or modification of any law."

This law has been a serious curb to free expression. The Prison Act of 1959 makes it an offense to publish "any information concerning any prisoner, ex-prisoner or the administration of any prison" without written authority. Regulations issued under the Extension of University Act of 1959 make it unlawful for students in the nonwhite university colleges to publish any material without permission.[50] The General Law Amendment Act, 1962, extends the restrictions that the government may impose upon persons under the Suppression of Communism Act, empowering it to prohibit persons from attending meetings and making it an offense to publish any speech or writing of any such banned person. It also provides that no new newspaper may be registered without the government's consent, except after making a deposit of up to $28,000.[51] Finally, under the Publications and Entertainments Act, 1963, the government has appointed a Publications Control Board, under the chairmanship of Professor G. Dekker of Potchef-

50 Hepple, *op. cit.*
51 *Survey of Race Relations*, 1962, pp. 37-39.

stroom University for Christian Higher Education, which may ban any book which is "undesirable," in the sense, inter alia, that it is "on any grounds objectionable." [52] Early in 1962 all the daily newspapers, which are members of the South African Newspaper Union, drew up a code of conduct and created a Board of Reference, with the purpose of ensuring that reports are accurate, and the code also provides that "Comment should take cognisance of the complex racial problems of South Africa and should also take into account the general good and the safety of the country and its peoples." [53] These newspapers are for the present exempt from the controls established by the 1963 act; but most periodicals are liable to be banned as "undesirable" by the Publications Control Board.

Under these laws the *Guardian* and its successors have all ceased publication. The liberal press has been harassed in various ways. In 1962 Peter Hjul, a director of *Contact,* a Liberal Party fortnightly, was prosecuted and fined under the emergency regulations in the Transkei and in 1963 he was banned and thereby prohibited from publishing. The owner and the editor of *Drum,* a magazine for Africans, were also charged under the emergency regulations; *Drum* subsequently ceased publication. Under the rules of the House of Assembly Anthony Delius, the distinguished political journalist of the *Cape Times,* was permanently banned from the precincts of Parliament in 1964. In May 1963, six newspaper men were detained under the Prison Act for taking photographs in Marshall Square, Johannesburg. The government also controls the access of journalists to the Bantu Areas and makes it extremely difficult for the press to obtain reliable information about them. For example, in May 1963 the *Star* was refused permission to send a reporter and photographer to Vendaland, a Bantu Area in the northeastern Transvaal whose inhabitants were suffering from prolonged drought and starvation.[54]

The result is that the most radical critics of the government have been silenced, the quasi-Communist press has been ex-

[52] *Ibid.,* 1963, pp. 68-73.

[53] *Ibid.,* 1962, pp. 58-59.

[54] *Ibid.,* 1962, pp. 63, 242, 1964, p. 48; *Star,* weekly edition, May 11, May 18, 1963; *House of Assembly Debates,* 1963, cols. 5966-67.

tinguished, the liberal press has been reduced to insecurity and near impotence, and the great English dailies are impeded from discovering and reporting the worst evils of apartheid and are under great pressure to refrain from fundamental criticisms of the government. Meanwhile, the Afrikaans press is expanding under the benign eye of a Cabinet, many of whose members hold directorships in publishing houses.[55]

Before 1963 foreign publications and films were liable to be excluded from South Africa under the Customs Act, 1955, which authorizes the Minister of the Interior to prohibit the importation of "goods which are indecent or obscene or on any ground whatsoever objectionable," and imposes severe penalties for possessing or offering for sale prohibited literature. In applying this law, the Minister consulted a Board of Censors and published lists of banned books from time to time in the *Government Gazette.* By 1963 there were 8,629 publications on the banned list. Many of these are pornographic; others are banned for political reasons. They include not only Communist publications, but also the writings of Dostoevsky and Tolstoy, Lawrence and Graves, Hemingway and Salinger, Faulkner and Caldwell, and Bertrand Russell, and works by South African authors such as Peter Abrahams and Harry Bloom. South African librarians are continually engaged in recalling and destroying books that have been banned; booksellers have a difficult task in deciding what foreign publications to order. Since the public libraries in South Africa are segregated, furthermore, the vast majority of the nonwhites, who cannot afford to buy books, have access to a most limited range.[56]

Films were formerly subject to censorship under the Entertainment (Censorship) Act of 1931, under whose terms the same

55 On official controls over the South African press, besides the works mentioned earlier, see Edgar H. Brookes and J. B. Macaulay, *Civil Liberty in South Africa* (Cape Town: Oxford University Press, 1958) chapter 6; International Commission of Jurists, *South Africa and the Rule of Law* (Geneva: International Commission of Jurists, 1961) pp. 75-78; and Elizabeth S. Landis, "South African Apartheid Legislation, II," *Yale Law Review,* LXXI, No. 3 (January 1962) 486-89.

56 Hepple, *op. cit.,* pp. 12-14, 24-25, 35-41; *Survey of Race Relations,* 1964, pp. 40-41.

Board of Censors advised the Minister which films were to be prohibited. Some films were rejected absolutely, others were cut, and others were not permitted to be shown to African audiences.[57] The Publications Control Board, established under the Publications and Entertainments Act, 1963, has succeeded the Board of Censors, and has powers over South African publications and films as well as increased powers over imported publications and films. It is empowered to prohibit films on moral, religious and political grounds, and appeals from the Board's decisions lie, not with the Courts, but the Minister, whose decision is final.[58]

The government has been concerned about the unfavorable reports of South African conditions that have appeared in the foreign press. It has deported foreign journalists (Basil Davidson, British, 1953, Henry Barzilay, British, 1959); withdrawn press credential cards (e.g., from those who protested against the expulsion of Barzilay); and refused visas (John Hatch, British, Doris Lessing, British, and Sven Oeste, Swedish). During the emergency of 1960 it suppressed reports and arrested and detained a Canadian journalist (Norman Phillips of the Toronto *Star*). In 1964 a Press Commission, after thirteen years' labor, produced a voluminous report criticizing dispatches sent to overseas news agencies and papers by South African "stringers," censuring leading overseas newspapers, including *The Times* of London and *The New York Times*, for showing hostility to Afrikaner Nationalists, and recommending that a Press Council be established "for the control and self-discipline" of the press and the registration of stringers.[59] However, these actions have not had the effect of intimidating foreign journalists, nor some courageous South African journalists, such as Stanley Uys, who act as correspondents of foreign newspapers.

Finally, the government has embarked upon a lavish propaganda campaign, both inside and outside South Africa, through

[57] Hepple, *op. cit.*

[58] *Survey of Race Relations*, 1963, pp. 68-73.

[59] Hepple, *op. cit.*, pp. 30-31; Norman Phillips, *The Tragedy of Apartheid: A journalist's experience in the South African riots* (New York: McKay, 1960); *Survey of Race Relations*, 1964, pp. 43-46.

the radio broadcasting system that it controls and through various publications. Even since 1936 the South African Broadcasting Corporation has been a public corporation with a monopoly of broadcasting in South Africa, controlled by a Board of Governors appointed by the Head of State on the advice of the Minister of Posts and Telegraphs. The SABC was originally modeled on the BBC and was politically neutral, providing parallel services in English and Afrikaans. In the last few years, it has been transformed. In 1961 Gideon Roos, the Director-General, resigned and so did other senior officials and news broadcasters. The present chairman is Dr. P. J. Meyer, who was formerly an officer in the *Ossewa Brandwag* and secretary of the *Federasie van Afrikaanse Kultuurverenigings,* and is reputed to be the present head of the *Broederbond.* J. J. Kruger, a former editor of the *Transvaler,* is cultural adviser, and Douglas Fuchs is director of programs. Under their direction the news reports and commentaries are now strongly impregnated with Nationalist propaganda. The liberal approach to race relations, anti-apartheid South Africans, the English South African press, the United Nations, and the independent States of Africa and Asia are persistently excoriated. After Mrs. Helen Joseph had been placed under house arrest under the General Law Amendment Act, a news commentary on October 31, 1962 implied that she was a dangerous Communist, notwithstanding the fact that in the treason trial the prosecution directed no arguments at Mrs. Joseph's position in relation to Communism and she was found not guilty of treason. On a more trivial plane, in January 1963 the SABC refused to broadcast a running report on the Natal Golf Championships, because an Indian golfer was participating; he eventually won. The SABC has instituted a Bantu Program Control Board, consisting of prominent supporters of the Nationalist Party. This Board has increased the amount of time given to Bantu programs. The SABC is also changing from medium and shortwave transmitters to VHF, with rediffusion stations. In due course it may be expected that most radio sets in South Africa will receive SABC broadcasts only.

There are more than a million radio licenses in South Africa. Most white householders have a license and the number of licenses held by nonwhites is rapidly increasing. The government's monopoly over radio services has now become an important instrument of political control. There is no television service in South Africa and it is the government's declared policy to refrain from creating one, on the grounds that the experiences of other countries have shown that television corrupts youth, promotes crime and is an unnecessary expense.[60]

Printed propaganda is conducted on a large scale by the Department of Information, a full-fledged government department created in 1962 in succession to a State Information Office in the Department of External Affairs. The duties of the department are to promote a favorable impression of government policy among all sections of the population, and also abroad. For this purpose it had a vote of $3,892,000 for the financial year 1963-1964. It publishes several journals for internal consumption, such as *Bantu* and the *Bantu Education Journal,* which it distributes free to African chiefs, teachers and others. Abroad, the Department has fifteen information officers, most of them in Britain, the United States and Western Europe. Large advertisements are placed in leading newspapers from time to time; the *South African Digest* and *Panorama* are published periodically and widely distributed. This propaganda is most sophisticated. It emphasizes the economic strength of South Africa and the material well-being of Africans in the Republic compared with Africans in other parts of Africa, and presents the Bantustan policy as being tantamount to African self-government.[61]

Nearly all the modern communications media in South Africa are controlled by whites. Those which are in the public sector, such as the radio services, are used as instruments of government propaganda. Those which are in the private sector, such as the daily and most of the periodical press, still reflect the variations of interest and opinion within the white caste, but the lead in circulation of the English-medium press

[60] On the SABC see *Survey of Race Relations,* 1959-60, pp. 260-62; 1961, p. 272; 1962, p. 49; 1964, pp. 48-49; *House of Assembly Debates,* 1962, cols. 7305-7401, and the *Star,* weekly edition, February 2, 1963.

[61] On printed propaganda see Hepple, *op. cit.,* pp. 57-60, and *House of Assembly Debates,* 1962, cols. 1877ff. and 7975ff., 1963, cols. 8394ff.

is gradually being narrowed and the capacity of the English-medium press to oppose the caste system is gradually being restricted by legislation. Nonwhite South Africans have to depend mainly on white-controlled media for their political information; but just as the English-medium press has never determined the political conduct of a significant number of its Afrikaner readers, so the white-controlled communications media are not likely to determine the political conduct of their nonwhite recipients. That is determined primarily by the realities of the daily life of nonwhites in the Republic. Nevertheless, the legislative restrictions on the privately-controlled media do have the effect of seriously impeding the flow of communication between nonwhite leaders and their followers — indeed, they make it extremely difficult for nonwhite leaders to emerge and to build up and maintain a following.

THE ARTICULATION OF INTERESTS

In South Africa the articulation of interests does not conform to the normal pattern of modern countries where the basic criterion of articulation is economic interest: in South Africa it is race. South African interest groups may be classified in three categories, distinguished by their ethnic scope. There are *community* groups, which are confined to members of only one community and which pursue the interests of that community (e.g., Afrikaner, Malay, Xhosa). There are *caste* groups which include members of the different communities within the same caste (white, Coloured, Asian, African). And third, there are a few *national* groups, extending to all the castes and communities in the country.

South African interest groups may also be classed according to the strengths of their channels of systematic influence over the authoritative political structures, especially Parliament, the Cabinet, and the bureaucracy. There are interest groups whose influence is dominant; others whose influence is slight; and others whose means of exerting systematic influence are virtually nil.

Afrikaner community groups are dominant in all areas in which they exist, and where they are lacking, white caste groups are dominant. Those of slight influence are white English-speaking community groups, and also white caste groups where they exist alongside Afrikaner community groups. All groups with nonwhite members — whether based on the community, the caste or the national principle — have virtually no systematic means of influencing the authoritative political structures. Therefore, systematic influence over the government of South Africa is monopolized by the white caste and dominated by its inner oligarchy — the Afrikaner community.

Afrikaner Associations

The primary political instrument of the Afrikaner community is the Nationalist Party, which will be considered in the next section. Besides this party there is a series of Afrikaner associations with direct or indirect political influence. Some of these associations are concerned with the interests of the entire Afrikaner community, and others are associations of particular groups within Afrikanerdom. The major associations which are concerned with the welfare of the entire Afrikaner community are the *Afrikaner Broederbond,* the *Federasie van Afrikaanse Kultuurverenigings* and the *Reddingsdaadbond.* The role of the *Broederbond* [Brothers' League] is hard to assess for it is a secret society.[62] Founded in 1918, it has operated in secret since 1922. Membership is by invitation and new members are believed to submit to elaborate rituals and pledges which emphasize its "tribal" character. Afrikaners of proven Nationalist fervor and talent are enlisted from a wide range of occupations — notably the schools, the universities, the churches, the civil service and (more recently) from business. The *Broederbond* is therefore a self-perpetuating association of Afrikaner elite. With a membership of perhaps between three and five thousand, its main concerns have apparently been to place zealous Afrikaner Nationalists in key positions and to found special organizations to meet new needs of the Afrikaner people. There are local cells, a general council, an Executive Council of "Twelve Apostles," and a "Trinity" headed by a Supreme Chief. It is probable that most Nationalist members of Parliament are members of the *Broederbond* and that Prime Minister H. F. Verwoerd, Min-

[62] On the *Broederbond* see Carter, *op. cit.,* pp. 250-56; Marquard, *op. cit.,* pp. 200-201; Munger, *op. cit.,* pp. 781-82.

ister of Economic Affairs N. Diederichs, and Minister of Posts and Telegraphs Albert Hertzog are Apostles; and Dr. P. J. Meyer, the Chairman of the Board of the SABC, is reputed to be the present Supreme Chief, in succession to the Rector of the University of Stellenbosch.

In 1935 Prime Minister J. B. M. Hertzog denounced the *Broederbond* as "a grave menace to the rest and peace of our social community," and in 1944 Prime Minister J. C. Smuts called it a "dangerous, cunning, political Fascist organisation" and ordered civil servants who were members to resign either from the *Broederbond* or from the service.[63] A committee of the Dutch Reformed Church (N.G.K.) was appointed to investigate the charges against the *Broederbond* in 1949 and according to its findings, which were published in 1951, the *Broederbond* was "wholesome and healthy, seeking only the progress and best interests of the Afrikaner nation." [64]

The *Broederbond* has continued to be a political issue. In August 1963 Professor A. van Selms, head of the department of Semitic Languages in the University of Pretoria and a member of the N.H.K., declared: "I view continued membership of the *Broederbond* of anyone who calls himself a Christian as a handicap to his moral judgments." [65] In 1963 and 1964 the *Sunday Times* published photostat copies of *Broederbond* documents and Sir de Villiers Graaff, Leader of the Opposition, pressed for a public enquiry by a judicial commission. The Prime Minister then appointed D. H. Botha, a judge of the Supreme Court, as a commissioner — but with instructions to sit in private and to investigate not only the *Broederbond,* but also the Sons of England and the Freemasons, which also conduct their affairs in secret. This was a typically astute response. In his report Judge Botha stated that he had found no evidence that any of the three organizations indulged in subversive or dubious activities, or exerted an undesirable influence.[66]

63 Carter, *op. cit.*, pp. 251-52.
64 *Ibid.*, p. 255.
65 *Star*, weekly edition, August 10, 1963.
66 *Survey of Race Relations*, 1964, pp. 20-22; *Africa Digest*, XII, No. 5 (London: April 1965) 133.

Conceivably the *Broederbond* is the ultimate center of power in South Africa, but it seems more likely that it had its greatest power before the 1948 election. Since that time the Cabinet as such has probably been the effective ruler of South Africa, and the *Broederbond* has become merely one of many supporting and overlapping organizations, though in the event of a political crisis within the Nationalist Party the Twelve Apostles, the Trinity and the Supreme Chief might yet exercise a decisive influence.

In 1929 the *Broederbond* was instrumental in founding the *Federasie van Afrikaanse Kultuurverenigings* [Federation of Afrikaner Cultural Associations] whose object is to preserve Afrikaner solidarity and to advance Afrikaner influence in every aspect of life.[67] The F.A.K. in turn has seen to the creation of exclusive Afrikaner associations in a wide variety of specific fields — in some cases by founding new associations, in others by capturing control of bodies that had previously embraced a wider membership and a wider ideal, and in others by seceding from such bodies.

During the 1930's there was a series of secessions. Typical was the secession leading to the establishment of an exclusive Afrikaner student association.[68] In 1924 Leo Marquard, an Afrikaner with wide loyalties who had recently returned from holding a Rhodes Scholarship at Oxford University, had convened a conference resulting in the founding of NUSAS (the National Union of South African Students). For some years NUSAS was supported by the student bodies in all the eight universities, but in 1933 an agitation commenced against NUSAS in the four Afrikaans-medium universities. Late that year Afrikaner students met in Bloemfontein under the chairmanship of P. J. Meyer, heard an address from D. F. Malan (later Prime Minister) on "Nationalism as an Outlook on Life," and founded A.N.S. (*Afrikaanse Nasionale Studentebond*), which soon received the support of the students' representative councils in the Afrikaans-medium universities.

[67] On the F.A.K. see Carter, *op. cit.*, pp. 256-58.

[68] Neville Rubin, *History of the Relations between NUSAS, the Afrikaanse Studentebond and the Afrikaans University Centres* (Cape Town: National Union of South African Students, 1960).

To the seceding Afrikaners NUSAS was not a truly national association, because it conveyed "nothing national in the Afrikaans sense," while to NUSAS the seceding Afrikaners were not national but merely sectional. During the Second World War, A.N.S. came under Nazi influence. In 1940 it issued a manifesto in favor of an authoritarian South African Republic, with Christian National Education, a state-controlled press and radio, and Afrikaans as the only official language. A.N.S. accepted the leadership of J. F. J. van Rensburg, head of a pro-Nazi sabotage organizations, the *Ossewa Brandwag,* and its branch in the University of Cape Town gave a platform to a *predikant,* Rev. J. D. Vorster, who applauded Hitler and *Mein Kampf* and looked forward to a "Christian National Republic . . . which would obey the rule of the blood." [69] With the defeat of Nazism, A.N.S. passed into oblivion.

However, in 1948 a new group, A.S.B. (*Afrikaanse Studentebond*), was founded. Its declared objects were combining all Afrikaner students in one organization, furthering their common interests, and maintaining and expanding "white Christian civilization in opposition to Communism." [70] The A.S.B. has the support of the overwhelming majority of Afrikaner university students — including the Afrikaner students in the English-medium universities — and it has steadfastly endorsed the government's racial policies.

On the other hand NUSAS, which had previously equivocated on the question of the admission of nonwhite student bodies, opened its membership to several nonwhite institutions after the Second World War. Later, NUSAS organized a series of spectacular demonstrations against the closure of the established universities to nonwhite students, and became one of the most forthright critics, not only of the Afrikaner Nationalist government, but of the entire system of white supremacy. Attempts have been made to heal the schism between NUSAS and the A.S.B., but they have failed because their attitudes towards nonwhites are irreconcilable. Today the A.S.B. is an Afrikaner community group with considerable influence over

69 *Ibid.,* p. 11.
70 *Ibid.,* p. 12.

the government; while NUSAS is a national group with a social philosophy diametrically opposed to that of the government, and the government is intimidating it and hoping to destroy it.

A similar secession led to the establishment of an Afrikaner association for the study of racial questions in South Africa. In 1929 a South African Institute of Race Relations had been created for this purpose, and during the 1930's it was building up a deserved reputation for open-minded scholarship and as an agent for the improvement of human relations across the community and caste lines, through its conferences, its publications and its casework. The Institute's membership was open to South Africans of all races, but in practice the bulk of its members were always English-speaking whites and its leadership lay mainly, but by no means exclusively, in the same community. In 1935 a group of Afrikaner intellectuals broke away from the Institute on the grounds that it was too liberal, and they founded a rival *Afrikaanse Buro vir Rassestudies*. This was the body which, in 1937, searching for a "slogan" different from "segregation" with which "to label the racial policy of the Afrikaners," coined the word "apartheid," and thereby played some part in the spadework that led eventually to the formulation of the policy of the Nationalist Party for the decisive election of 1948.[71] By the time of that election, however, the *Buro* itself was moribund.

Four months after the election another group of Afrikaner intellectuals founded the *Suid-Afrikaanse Buro vir Rasse-Aangeleenthede* [South African Bureau for Racial Affairs], with financial aid from the *Federasie van Afrikaanse Kultuurverenigings*. Among the founders were Professor N. J. J. Olivier of Stellenbosch University, Professor W. W. M. Eiselen of Pretoria University (soon to become secretary of Native Affairs), Professor J. C. van Rooy of Potchefstroom University (then head of the *Broederbond*), and Professor H. B. Thom of Stellenbosch University (a later head of the *Broederbond*). Thus this important sphere of activity has become divided on

[71] N. J. Rhoodie and H. J. Venter, *Apartheid: A socio-historical exposition of the origin and development of the apartheid idea* (Cape Town: HAUM, 1959) p. 171.

typical South African lines. The Institute remains open to
people of all races and pursues its basically humane and empirical course, collecting and publishing data on South African
affairs, but without the means to exert any appreciable influence over the government, while SABRA, applying a strict
color bar and with an almost exclusively Afrikaner membership, has close contacts with the government.[72]

Other exclusive Afrikaner associations that have been
founded by secession from more broadly-based associations are
the *Voortrekkers* (from the Boy Scouts), *Noodhulpliga* (from
the Red Cross), an Afrikaner institute of international affairs,
and Afrikaner teachers' associations.

The *Reddingsdaadbond* [Savings Association], which was
founded at the time of the celebrations of the centenary of the
Great Trek in 1938 to aid the Afrikaners in their second Great
Trek, from the rural areas to the industrial towns, has carried
the process of fission into the economic field.[73] A generation
ago Afrikaners controlled a very small proportion of the wealth
of South Africa, for most of the powerful enterprises were of
British or Jewish origin and remained under the control of
South Africans of British or Jewish descent. However, there already were a small Afrikaner life assurance society and a small
Afrikaner trust and assurance society. The R.D.B. has seen to
the founding of other Afrikaner financial institutions and to the
channeling of Afrikaner business into the Afrikaner institutions.

By 1963 the five leading Afrikaner financial enterprises had

[72] On SABRA see Carter, *op. cit.,* pp. 266-72; Marquard, *op cit.,* pp.
199-200; Munger, *op. cit.,* pp. 503-50; and Rhoodie and Venter, *op. cit.,* pp.
169-75. SABRA publishes the *Tydskrif vir Rasse-aangeleenthede* [Journal
of Racial Affairs] and a *Nuusbrief* [*Newsletter*], both of them bimonthly
since 1949, and a number of monographs. On the South African Institute
of Race Relations see Carter, pp. 336-37 and Munger, pp. 479-84. The
Institute publishes *Race Relations News* (monthly, 1938ff.) and *A Survey
of Race Relations in South Africa* (annually, 1929ff.). Its other publications include Ellen Hellmann, ed., *Handbook on Race Relations in South
Africa* (Cape Town: Oxford University Press, 1949), and a considerable
number of monographs.

[73] On the R.D.B. see Carter, *op. cit.,* pp. 255-61 and Munger, *op. cit.,* pp.
551-59.

total assets of about $1,070 million.[74] The most powerful are the *Volkskas* [Peoples' Bank], Sanlam (a life assurance society), the Trust Bank, Saambou (a building society), and Santam (a trust and assurance society). Afrikaner companies are also making headway in the mining and industrial sectors — the rise of the Rembrandt Tobacco Company under Anton Rupert, with ramifications in four continents, is a striking example of Afrikaner enterprise.[75] The total share of exclusively Afrikaner enterprise in the national economy is estimated to have risen from 5 percent in 1938-1939 to 11 percent in 1948-1949,[76] and it had probably reached between 15 and 20 percent by 1964. These Afrikaner enterprises and Afrikaner chambers of commerce and industry are able to exert considerable influence over the government, especially since most Afrikaner politicians have become directors of companies. Nevertheless, English-speaking white South Africans still control the bulk of the economy, and the government is also influenced by industrial organizations that are predominantly under their control. Of these, the Transvaal and Orange Free State Chamber of Mines is by far the most powerful, embracing as it does all the great gold-mining corporations in the country.

Trade Unions

In the field of labor, professional and sports associations, the primary problem confronting Afrikaner Nationalists has not been British influence as such, but rather the problem of non-white infiltration into associations that in virtually every case were initially confined to the white caste. Here Afrikaner Nationalists have given priority to transforming national groups into caste groups, and preventing caste groups from developing into national groups, for the caste line has been even more important to them than the community line, though in some cases (as we shall see) Afrikaner community groups have been sponsored.

[74] This figure represents the total assets of *Volkskas*, Sanlam, the Trust Bank, Saambou and Santam, per companies' balance sheets published in Beerman's *Financial Year Book of Southern Africa*, 1964, E. Landsberg, ed.

[75] Munger, *op. cit.*, pp. 554-58.

[76] *Burger*, February 25, 1960.

Trade unionism was introduced to South Africa at the turn of the century by white immigrants from Europe and Australia. From an early stage most white South African trade unionists were more concerned to maintain their caste privileges than they were to create a united workers' front against management, and successive governments responded to their demands. Consequently, serious legal impediments were placed in the way of nonwhite — and especially African — trade unionists: the pass laws (in conjunction with endemic under-employment of Africans) have meant that African workers have always had to weigh the advantages of joining trade unions against the danger that they would thereby lose their jobs and their access to the towns; breaches of contract and strikes by African workers have generally been held to be criminal offenses; and the definition of "employee" in the industrial conciliation legislation has excluded most African workers, so that African trade unions have not been able to participate in the national system of collective bargaining. The result was that by 1948 there were segregated white unions, segregated Coloured, Asian and African unions, and a few mixed unions in which Coloured, Asian and even in some cases a few African members had equal rights with whites; among the trade union leaders were a few who were committed to the idea of uniting the industrial workers of all races.[77] This confused situation was anathema to the Nationalist Party, which has striven to prevent the rise of a working-class movement transcending the color bar.

During the 1930's ardent Afrikaner Nationalists founded a *Blankewerkersbeskermingsbond* [White Workers' Protection Association] and launched a vitriolic campaign against the radical trade union leaders, whom they denounced as Jews, Communists and *Kaffer-Boeties* [literally: Kaffir-brothers]. Thus the newly urbanized Afrikaners, who were becoming the majority of the white workers in most industries, found it necessary to choose between the race principle and the class principle. Until 1948 the struggle was bitter and inconclusive, but since then the racial principle has triumphed, thanks largely to government support. Within a year of coming into power the Na-

[77] On trade unionism before 1948 see H. J. Simons, "Trade Unions," in Ellen Hellmann, *op. cit.*, chapter 6.

tionalists gained control of the important Mine Workers Union. Other unions were purged of their radical leaders under the Suppression of Communism Act and its amendments, which empowered the government to impose severe restrictions on Communists and defined a Communist so loosely as to include anyone who encouraged in any way the achievement of *any* of the objects of Communism, which was also loosely defined. By 1956, fifty-six trade union leaders had been ordered to resign from their unions, and the back of the radical leadership of the trade unions had been broken.[78]

The Industrial Conciliation Act, 1956, struck powerfully at the very existence of mixed trade unions. No mixed unions that did not exist in 1956 may be registered; the existing mixed unions are encouraged to split into uniracial unions; and those that remain mixed are compelled to have separate branches for white and for nonwhite members and to have all-white executive committees, and are prohibited from holding mixed meetings, conferences or congresses. The same Act places still further obstacles in the way of African trade unionists by prohibiting Africans from representing employees in industrial councils or in disputes referred to conciliation boards, and prohibiting employers from collecting trade union dues from African employees. Under these pressures several of the mixed unions have split. In 1956 there were fifty-nine mixed unions, and by 1961 sixteen of them had split or were about to do so. On the other hand, notwithstanding the government's wish to prevent such contacts and the existing legal impediments, cooperation between white and nonwhite branches continues in the surviving mixed unions and there are also several cases of cooperation between white and nonwhite unions.

Analysis of the coordinating bodies shows that the government has gone a long way towards weakening and dividing its opponents in the trade union movement. On the rightist side, there is the South African Confederation of Labour (SACOL), virtually an all-white body with a predominantly Afrikaner

[78] On trade unionism since 1948 see Muriel Horrell, *South African Trade Unionism: A study of a divided working class* (Johannesburg: South African Institute of Race Relations, 1961); *Survey of Race Relations,* 1961, pp. 202-208; 1962, pp. 161-63; 1963, pp. 213-15; 1964, pp. 262-66.

membership. In the middle is the Trade Union Council of South Africa (TUCSA), which has always admitted all types of registered unions but did not admit unregistered (i.e., African) unions until 1962, and which has a majority of white and significant minorities of Coloured and Asian members. On the left, there is the South African Congress of Trade Unions (SACTU); this movement, which has always admitted unregistered unions equally with others, allied itself to the African National Congress and was thereby committed to political action against discriminatory laws and practices; its membership is predominantly African. Some other African unions are associated in a Federation of Free African Trade Unions of South Africa (FOFATUSA); there are also many unaffiliated unions of all types. The strengths of these bodies in 1961 were estimated as follows:

TABLE IV.3   *Trade Union Coordinating Bodies* [79]

| | No. of Unions | Number of Members | | | | Total |
		White	Coloured	Asian	African	
SACOL	28	150,158	175			150,333
TUCSA	49	110,427	44,726	11,850		167,003
SACTU	46	498	12,384	1,650	38,791	53,323
FOFATUSA	17				18,385	18,385
Subtotal	140	261,083	57,285	13,500	57,176	389,044
Unaffiliated	108	49,344	19,444	4,233	2,776	75,797
Total	248	310,427	76,729	17,733	59,952	464,841

Professional and Scientific Associations

When most South African professional and scientific associations were founded, the color question was not an issue because nonwhites has not yet obtained the qualifications for membership. Later, when the first nonwhites began to qualify, they were often admitted to the associations on the same basis as whites; but this sort of contact, too, the Nationalist government has tried to stop.

[79] Adapted from Horrell, *Trade Unionism*, p. 89.

In the case of the nursing profession, the government found it necessary to resort to legislation.[80] Under pre-1948 legislation there was a Nursing Council, which dealt with the registration, training and discipline of nurses, and a Nursing Association which looked after their group interests. Nonwhite nurses voted equally with whites in the elections of nurses' representatives on the Council and of members of the Board of the Association; nonwhites equally with whites were eligible for election to the Council and the Board, though in fact no nonwhite ever was elected. Conditions in the branches of the association varied. In some branches meetings were mixed, in others nurses of the different races met separately. The nursing profession was split on racial lines by the Nursing Act of 1957. The Nursing Council may now consist of white persons only — including one selected by an "Advisory Board" elected by Asian and Coloured nurses, and an individual picked by an "Advisory Board" elected by African nurses. The Council is required to keep separate registers of nurses according to their racial groups and empowered to prescribe different qualifications and different uniforms for the different races. Similarly, the Board of the Nursing Association may be comprised only of white persons, among them one named by an "Advisory Committee" elected by Asian and Coloured nurses and another chosen by an "Advisory Committee" elected by African nurses. The act also provides that, except in an emergency, no white nurse may be placed under the authority of a nonwhite nurse.

There was considerable opposition to the enactment and enforcement of this law. Some nonwhite nurses left the country; others formed a non-racial Federation of South African Nurses and Midwives in the hope that it would be recognized by the International Nursing Council; and others have accepted the new situation. In 1960 the government was able to announce that 17,154 white, 903 Coloured and Asian, and 4,633 African nurses were registered with the reconstituted South African Nursing Council, leaving perhaps three or four thousand nonwhite nurses unregistered.

[80] On the introduction of apartheid in the nursing profession see *Survey of Race Relations*, 1955-56, pp. 173-75; 1956-57, pp. 157-60; 1957-58, pp. 178-80; 1959-60, pp. 208-209; 1961, pp. 221-22.

In other professions effective cooperation across the color bar has been impeded by rigorous application of basic apartheid laws. For example, in 1956 Duma Nokwe, the first African to obtain an LL.B. degree and be admitted to practice before the Transvaal Division of the Supreme Court, was denied permission by H. F. Verwoerd, in his capacity as Minister of Native Affairs, to occupy an office in the Johannesburg building used by the white advocates. This made it impossible for Nokwe to pursue a legal career in Johannesburg, whereupon he became full-time secretary-general of the African National Congress.[81] Similarly in 1958 C. M. Kobus, an African attorney, and A. Ndlovu, an African advocate, were ordered to vacate their chambers in Cape Town. Kobus tried to continue his legal career in the African township of Langa, but in 1960 he gave up his professional independence because he could not conduct an efficient business in a segregated township at a considerable distance from the court and the barristers' chambers; Ndlovu migrated to the United Kingdom.[82]

In 1962 the South African Psychological Association decided to admit qualified nonwhites as members, whereupon a group of Nationalist members seceded and founded an all-white Psychological Institute.[83] The government has been able to apply economic pressure to other professional bodies. On March 5, 1963, the government declared that the eleven scientific organizations receiving financial aid from the Department of Education, Arts and Science had been

> . . . requested to comply with Government policy, by amending their Constitutions if necessary, to provide for separate societies. Nonwhite societies could, by means of affiliation, be combined in national societies which could then send representatives to specific executive meetings of national societies for whites. In this way channels could be created not only for the exchange of views but also for the flow of knowledge gained at congresses and conferences of white scientists to nonwhite scientists. [The statement added] . . . the implementation of

81 *Ibid.*, 1955-56, p. 172.
82 *Ibid.*, 1957-58, pp. 177-78; 1959-60, p. 208.
83 *Ibid.*, 1962, p. 169.

this policy will be necessary to ensure that the societies will continue to qualify for financial aid from the government.[84]

Sports Associations

The government is also trying to prevent inter-racial contacts on sports fields.[85] J. de Klerk, Minister of the Interior, has declared his policy to see that there shall be no mixed teams and no competitions between teams of different races in South Africa, that mixed teams shall not represent South Africa abroad, and that each sport shall be controlled by an all-white organization.[86] There is still no legislation specifically designed to give effect to this policy, but the government can go a long way towards enforcing it under the Group Areas Act and by its power over entry and exit, so that foreign sportsmen are prevented from entering the Republic and South African sportsmen from leaving it unless they comply with the policy.

White South Africans are extremely proud of their sportsmen's achievements in international competition, so that this aspect of the government's policy is peculiarly vulnerable to international pressure. The International Table Tennis Federation has already switched its recognition from the all-white South African Association to the non-racial and predominantly nonwhite South African Table Tennis Board; the Federation of International Football Associations has suspended its recognition of the all-white Football Association of South Africa; and the New Zealand Rugby Union has decided that all future New Zealand touring teams shall be fully representative (i.e., shall include Maoris on equal terms with whites). The rugby

[84] *House of Assembly Debates,* 1963, cols. 2140-41. The eleven organizations named are: Entomological Society of S. A., Royal Society of S. A., Nutrition Society of Southern Africa; Geological Society of S. A., S. A. Geographical Society, S. A. Society for the Advancement of Science, S. A. Biological Society, S. A. Archaeological Society, Zoological Society of S. A., Ornithological Society of S. A., Tree Society of S. A.

[85] On this question see Muriel Horrell, *Sport and Race in South Africa* (Johannesburg: South African Institute of Race Relations, 1963); also *Survey of Race Relations,* 1963, pp. 283-301; 1964, pp. 330-50.

[86] The Bloemfontein City Council goes so far as to prohibit nonwhites from watching sports in the Orange Free State stadium, even in segregated seating. *Survey of Race Relations,* 1963, p. 290.

issue is of particular popular concern because rugby is white South Africa's premier sport and New Zealand is South Africa's traditional rival.

Similar crises are pending in other sports. The all-white South African Boxing Association cooperated with the Non-European Boxing Association in sending five white and three nonwhite boxers to the 1963 United States championships, where one of the nonwhites, Lucas Matseke, won the flyweight title. The government granted the exit permits on the ground that the South Africans were competing as individuals and not as a team. This is not a formula that can readily be applied to many other types of sports contests. Perhaps the future relations between South African and foreign and international sports bodies will be influenced by developments in the dispute concerning the Olympic Games. The Afro-Asian members of the International Olympic Committee seem determined to continue to withhold recognition from the all-white South African Olympic and National Games Association, and perhaps to grant recognition to the South African Non-Racial Olympic Committee, which is predominantly nonwhite. If South Africa's exclusion from the 1964 Games is repeated in 1968, other international sports bodies are likely to follow suit.

A Racial Hierarchy of Associations

The dominant interest groups in South Africa are, therefore, the three general Afrikaner community groups — the *Broederbond,* the F.A.K. and R.D.B.; a large number of specific Afrikaner community groups, such as the A.S.B. and SABRA, the *Blankewerkersbeskermingsbond* and SACOL, and the Afrikaner financial houses and chambers of commerce and industry; and specific white caste groups operating in areas where there are no Afrikaner community groups, such as many of the professional and sports associations and some industrial associations, like the Chamber of Mines. These groups monopolize all the regular channels of political influence in South Africa, not only because they are the beneficiaries of discriminatory legislation, but also because all significant political decision-making roles in the country are performed by whites, and most of them by Afrikaners.

This fact is as true of the army and the navy, the police and the bureaucracy, as it is of the Cabinet, the judiciary and the central and provincial legislatures. Indeed, the elite of the Afrikaner community includes the leaders of most of the Afrikaner interest groups and the decision-makers in most of the authoritative governmental structures; together they form a single social unit. So compact is this unit that effective pressures are often, perhaps usually, transmitted in the course of normal social contacts, though when formal contacts are requested, access is readily granted. Thus the process of interest articulation in South Africa is dominated for the most part by the overriding ethnic interest of the Afrikaner community, although within that community there is a proliferation of associational interest groups, all dedicated to the proposition that the political *summum bonum* is the welfare of the Afrikaner community.

For British community groups, and for white caste groups that stand in opposition to Afrikaner community groups, effective access to governmental decision-makers is much more difficult. They do not have normal social access because their leaders are not part of the self-consciously Afrikaner community, but they are not suppressed or entirely ignored, because they are members of the white caste, and voters. On some issues, where the interests of such groups coincide with the interests of corresponding Afrikaner community groups, their claims are effectively transmitted to the government by the Afrikaner group leaders. For example, the claims of English-speaking white teachers' associations for salary increases and improvements in conditions of service are effectively transmitted by the Afrikaner teachers' associations, whose interests on these issues are virtually identical. On the other hand, in cases where the interests of such groups conflict with those of Afrikaner groups, the former have to resort to indirect methods to make their influence felt at all.

Consequently English-speaking white interest groups have become expert organizers of public statements, mass meetings, petitions, solemn processions and symbolic devices, designed to draw the attention of the government and the electorate to objections to contemplated legislation. The English-medium universities resorted to most of these methods, including processions of their governing bodies, their faculties and their students through the streets of Cape Town, Johannesburg and Durban, in attempting to dissuade the government from enacting the legislation that made it unlawful for them to admit nonwhite students; the students of those universities organized a series of ceremonies in which a torch was used as the symbol of freedom.

South African conditions have brought into being an organization that has resorted to original techniques of protest — the Black Sash. This is an organization of white women, founded to protest a particular piece of legislation — the Senate Act which led to the removal of the Cape Coloured voters from the common roll. When the Senate Act passed the Black Sash did not dissolve, but remained in existence to serve as a reminder to the government and the electorate of what had been done and to protest later legislation restricting the liberties of South Africans. Wearing white dresses and black sashes, standing silently with bowed heads in public places, such as the entrance to the Parliament buildings, the members of the Black Sash certainly succeeded in producing reportable news. However, it is doubtful whether these pacific but extra-parliamentary techniques materially influenced the course of events in South Africa. Over the years their thrust became blunted through continual use without appreciable success, and the Black Sash now concentrates on helping individual victims of oppressive laws.[87a]

The government steadfastly restrains all groups with nonwhite members (whether national groups or nonwhite caste or community groups) from exerting effective influence through normal channels. It has banned the multi-racial Communist Party and Congress of Democrats, and also the African National Congress and the Pan-Africanist Congress. It excludes Africans from the collective bargaining process; bars nonwhites from virtually all groups that feed directly into the political system, other than those groups which it controls; harasses and intimidates systematically individuals who oppose the political system, by bannings and arrests. The result is that most nonwhite associations, seeking to remain within the framework of the law, profess to be apolitical.

[87a] In 1963 the Black Sash opened its ranks to nonwhite women. It publishes a monthly journal, *The Black Sash*.

While most white opposition groups use methods that, however flamboyant, are legal and pursue goals that, however radical, are reformist, nonwhite groups, if they are to provide any outlets for political expression, have to use illegal methods because their scope for legal action is more limited, and pursue revolutionary goals because reformism has not produced discernible results. Their means include the printing and dissemination of subversive literature, the creating and maintaining of subversive organizations, the calling of illegal strikes, and the commission of calculated acts of sabotage. But these methods, too, have proved unfruitful, so nonwhite political frustrations produce much anomic conduct — spontaneous, unpredictable, and often uncontrollable outbursts of irrational mob action.

Thus, the mode of articulation of interest reflects the structure of South African society. The picture is not a tidy one, for there are divisions of interest even within the Afrikaner community and by no means all the members of the nonwhite castes are completely cowed. Though South Africa is the nearest approach to a pigmentocracy which has existed in an industrialized society, it remains to be seen whether industrialization and pigmentocracy are compatible. The historian of the future may find that the most significant associations in South Africa in the 1960's are not the Afrikaner community associations that are interwoven with the present political system, but the plethora of African associations that profess to be apolitical and seem to be impotent today, but possibly carry the germs of South Africa's political system of tomorrow.

THE AGGREGATION OF INTERESTS

If a South African were asked to classify his party system, his answer would probably depend upon his prescribed status in South African society. An Afrikaner would probably label it a two-party system, pointing out that South Africa is ruled by a Cabinet responsible to an elected legislature, and that the Opposition of today has the prospect of becoming the Government of tomorrow. An English-speaking white South African would be inclined to state that though the forms of a two-party system do exist, in reality South Africa has become a one-party state, in the sense that since 1948 the Nationalist Party has entrenched itself in power by legislation and administrative action, that it has increased its majority in every election, and that it seems *de facto* to be irremovable by constitutional means. A nonwhite South African would probably say that South Africa is an authoritarian state, ruled by a government responsible to an ethnic oligarchy, and that the existence and maneuvers of the political parties within the oligarchy are of relatively trivial importance. There is some truth in each statement, and a comprehensive definition should certainly include each of the three ingredients. South Africa has a two-party system, tending towards a one-party system, within an ethnic oligarchy or pigmentocracy.[87b]

The Nationalist Party

The ruling party is the party of the Afrikaner nation, born in rejection of fusion with the South African Party, nourished in anglophobia and negrophobia, and elevated and sustained by the whole network of exclusive Afrikaner associations and institutions.[88] J. C. Greyling, Nationalist Member of Parliament for Ventersdorp, declares that "The National Party is no party; it is the personification of the efforts and thought of the whole

[87b] In April 1965 Minister of Justice B. J. Vorster suggested that South Africa might become a one-party state. Much discussion followed in the press. *Press Digest* (Johannesburg), April 15 and 29, 1965.

[88] On the Nationalist Party—its historical origins, its ideology and its structure—see Carter, *op. cit.*, especially chapter 8; J. Albert Coetzee, *Politieke Groepering in die Wording van die Afrikanernasie* (Johannesburg: Voortrekker Pers, 1941); G. Cronjé, *'n Tuiste vir die Nageslag: Die blywende oplossing van Suid-Afrika se Rassevraagstukke* (Johannesburg: Publicité Handelsreklamediens, 1945), *Afrika sonder die Asiaat* (Johannesburg: Publicité Handelsreklamediens, 1946), and *Regverdige Rasse-Apartheid* (Cape Town: Citadel Press, 1947); D. W. Krüger, *The Age of the Generals* (Johannesburg: Dagbreek, 1958), and *South African Parties and Policies, 1910-1960: A select source book* (Cape Town: Human and Rousseau, 1960); D. F. Malan, *Afrikaner-Volkseenheid en my Ervarings op die Pad Daarheen* (Cape Town: Nasionale Boekhandel, 1959); Marquard, *op. cit.*; Sheila Patterson, *The Last Trek* (London: Routledge and Kegan Paul, 1957); Oswald Pirow, *James Barry Munnik Hertzog* (Cape Town: Howard Timmins, 1957); Rhoodie and Venter, *op. cit.*; Michael Roberts and A. E. G. Trollip, *The South African Opposition, 1939-1945* (London: Longmans, 1947); P. van Biljon, *Grensbakens tussen Blank en Swart in Suid-Afrika* (Cape Town: Juta, 1947); F. A. van Jaarsveld, *The Awakening of Afrikaner Nationalism, 1868-1881* (Cape Town: Human and Rousseau, 1961).

nation." [89] He is correct in two senses. In one sense the Nationalist Party is more than a party. It deems itself to be the only legitimate political home for an Afrikaner, irrespective of wealth, occupation or class. The Afrikaner who does not support the Nationalist Party is not a true Afrikaner, but a traitor.

D. F. Malan taught the Afrikaner people the lesson of political solidarity. Disunited, they were the prey of the British government, of British South Africans and of traitors; united they rule South Africa.[90] That lesson has sunk deep into the Afrikaner mores and is transmitted not only by the party itself, but also by many organs of the state, notably the public schools, and by the whole gamut of Afrikaner organizations, from the Dutch Reformed Churches to the voluntary associations. Many families that were Smutsite in the previous generation have become Verwoerdian in the present generation. Rebels are few, because the rebel faces the terrible punishment of ostracization by his community, and the punishment is applied to his entire family. Of those who do rebel, some return, chastened, to the fold; others, smeared and derided, are ejected from the entire complex of Afrikaner institutions and associations — indeed from the *volk* itself — and they have either to live in social isolation or to essay the difficult and often uncongenial task of integration into the English-speaking white community. Consequently, only the exceptionally noble or the exceptionally frustrated Afrikaner has the courage to rebel and the stamina to persist in a state of public rebellion against organized Afrikanerdom.

In another sense the Nationalist Party is less than a party, because the "nation" for which it stands is only a fraction of the population of South Africa. It has never made any attempt to identify itself with the nonwhites, and towards the English-speaking whites it has always been ambivalent. On the one hand it is concerned to preserve Afrikanerdom, pure and unsullied by alien influences; on the other hand it requires white allies against the nonwhites. In practice, until the end of the Second World War the primary emphasis was given to the reestablishment of *Afrikaner* unity, and little more than lip serv-

[89] *House of Assembly Debates,* 1963, col. 6136.
[90] Malan, *op. cit.*

ice was paid to the idea of *white* unity; but since that time the latter idea has been more urgently expressed.

There are two reasons for this change of emphasis. Afrikanerdom's very success in gaining control of the political machinery, in increasing its share of the national economy and in severing South Africa's last political links with Britain has enabled it to view with equanimity the prospect of white unity. A generation ago white unity might have spelt the absorption of Afrikaners by British South Africans; today it is more likely to involve the absorption of British South Africans by Afrikaners. Furthermore, the unity of all white South Africans now seems essential if they are to survive the internal and external challenges to white supremacy. Consequently, though anglophobia persists as a deep-rooted element in the Afrikaner psyche and it still breaks surface from time to time, most of the leaders, including Prime Minister Verwoerd, present the party as the only true political instrument for all white South Africans.

Before 1965 very few English-speaking voters actually supported the Nationalist Party. The results of the republican referendum of 1960 and the general election of 1961 are probably to be interpreted as meaning that the party had the support of nearly 85 percent of the Afrikaner voters and less than 10 percent of the English-speaking voters. However, the results of the Provincial Council elections of March 1965 suggest that appreciable numbers of the English-speaking whites then voted Nationalist, at least in Natal.[91] In any case, the Nationalist Party is drawing dividends from its claim to embody the will of a united white nation, in the sense that the official opposition has become a cautious and selective critic, almost as anxious as the government itself to present a favorable image of the South African political system to the outside world. What could be more satisfactory to a ruling party firmly entrenched in power than an opposition which endorses the principles of some of its most far-reaching legislation in the name of national

91 Munger, *op. cit.*, pp. 707-32, for an analysis of the referendum; and Newell M. Stultz and Jeffrey Butler, "The South African General Election of 1961," *Political Science Quarterly*, LXXVIII No. 1 (March 1963) 86-110. See also footnote 85, chapter III.

security, and whose very existence seems to refute the allegations of authoritarianism! [92]

Membership in the Nationalist Party is open to white South Africans who are at least eighteen years of age (seventeen in Natal), who accept the party's statement of principles, and who pledge themselves to accept party discipline. A high proportion of the Afrikaner people — probably between a third and a half of those who are qualified — are members. The inducements are many. Only members may participate in primaries or be elected to party offices, and party membership is often a recommendation for employment, as well as a satisfaction of the indivdual's need to belong to a prestigious, corporate group. Indeed, the party is a manifestation of the Afrikaner community, organized for political purposes. For many Afrikaners it is as natural to belong to the party as it is to belong to a Dutch Reformed Church.

The party is efficiently structured, with a particularly strong grass-roots organization. There are local groups or cells of about ten members under elected group leaders; successively above them are the branches (usually corresponding with polling districts), the divisions (corresponding with parliamentary constituencies), and the provinces. At each of these levels there is political activity of a far more continuous character than is to be found in countries with a homogeneous population; before an election there is intense activity for several weeks, absorbing the time and the energy, not merely of a few zealots, but of a high proportion of the members. Indeed, Afrikaner Nationalists have a rare degree of political dedication, verging on obsession. It is true that the unbroken series of electoral gains since 1948 has diminished the need for political effort; it has become a foregone conclusion that the party will acquire a large parliamentary majority and in the 1961 election there were many uncontested seats. But tension is maintained by other factors: the desire to break previous records of seats and majorities, the anxiety to discredit the latest crop of rebels, and, above all, the deepening consciousness of the hostility of the nonwhites and of the outside world. The tension is also promoted by the

[92] E.g., the United Party supported the Second Reading of the General Law Amendment Bill, 1963.

Afrikaans press, which devotes a high proportion of its space, year in and year out, to party polemics.

We have already seen how numerous organizations act as agents for the promotion of Afrikaner self-consciousness in every sphere of human activity. The party itself has one important subsidiary — the *Nasionale Jeugbond* [National Youth League], which draws young Afrikaners into the party and trains them for party service so successfully that many of the younger Nationalist members of Parliament received their political initiation in the *Jeugbond*. That the young Nationalists of today are more intolerant than their elders and have more than a trace of sheer fanaticism is largely to be attributed to the *Jeugbond*.

The structure of the Nationalist Party is federal, the organizations in each province and in South-West Africa having great autonomy. The body electing all office-holders and laying down policy is the provincial party congress, whose meeting is the peak of the annual party activity, bringing the representatives of the divisions or the branches into contact with the provincial leaders in an atmosphere of cordial camaraderie. Between congresses, control over the provincial party is exercised by the provincial leader and the provincial steering committee, elected by the congress. They determine the extent, the manner and the timing of the application of the policy laid down by congress and operate the party machinery — appointing and dismissing officials, disciplining individuals, determining whether candidates are eligible for office and (in the Transvaal) repudiating the decisions of branches at their discretion.

Linking the provincial organizations is a Federal Council, comprising seven representatives from each province and from South-West Africa, appointed by the congresses, one representative of the *Jeugbond,* and the national leader. But this unwieldy body rarely meets, and it has only a small office establishment whose main function is to produce the party organ, the *Kruithoring* [Powder-horn]. The coordinating power between the provincial organizations is *de facto* exercised by a Steering Committee of the four provincial leaders — consisting, in 1963, of H. F. Verwoerd (Transvaal), T. E. Dönges (Cape), J. J. Serfontein (Orange Free State) and W. A. Maree (Natal) — who meet informally as requisite to deal with over-all problems of strategy and tactics, subject, when possible, to confirmation by the provincial congresses.

The other coordinating body is the parliamentary caucus, consisting of the Nationalist Party members of the Senate and the House of Assembly. This group meets weekly during parliamentary sessions, under the control of the whips whom it elects, to determine the attitude to be adopted towards questions due for debate in Parliament. It also has the crucial power of electing the national Leader, and for this purpose it is convened out of session if necessary.

In form, therefore, the Nationalist Party is federal and democratic. In recent years, however, there has been a centralizing and authoritarian trend within the party. The continuity of Nationalist rule since 1948 has promoted a shift of power from the organs of the party, as such, to the Cabinet; this shift has been accentuated by the personalities of the Prime Ministers and the deepening crisis of the regime.

During his premiership D. F. Malan had tremendous prestige as the man who had reunited national Afrikanerdom and led it to the unexpected electoral victory in 1948; throughout the party it was acknowledged that Malan was without peer as tactician and debater. With J. G. Strijdom the center of gravity in the party began to move from the Cape to the Transvaal — from the Afrikaner community that had experienced a continuity of political development ever since 1806 and had become conditioned to the process of discussion and compromise, to the community with a stormy political history and in which the authoritarian leadership of Paul Kruger was regarded as a model. This movement has continued under H. F. Verwoerd.

Verwoerd was born near Amsterdam in 1901 and migrated to South Africa as a child. It will be for a future biographer to determine whether it was his experiences as a foreign boy in an ultra-English colonial school in Southern Rhodesia that instilled in him a potent anglophobia. After studying at Stellenbosch University he declined a scholarship to Oxford, giving preference to study in German universities. In 1927 he returned to Stellenbosch as professor of applied psychology — a science of which he has become a superb exponent. His first political activities were as organizer of a national conference on the poor white problem and as leader of a deputation to ask Prime Minister Hertzog to refuse admission to Jewish refugees from Nazi Germany. In 1937 he followed in the footsteps of D. F. Malan by leaving his profession to become the founder-editor of a newspaper, the *Transvaler,* in which he was an uncompromising advocate of Afrikaner nationalism and a supporter of the Nazi cause in the Second World War. He entered the Senate in 1948 and two years later acquired the key portfolio of Native Affairs; he then proceeded to lay the legislative and administrative foundations of the policy of apartheid. By 1958 Verwoerd was the natural candidate of the Transvaal Nationalists for the succession to J. G. Strijdom, and in the second ballot in the caucus he defeated T. E. Dönges by ninety-eight votes to seventy-five. He attributed that victory and his survival after an assassination attempt in 1960 to the will of God.[93]

Verwoerd's power over the party has increased immensely since he became Prime Minister. Where his predecessors hesitated at the brink, he staked his reputation on the achievement of the Republic and acquired great prestige. The growth of his power is also due to the fact that his talents seem to be greatly superior to those of his colleagues. Where a Dönges gives an impression of *slimness* (a South African term for cunning), Verwoerd seems frank and sincere. Where a Vorster seems to relish violence, Verwoerd wears a velvet glove. Where a Louw is bitterly polemical, Verwoerd combines effective criticism with constructive analysis. Where a Sauer inclines to compromise under pressure, Verwoerd is consistently unyielding. These qualities have been particularly impressive in a period when the increasing challenge to the regime has created a widespread yearning among Afrikaners for a sense of security. It is he who has been adamant in refusing to give concessions to nonwhites in the towns; and it is he who has pressed ahead with the Bantustan program.

Among the tangible sources of his strength are his chairmanship of Voortrekker Pers and Afrikaanse Pers, two of the largest

93 Information from the *Cape Times* library, Cape Town. There is no biography of Prime Minister Verwoerd.

Afrikaans publishing houses, and the fact that since 1961 over half the Cabinet have owed their appointments as Ministers to him, and the twenty or more members of Parliament who were formerly party employees are his loyal supporters. He also cultivates his leadership by appearing and speaking at the congresses not only of his own Transvaal section of the party, but also the other provincial sections, where he makes most effective use of his opportunities. As a result, it seems that Verwoerd dominates the party, the caucus and the Cabinet to a greater extent than any of his predecessors. He probably makes every important policy decision, which in turn is endorsed and applied by the organs of the government and the party. When J. D. du P. Basson began to break with the Nationalist Party in 1959 he accused the Prime Minister of introducing the legislation eliminating the representatives of Africans from Parliament without consulting the caucus or any of the governing bodies of the party, and the charge seems well-founded.[94]

Nothing more clearly demonstrates the power of Verwoerd, not only within the party but within the Afrikaner nation as a whole, than the disputes that took place in the Dutch Reformed Churches and SABRA in 1960 and 1961.[95] The Sharpeville shootings (March 1960), the attempted assassination of the Prime Minister (April), and the withdrawal of much foreign capital from South Africa caused heartsearchings in every Afrikaner organization. For a brief moment, while the Prime Minister was on the danger list, there seemed to be a collapse of political authority, with senior police officers apparently ordering widespread arrests without the knowledge of Cabinet Ministers.

Thereafter, for about a year, a series of demands for political concessions emanated from within the most influential Afrikaner organizations. In July the political commentator of *Die Burger* suggested allowing the Coloured voters to elect Coloured people to represent them in Parliament and several Afrikaner professors and theologians hinted at the need to consult both African and Coloured leaders with a view to instituting other

[94] *House of Assembly Debates*, 1959, col. 9498.

[95] *Survey of Race Relations*, 1959-60, pp. 89-106; 1961, pp. 9-13, 63-73, 79-80; 1962, pp. 4-6, 10-11.

reforms. In November eleven leading Afrikaner theologians, drawn from all three Dutch Reformed Churches, published *Vertraagde Aksie* (which was soon issued in an English translation under the name *Delayed Action*), denouncing racial discrimination and calling for a new approach.[96] In December delegates of the World Council of Churches and its eight member churches in South Africa, including the N.G.K. of the Cape Province, the N.G.K. of the Transvaal, and the N.H.K. of South Africa, conferred at the Cottesloe residence of the University of the Witwatersrand. The Cottesloe conference prepared and published a statement, each paragraph of which had been endorsed by four-fifths of the delegates (i.e., by at least some of the Dutch Reformed delegates), rejecting unjust discrimination and the exclusion of Christians from churches on racial grounds; denying the existence of a scriptural basis for the prohibition of mixed marriages; condemning job reservation, the prevailing nonwhite wage rates, and the disintegrating effects of migrant labor on African family life; recommending consultation between the government and leaders accepted by the nonwhite peoples; and declaring that the rights to own land wherever he is domiciled and to participate in the government of his country are part of the dignity of an adult man.[97] Then early in 1961 a group of Afrikaner intellectuals, most of them connected with SABRA, held discussions with Coloured and African leaders and organized groups of Afrikaners with a view to exerting pressure on the government to moderate its policies. So sincere and so determined were these Afrikaner rebels against the Verwoerd line that some foreign observers reached the conclusion that a radical change of policy would be produced by this liberal movement within Afrikanerdom.

Such a conclusion was based on wishful thinking. The reaction of Verwoerd was uncompromising and overwhelmingly successful. In his first statement after recovering from his gun-

[96] B. B. Keet, *et al.*, *Delayed Action: An ecumenical witness from the Afrikaans-speaking Church* (South Africa: privately published, 1960).

[97] Leslie A. Hewson, ed., *Cottesloe Consultation: The Report of the Consultation among South African Member Churches of the World Council of Churches, 7-14 December 1960, at Cottesloe, Johannesburg* (Johannesburg: South African Institute of Race Relations, 1961).

shot wounds the Prime Minister made his position abundantly clear: any concessions would only pave the way for racial integration, culminating in biological assimilation.[98] In November 1960 Verwoerd declared that Nationalist leaders must stand like "walls of granite" on their color policy, because the existence of the nation was at stake; in the same month he convened the Federal Council of the Nationalist Party, which endorsed his attitude.[99] In February 1961 SABRA announced the indefinite postponement of a congress to have been held in April to discuss the position of the Cape Coloured people. In April Verwoerd elaborated his proposal to give Africans political rights in the Bantu Areas and there alone, and to provide the Coloured and Asian peoples with opportunities for development through participation in special councils. In May he talked about people "playing with fire" and declared that "the state of the nation will remain healthy only so long as the policy of this government is supported *in all respects.*" [100]

By then SABRA and the Dutch Reformed Churches were stepping into line. The N.H.K. synod met in March 1961, denounced *Vertraagde Aksie* and the Cottesloe resolutions, and withdrew from the World Council of Churches. Soon afterward the synodal commission of the N.H.K. summoned Professor A. S. Geyser, one of the authors of *Vertraagde Aksie,* ordered him to resign from the chair of New Testament Theology at Pretoria University — a chair which was subsidized by the N.H.K. — and tried him on charges of heresy laid by three of his students at the university, eventually finding him guilty on one charge, involving a departure from the church's position on Christology. By the end of 1961 the N.G.K. synods of the Transvaal and the Cape Province had also repudiated the Cottesloe resolutions and withdrawn from the World Council of Churches.[101] As for SABRA, Professor N. J. J. Olivier of the University of Stellenbosch, its vice-chairman and principal organizer for twelve years, was the leader of the reform movement. When the annual conference approached, he became the ob-

[98] *House of Assembly Debates,* 1960, cols. 8337-43 (May 20). The Prime Minister's statement was read by the Minister of Finance.

[99] *Survey of Race Relations,* 1961, p. 10.

[100] *House of Assembly Debates,* 1961, cols. 6947-48.

[101] *Survey of Race Relations,* 1961, pp. 66-70.

ject of personal denunciation and at the conference he was defeated by a conformist in the vice-chairmanship election, whereupon the other reformers withdrew when nominated as committee members.[102] The conference also refused to consider the reports of commissions that had been sounding Coloured and African opinion. Thus, the one Afrikaner lay organization showing a capacity for independent thought and action on racial questions (albeit with a strong bias towards some system of apartheid) was reduced to conformity. Within Afrikanerdom as a whole there seems to have been a shift of power from the parts to the center, from the caucus to the leader, from the Cape to the Transvaal.

Criticisms of the political leadership are still to be heard from within the Afrikaner community. In 1963, for example, several ministers of the Dutch Reformed Churches, including the Rev. C. F. Beyers Naudé of the N.G.K. and Professor A. S. Geyser (who had applied to the Supreme Court for the findings of the synodal commission to be set aside, obtained a favorable settlement, and was readmitted as a minister of the N.H.K.), founded a Christian Institute of Southern Africa, in conjunction with white and nonwhite ministers of other churches, with the aim of uniting all South African Christians and making Christianity a living force in South Africa.[103] Nevertheless, the teeth had been removed from the reform movement, which seemed incapable of gaining control over the party or even of causing a significant secession from the party. Indeed, the next serious challenge to the leadership may come from the reactionary side, for there are Nationalists who consider that Verwoerd is devoting too much time and money to the Bantu Areas and too little to the interests of the white urban workers.

Opposition Parties

The current United Party is a pale reflection of the United Party of J. C. Smuts.[104] In Smuts's day it was wholeheartedly supported by virtually all the English-speaking white organiza-

---

102 *Ibid.*, pp. 79-80.

103 *Ibid.*, 1963, pp. 6-7.

104 On the United Party see Carter, *op. cit.*, chapter 11 and pp. 472-74; Krüger, *Parties and Policies*, pp. 85-88, 337-53, 452-58; and J. C. Smuts, Jr., *Jan Christiaan Smuts* (London: Cassell, 1952).

tions in the country, by most of the great commercial, industrial and financial houses, and by a small but devoted minority of the Afrikaners. Today its Afrikaner support has dwindled and its English-speaking support is at best halfhearted. Many business leaders find it expedient to refrain from giving it overt support, for fear of reprisals from the government. Having suffered a continuous and increasingly disastrous series of defeats at the polls and having been eroded by many secessions on both flanks, the United Party lacks drive and energy. Its old ideological appeal to white South Africans to unite on a basis of Anglo-Afrikaner equality is no longer effective, because about half of the electorate prefers the Nationalist Party's uncompromising appeal to Afrikaner sentiment, and scarcely any of the voters are wholly immune from the Nationalist Party's appeal to white sentiment. As the challenge to the political system has developed both inside and outside South Africa, the United Party has been driven to the defensive. It tends to look to the past for inspiration and has failed to produce a dynamic forward-looking policy, related to the facts of contemporary South African life and clearly distinguishable from the policy of the government. In addition, it has no leader comparable with Verwoerd. On the other hand, the failure of the Progressive Party and the Liberal Party to attract significant electoral support shows that the white electorate of South Africa is incapable of terminating the caste system of its own volition.[105]

Consequently, so long as the system is not destroyed by economic disaster, or by revolution from within, or by attack from without (or some combination of these forces), the Nationalist Party seems likely to rule South Africa. With its highly articulated supporting organizations, its control of the bureaucracy, the police and the army, and its tough, experienced leadership, it appears impregnable. Indeed, whatever our viewpoint may

[105] On the Progressive Party see Z. J. de Beer, *Multi-Racial South Africa: The reconciliation of forces* (London: Oxford University Press, 1961); Krüger, *Parties and Policies,* pp. 105-11, 459-64; and Donald Molteno, *et al., A Report prepared for the Progressive Party by a Commission of Experts* (2 vols., Johannesburg: Progressive Party, 1960-62). On the Liberal Party see Carter, *op. cit.,* pp. 347-52; Liberal Party, *Non-Racial Democracy: The Policies of the Liberal Party of South Africa* (Pietermaritzburg: Liberal Party, 1962); and the monthly journal *Contact.*

be regarding the morality, the wisdom, and the long-term practicability of making the preservation of white supremacy the primary goal of politics in an industrialized state in the second half of the 20th century, we should recognize that in the South African context the Nationalist Party is a remarkably efficient instrument for that purpose.

CHAPTER V

The Internal Opposition
to the System

OPPOSITIONS TO a caste system vary in scope, in objective and in method. In scope, an opposition may be national or sectional. A national opposition, in the fullest sense, derives support not only from all the castes but also from all the major classes within each caste, whereas a sectional opposition is limited in terms of caste, or class, or both. In objective, an opposition may be reformist or revolutionary. A reformist opposition is concerned in the short run to ameliorate the condition of the subject castes and in the long run to persuade the members of the ruling caste, operating through the existing constitutional machinery, to admit members of the other castes to a share in power, and thus gradually to erode the caste system by a process that maintains the institutional continuity of the state. In contrast, a revolutionary opposition is concerned not with mitigating the effects of the caste system but with destroying the system, and not operating through the established constitutional machinery (whose legitimacy it denies), but overthrowing it and starting again with a clean slate. Finally, a revolutionary opposition may confine itself to nonviolent methods for advancing its purposes — such as strikes and passive resistance to caste laws and customs — or it may resort to organized violence.

During the last fifty years there have been three main phases in the opposition to the caste system in South Africa. For a long while the principal opposition was sectional in scope (being limited to elite groups in each caste), reformist in objective, and nonviolent in method. Then between about 1948 and 1960, while remaining nonviolent, it became revolutionary in objective and very nearly truly national in scope. Since 1960 the principal opposition has been an underground and essentially African movement, pursuing revolutionary goals by violent as well as nonviolent means.

The two great changes in the character of the principal opposition were both reactions to the persistent and increasingly unequivocal determination of the controllers of the authoritative governmental institutions to maintain white supremacy at all costs. The postwar shift from a sectional to a national scope and from a reformist to a revolutionary objective was a reaction to the prolonged refusal of South African governments to grant any of the reforms that had been demanded, culminating in the 1948 election of a government committed absolutely to the maintenance of white supremacy. The shift to go-it-alone Africanism and violence was a reaction against the government's systematic and violent suppression of all forms of African protest, climaxing with the banning of both the major African political organizations in 1960.

OPPOSITION BEFORE 1948

The sectional, reformist opposition to the caste system had roots in the Cape Colony, where the laws had been for the most part color-blind and nonwhites had been admitted to the franchise on the common voters' roll, subject to economic and educational qualifications, equally with whites. After 1910, as segregationist laws and practices become more and more pervasive in the Cape Province and the other three provinces of the Union, whites as well as nonwhites opposed the trend.

Among the whites, opposition was generally confined to the professional classes in the major cities, especially to lawyers, clergy and university teachers in Cape Town and Johannesburg. In 1929 some of them founded the South African Institute of Race Relations to collect and publish information about race relations in South Africa and to arrange conferences for the discussion of South Africa's racial problems. Thus sophisticated people who were anxious about the segregationist trend were drawn into regular contact with one another and a body of relevant empirical data was accumulated.

In 1939, R. F. A. Hoernlé, a former professor of philosophy at Harvard University who had been head of the department of philosophy at the University of the Witwatersrand since 1923, analyzed the segregation policy of the government of the day:

> . . . "Segregation" stands for a policy offensive to all non-Europeans in South Africa, viz., for a policy of exclusion, forced upon them by the White group, from the status and privileges which the White group insists upon reserving for itself. This is segregation as an instrument of domination; segregation *which retains the segregated in the same social and political structure with the dominant White group,* but subjects them to the denial of important rights and keeps them at a social distance implying inferiority.[1]

The whites who represented Africans in Parliament under the Representation of Natives Act of 1936 — notably, Senator Edgar H. Brookes, Margaret Ballinger and Donald B. Molteno — persistently exposed the harshness of the laws as they bore upon the nonwhite peoples. There were even leading white politicians, responsible to white electorates, who were uneasy about the segregation policy. When he was out of office in 1929, J. C. Smuts himself admitted that the entire basis of that policy would fall away if significant numbers of Africans were incorporated in the industrial process in the cities; in 1945 J. H. Hofmeyr, Jr., Deputy Prime Minister of South Africa, advocated "an unwearying activity towards the removal of inequalities of opportunity." [2]

[1] R. F. Alfred Hoernlé, *South African Native Policy and the Liberal Spirit* (Johannesburg: Witwatersrand University Press, 1945) p. 168. Italics as in the original. See also the same author's *Race and Reason* (Johannesburg: Witwatersrand University Press, 1945).

[2] Jan C. Smuts, *Africa and Some World Problems* (Oxford: Clarendon Press, 1930) pp. 94-98; Jan H. Hofmeyr, *Christian Principles and Race Problems: Hoernlé Memorial Lecture, 1945* (Johannesburg: South African Institute of Race Relations, 1945) p. 31.

Doubts about the segregation policy were also expressed in a series of reports by government commissions. In 1932 the Holloway Commission reported that to treat all Africans as residents of the reserves, with no rights other than those of visitors in the white areas, was "impracticable" and "unfair." [3] In 1946 the Social and Economic Planning Council reported that there would always be large numbers of Africans in the white areas, however efficiently the economy of the reserves might be developed.[4] The Fagan Commission reported in 1948 that "the idea of total segregation is utterly impracticable" and that the process of urbanization of Africans was an inevitable and irreversible phenomenon.[5]

Despite these doubts, up to the crucial general election of May 1948 all governments had maintained far-reaching legal discriminations against Africans in the white areas, and no white political organization existed which presented a clear-cut challenge to the system. The white liberals were equivocal when it came to propounding policies. Continuously preoccupied with the business of trying to ameliorate the effects and to expose the fallacies of the existing system, they failed to create a picture of their ultimate goal for South African society or to suggest how radical reforms might be realized.

Political activity among the subordinate castes began towards the end of the 19th century.[6] Before 1948 the principal organ-

[3] Union of South Africa, *Report of Native Economic Commission, 1930-1932: U.G. 22/1932* (Pretoria: Government Printer, 1932) p. 101.

[4] Union of South Africa, *Social and Economic Planning Council Report No. 9: The Native Reserves and their place in the economy of the Union of South Africa: U.G. 32/1946* (Pretoria: Government Printer, 1946) p. 3.

[5] Union of South Africa, *Report of the Native Laws Commission, 1946-48: U.G. 28/1948* (Pretoria: Government Printer, 1948) p. 19.

[6] On nonwhite political activity before 1948 see Mary Benson, *The African Patriots: The story of the African National Congress of South Africa* (London: Faber, 1963); Gwendolen M. Carter, *The Politics of Inequality: South Africa since 1948* (London: Thames and Hudson, 1958) chapter 14 and pp. 481-84; René M. de Villiers, "Politics," in Ellen Hellmann, ed., *Handbook on Race Relations in South Africa* (Cape Town: Oxford University Press, 1949) chapter 21; P. S. Joshi, *Verdict on South Africa (The Tyranny of Colour)* (Bombay: Thacker, 1945), and *The Struggle for Equality* (Bombay: Hind Kitabs, 1951); Edward Roux, *Time Longer than Rope: A history of the Black Man's struggle for freedom in South*

izations were the African National Congress (founded in 1912), the South African Indian Congress (founded in 1920 as an amalgamation of pre-existing Natal and Transvaal organizations), and the African Political Organization (whose members were Coloured people). All three organizations comprised small groups of Western-oriented middle-class elements and lacked mass support. Their purpose was to realize the promise inherent in the Cape liberal tradition, first, by gaining full equality with whites for the nonwhite middle classes which they represented and, later, by extending the benefits of equality to the masses of the people. The precedent they had in mind was the step-by-step extension of the parliamentary franchise to all classes and both sexes in Britain. By rational argument and pressure within the framework of the constitution they sought to persuade the existing electorate to reverse the segregationist tide. Throughout this period the African National Congress remained under the control of lawyers, clergy and journalists and had the professed objects of educating the white electorate concerning "the requirements and aspirations of the Native people," enlisting the support of sympathetic white organizations, promoting unity among all African peoples and, above all, redressing African grievances "by constitutional means." [7] The A.N.C. adhered scrupulously to these cautious methods and modest objectives. It protested each installment of segregationist legislation from the Land Act of 1913 through the Representation Act of 1936, usually making its protests in South Africa but sometimes sending delegations overseas — to England in 1913 and to Versailles in 1919. Though the A.N.C. usually acted alone, its leaders were as a rule in close touch with white liberals and on occasion they sponsored multi-racial conferences, as in 1926.

By 1948 it was clear that this type of opposition was barren. Instead of being admitted to equality, the nonwhite middle classes were being subjected to additional forms of discrimina-

---

Africa (London: Gollancz, 1948); I. B. Tabata, *The All-African Convention: The awakening of a people* (Johannesburg: People's Press, 1950).

[7] *The Constitution of the African National Congress,* 1919, "Objects," clauses 4, 6, and 11, cited in Carter, *op. cit.,* pp. 482-84.

tion. All the reformist opposition had achieved was a succession of rearguard actions, each ending in defeat.

Sporadic efforts were also made to create revolutionary movements. The most spectacular was founded by Clements Kadalie, an African from Nyasaland, who created an Industrial and Commercial Workers Union with the help of a small group of white Socialists and organized a series of industrial strikes starting in 1919.[8] Like its exact contemporary, the Universal Negro Improvement Association of Marcus Garvey in the United States, however, the I.C.U. was poorly organized and it disintegrated in the late 1920's, partly from internal weaknesses and partly in consequence of official suppression.

The Communist Party of South Africa was founded in 1921 by a small group of whites. It was the only political organization in South Africa that recruited members from all the racial groups and had a multi-racial executive. But it suffered from ill-judged directives from Moscow, like other Communist Parties outside Russia, and from a series of internal schisms; it never gained a wide following. Nevertheless, it exerted a considerable influence on the I.C.U., and by 1948 Communist ideas were attracting several of the younger and most frustrated members of the A.N.C. and the S.A.I.C.[9]

WHITE OPPONENTS OF THE SYSTEM

In May 1948 the white electorate rejected any possibility of seeking an accommodation with the reformist opposition to the caste system along the lines that had always been demanded by the reformers, in favor of the doctrine of "apartheid" or "separate development" as propounded by the Nationalist Party — that is to say, in favor of the perpetuation of the caste system within the white areas of South Africa on the grounds that nonwhites would be able to fulfill their legitimate aspirations in their own areas.[10] Since then, as the tensions within South African society have mounted, an ever-higher proportion of the white electorate has supported the Nationalist Party; at

8 Roux, *op. cit.*, pp. 161-205, 251-63.

9 *Ibid.*, chapters 15ff.

10 See *National News* (the official election newspaper of the Nationalist Party), May 19, 1948.

the same time, a small but continuously augmented stream of white people has become fundamentally critical of the official policy. These critics are drawn from both the Afrikaner and the English-speaking communities and many of them are professional men of high standing. They point to the glaring gulf between the theory and practice of apartheid, to the continuous increase in the number of Africans in the white areas, to the absence of any adequate substitute for participation in the political process for Coloureds and Asians, and to the harshness of the methods employed to maintain the caste system. They conclude that the government's policy is morally indefensible and, in the long run, disastrous. Though they have been almost completely ineffective in creating voting power, they have built up an impressive critique, not only of the day-to-day performance of the government, but also of the caste system.

Among the academic critics of the caste system is P. V. Pistorius, professor of Greek in the Afrikaans-medium University of Pretoria. Pistorius has written a book with the thesis that there is *No Further Trek* for the Afrikaner, for "the hard fact is that the integration of white and black in South Africa has passed the point of no return." [11] Leo Marquard, a historian, compared the situation in South Africa with the postwar situation in tropical Africa:

> Our problem is fundamentally the same as that of any other colonial power: how to terminate colonialism reasonably and peacefully. Our problem is not unique unless we want to make it so. Nor is the solution unique. It is to renounce political power over colonial subjects. For Europe, this takes the form of withdrawing political authority; for us it must take the form of sharing political authority with our colonial subjects.[12]

Edgar H. Brookes, when he was professor of history and political science in the University of Natal, emphasized the illusory nature of the official policy:

> This is the evil in pipe-dreams of *apartheid* which cannot stand the tests of a map, a balance-sheet, or an honest election

---

[11] P. V. Pistorius, *No Further Trek* (South Africa: Central News Agency, 1957) p. 38.

[12] Leo Marquard, *South Africa's Colonial Policy* (Johannesburg: South African Institute of Race Relations, 1957) pp. 25-26.

with all the facts laid before the people. We enable ourselves to remain hopeful because we think that the Africans will accept "heartlands" which have no adequate boundaries on any map, will be satisfied with a "self-government" in those "heartlands" which is ill-defined and incomplete, will be content to remain under the control of a Union in whose ultimate and sovereign decisions they will have no share. We remain hopeful, difficult though it may be, when we have no real plan at all to deal with the Coloured people, the Indians, or those many Africans who can never be accommodated in the "heartlands." Perhaps we do not like them, perhaps it is all too difficult. But, in the name of God, when are we going to grow up and face our difficulties maturely, incisively and clearly, and to see truth as it is? [13]

D. V. Cowen, when he was professor of comparative law in the University of Cape Town, concluded that "in South Africa the values of civilized life are being corrupted and swept away in the determined pursuit of an impracticable ideal, against the wishes of the majority of the people." [14] Dr. Monica Wilson, professor of anthropology in the University of Cape Town, argues for interracial cooperation:

The God-given opportunity in South Africa, and our real achievement, lies in the close cooperation of Black and White, not in isolation and partition. That cooperation has in fact been closer here than anywhere else in Africa; we have a long tradition of common schools and open universities; of participation in municipal and provincial councils, and of voting on a common roll. This sort of equal cooperation and not the timid withdrawal into a laager, is the growing point in the South African tradition. [15]

Dr. H. M. Robertson, professor of economics in the University of Cape Town, makes a similar point:

It is all very well to look forward to a golden age when there are no occasions for interracial tension once *apartheid* is com-

---

[13] Edgar H. Brookes, "South Africa and the Wider Africa, 1910-1960," *Race Relations Journal*, XXVII, No. 1 (January-March 1960) 8.

[14] D. V. Cowen, *Liberty, Equality, Fraternity—Today: The Alfred and Winifred Hoernlé Memorial Lecture, 1961* (Johannesburg: South African Institute of Race Relations, 1961) p. 12. See also the same author's *The Foundations of Freedom* (Cape Town: Oxford University Press, 1961).

[15] Monica Wilson, "The Principle of Maintaining the Reserves for the African," *Race Relations Journal*, XXIX, No. 1 (January-March 1962) 8-9.

plete. But it is quite another matter if, in fact, the measures progressively applied both in the legislative and the administrative fields in order to achieve *apartheid* raise those very resentments and occasions of conflict which it is the avowed intention of *apartheid* finally to resolve. This shows only too clearly the dangers of doctrinaire attempts to reverse a process which has operated throughout the three hundred years since white men first settled in South Africa, in which, in spite of conflict, there has also been a steady intertwining of the daily lives of those of different races, through ties of mutual benefit in interdependence.[16]

Finally, Professor Philip V. Tobias, President of the Institute for the Study of Man and head of the department of anatomy in the University of the Witwatersrand, has declared bluntly that "Science provides no evidence that any single one of the assumptions underlying South Africa's racial legislation is justified." [17]

The Christian churches in South Africa, other than the Dutch Reformed Churches, have all made official pronouncements critical of the caste system. The long line of outspoken Anglican critics includes the last two archbishops of Cape Town — Dr. Geoffrey H. Clayton and Dr. Joost de Blank — a former bishop of Johannesburg, Ambrose Reeves, and Father Trevor Huddleston whose book, *Naught for Your Comfort,* was based on his experiences as priest-in-charge of a mission in an African township near Johannesburg. Huddleston deplored the ignorance of white South Africans of the realities of life for Africans:

> The truth is that the overwhelming majority of South Africans of the "white" group have no conception whatever of human relationships except that based on racial domination. The only Africans they know, they know as servants or as employees. Whilst the centre of the South African scene has shifted inevitably to the cities and their industrial areas, the vast majority of "Europeans" have no knowledge whatever of the urban Afri-

[16] H. M. Robertson, *South Africa: Political and Economic Aspects* (Durham: Duke University Press, 1957) pp. 32-33.

[17] Philip V. Tobias, *The Meaning of Race* (Johannesburg: South African Institute of Race Relations, 1961) p. 22.

can and his background. The greatest tragedy, in one sense, of the present situation is the total ignorance of those in responsible positions of government of the way in which young Africa thinks, talks and lives.[18]

There are also Dutch Reformed clergy who have had the courage to stand out against the caste system, notably C. F. Beyers Naudé, editor of *Pro Veritate,* and the eleven leading theologians who contributed to *Delayed Action,* in which the Rev. M. Redelinghuys of the Hervormde Kerk wrote:

. . . Apartheid, with everything it entails, must be carried out by force; force, where power exceeds justice, thus paving the way for violence. What else can be expected if there is not mutual agreement between the races to live in separate territories? What outcome can there be but that we will have to fight for dictatorial powers in order to enforce our will on others; that we will, as far as we are allowed, move in the direction of a police state? [19]

Several of the most distinguished South African judges, after retirement from the bench, have also become forthright critics of the caste system, notably ex-Chief Justice Albert van de Sandt Centlivres [20] and former Appeal Judge O. D. Schreiner.[21] Likewise several of South Africa's most talented writers and journalists, such as Mary Benson [22] and Colin Legum,[23] who now live outside South Africa, and Anthony Delius,[24] René M. de

---

18 Father Trevor Huddleston, C.R., *Naught for Your Comfort* (London: Collins, 1956), p. 19.

19 Rev. M. Redelinghuys, "The Church in South Africa," in B. B. Keet, *et al., Delayed Action: An ecumenical witness from the Afrikaans-speaking Church* (South Africa: privately published, 1960) p. 88.

20 E.g., A. van de Sandt Centlivres, *Thomas Benjamin Davie: The First T. B. Davie Memorial Lecture* (Cape Town: University of Cape Town, 1961).

21 E.g., O. D. Schreiner, *South Africa — United or Divided?* (Johannesburg: South African Institute of Race Relations, 1964).

22 Mary Benson, *The African Patriots: The story of the African National Congress of South Africa* (London: Faber, 1963).

23 E.g., Colin Legum and Anthony Sampson, "The Case for Blockading South Africa," *The Observer,* April 12, 1964.

24 Anthony Delius, *The Last Division* (Cape Town: Human and Rousseau, 1959). This long poem is a striking political satire.

Villiers,[25] Alan Paton and Stanley Uys,[26] who remain in South Africa. Alan Paton's *Cry the Beloved Country* and *Too Late the Phalarope* are among the best-known examples of South African protest literature. This is what Paton wrote about the Group Areas Act:

> The Group Areas Act is an evil instrument, repugnant to all true religion and morality, and contemptuous of human rights.
>
> It is false to religion in that it exalts the welfare of groups above the welfare of persons, and indeed treats persons as of less account, *and in many cases as of no account at all.*
>
> It has given the advantage, *almost without exception,* to the ruling group in the country. . . .
>
> The Act has purported to aim at racial harmony, but in fact it had done immeasurable harm to race relations. One might forgive fear, but it is hard to forgive those evil companions that exploit it, avarice, cruelty, and hypocrisy. . . .
>
> God save us all from the South Africa of the Group Areas Act, which knows no reason, justice, or mercy.[27]

All the politicians who were elected to Parliament by African voters under the Representation of Natives Act were critical of the caste system. Margaret Ballinger, who was a Native representative from the introduction of the system in 1937 until its abolition in 1960, regarded the government arguments in justification of its policy as grossly misleading: "It is bad enough to tell the world that you are doing things that you are not doing, but it is a shameful revelation of our cultural standards to try to support that sort of case with arguments which everybody can see through with half an eye." [28] Helen Suzman, the solitary Progressive Party member of the Parliament elected in 1961, has vigorously opposed every major racial bill. In 1963 Hamilton Russell resigned from the United Party of which he had been a longtime parliamentary member, after the party

---

[25] E.g., René M. de Villiers, "Dialogue degenerates into Rubbish," *Star,* weekly edition, January 25, 1964.

[26] E.g., Stanley Uys, "The Golden Limb," *The Spectator,* January 3, 1964.

[27] Alan Paton, *The People Wept* (Kloof, Natal: privately published, 1958) pp. 43-44.

[28] *House of Assembly Debates,* 1959, col. 92.

caucus had endorsed the General Law Amendment Bill empowering the government to commit people to jail without trial. In his letter of resignation Russell wrote: "It seems to me that the public of South Africa have had their minds so battered by persistent arbitrary assaults upon their liberties and lives that they have become punch-drunk." [29]

Comments such as these — and only a few examples from a vast mass of criticism have been given — are symptomatic of the fact that the ruling caste carries within itself a responsible, rational element that is deeply shocked by the excesses of the regime. Though the critics include some of the most distinguished white South Africans and though their views may be logically irrefutable, in electoral terms they have been of very little consequence and in legislative terms they have sustained an unbroken series of defeats. Their political weight would probably have been negligible in any case, for ruling castes do not voluntarily surrender their power. The critics have accentuated their weakness by failure to agree among themselves upon a positive program. Some are mild reformers; most of them, including the supporters of the Progressive Party, are radical reformers of various hues; others, such as the supporters of the Liberal Party, are ambiguously poised between radical reform and nonviolent revolution; and a few, including the handful of Communists, are committed to violent revolution.

Between these white opposition groups there are deep gulfs, and within each group a great deal of energy is dissipated in internal dispute. Moreover, as other South Africans have succumbed to the polarizing process, nearly all the white critics have become isolated from both poles. All but the mildest of reformers have become separated from the mainstream of white political activity and are now regarded as traitors to the white race, or at least dangerous extremists, by the United Party as well as the Nationalist Party; and all but a few dedicated revolutionaries have become isolated from the mainstream of nonwhite political activity, as it in turn has moved from reformist to revolutionary objectives, and from nonviolent to violent methods. In short, the white critics of the caste system have

[29] *Star*, weekly edition, May 11, 1963.

made an impressive diagnosis of the malady affecting South Africa, but they cannot agree among themselves which remedy to prescribe and they lack the means to apply any remedy at all.[30]

AFRICAN NATIONALISTS AND THEIR ALLIES

The origins of a firmer policy in the principal nonwhite organizations may be traced to the war years, when a new generation of African intellectuals began to lose patience with the established leadership and to form a pressure group within the African National Congress.[31] The core of the group were four Africans who were working in Johannesburg: Anton Lembede from Natal, who had obtained a B.A. degree by correspondence and worked as a teacher and a law clerk; Walter Sisulu from the Transkei, who was a laborer; Oliver Tambo from Pondoland who, after taking a B.A. degree at Fort Hare, was working as a teacher and later qualified in law; and Nelson Mandela, the son of a Transkei chief, who also obtained a law qualification and went into practice with Tambo in 1952. Forming a Youth League in 1944, these men gained control of the A.N.C. in 1949 when the national conference adopted their program; this included the use of strikes, civil disobedience and non-cooperation to coerce the government to remove discriminatory laws. At the same time they secured the election of Walter Sisulu as secretary-general of the A.N.C. and they caused the president-general, Dr. A. B. Xuma, to be replaced by Dr. J. S. Moroka. In 1952 they came to the conclusion that Moroka was not the dynamic leader they were looking for and they succeeded him with Albert J. Luthuli, a devout Christian, who had been a teacher and then the elected chief of an African

[30] For a sympathetic analysis of the dilemma of the white South African liberals see C. W. de Kiewiet, "Loneliness in the Beloved Country," *Foreign Affairs* (April 1964) pp. 413-27.

[31] Benson, *op. cit.*, chapters 9-15; Edward Feit, *South Africa: The dynamics of the African National Congress* (London: Oxford University Press, 1962) chapter 1; John Laredo, *African Political Organisation* (Johannesburg: South African Institute of Race Relations, 1961); Albert Luthuli, *Let My People Go: An autobiography* (London: Collins, 1962) chapters 9-10; Ronald Segal, *Political Africa: A Who's Who of personalities and parties* (London: Stevens, 1961).

community at Groutville, Natal. The South African Indian Congress had already undergone a similar change, with the emergence of Dr. G. M. Naicker as president of its Natal section and Dr. Y. M. Naidoo as president of its Transvaal section.

The first systematic campaign against the Afrikaner Nationalist government was undertaken by the African and the Indian congresses in concert in 1952, when large numbers of volunteers went out of their way to defy discriminatory laws and some eight thousand were arrested. By the end of the year, however, rioting occurred in Port Elizabeth, East London, Cape Town and Johannesburg, contrary to the intentions of the organizers, who called the campaign off in 1953 when Parliament had enacted severe penalties for protest actions.[32]

The next major campaign was almost national in scope. The African National Congress, the South African Indian Congress, the South African Coloured People's Organization, the predominantly white Congress of Democrats and the multi-racial South African Congress of Trade Unions cooperated in a campaign designed to enlist the support of the nonwhite masses and the sympathy of the outside world. Throughout the country, local groups compiled lists of grievances and elected delegates to a "Congress of the People." On June 26, 1955, three thousand delegates (over two thousand Africans and two to three hundred each of Coloured people, Asians and whites) met at Kliptown near Johannesburg and adopted a "Freedom Charter," which begins:

> We, the people of South Africa, declare for all our country and the world to know:
>
> that South Africa belongs to all who live in it, black and white, and that no Government can justly claim authority unless it is based on the will of all the people;
>
> that our people have been robbed of their birthright to land, liberty and peace by a form of Government founded on injustice and inequality;
>
> that our country will never be prosperous or free until all our people live in brotherhood, enjoying equal rights and opportunities;

[32] Leo Kuper, *Passive Resistance in South Africa* (London: Jonathan Cape, 1956). See also Benson, *op. cit.,* chapters 16-17, and Luthuli, *op. cit.,* chapters 11-13.

that only a democratic state, based on the will of all the people, can secure to all their birthright without distinction of colour, race, sex or belief;

And therefore, we the people of South Africa, black and white together — equal, countrymen and brothers — adopt this Freedom Charter. And we pledge ourselves to strive together, sparing nothing of our strength and courage, until the democratic changes here set out have been won.[33]

The government responded by enacting further repressive legislation and, in December 1956, by arresting 156 persons, including the leaders of the organizations forming the Congress alliance, and charging them with high treason, in the form of a conspiracy to overthrow the state by violence and replace it with a state based on Communism. Although sixty-five of those arrested were released after the preliminary examination, although thirty of the accused were acquitted and discharged on March 29, 1961, and although the case against the remaining sixty-one accused was then withdrawn, the arrests and the prolonged trial on a capital charge had a deterrent effect on other opponents of the caste system.[34]

The failure of both the passive resistance campaign of 1952-1953 and the Congress of the People campaign of 1955-1956 led to new divisions within the A.N.C. There were those who agreed with Albert Luthuli, Walter Sisulu and Nelson Mandela that the Congress should continue to cooperate with other bodies and to confine itself to nonviolent methods; others contended that the alliance with the Indian, Coloured and white congresses had weakened and distracted the A.N.C. and that there were excessive Communist influences in each of the congresses. What was needed, they believed, was a pure African movement, dedicated simply and solely to the emancipation of the African majority of the population of South Africa by

[33] Full text in Carter, *op. cit.*, pp. 486-88. On the Congress of the People campaign see also Benson, *op. cit.*, chapter 18; Feit, *op. cit.*, chapters 3-5; Luthuli, *op. cit.*, chapter 15; Segal, *op. cit.*, pp. 427-32.

[34] On the treason trial see Benson, *op. cit.*, chapter 20; Lionel Forman and E. S. Sachs, *The South African Treason Trial* (London: Calder, 1957); Muriel Horrell, compiler, *A Survey of Race Relations in South Africa* (Johannesburg: South African Institute of Race Relations) 1956-57, pp. 41-45, 1957-58, pp. 34-38, 1958-59, pp. 44-47, 1959-60, pp. 37-39, 1961, pp. 62-63; Luthuli, *op. cit.*, chapter 16.

whatever means necessary. Failing to obtain control of the A.N.C., the more radical group seceded in 1959 and founded the Pan-Africanist Congress. The P.A.C. leaders were younger than the A.N.C. leaders. The president of the P.A.C. was Robert Sobukwe, who was born in the eastern Cape Province in 1924, educated at Fort Hare and, since 1953, had been a Languages Assistant in the Department of Bantu Studies in the University of the Witwatersrand; the secretary was Potlako Leballo, who was born near the Basutoland and Orange Free State border in 1922 and, since 1954, had been a full-time politician and chairman of the A.N.C. branch in Orlando township near Johannesburg.[35]

Attempting to keep the initiative, the A.N.C. planned a new campaign against the pass laws, which was to have started at the end of March 1960. But the P.A.C. forestalled the A.N.C., taking the first step in its national campaign on March 21, 1960. On that day large numbers of Africans presented themselves at police stations in different parts of the country without passes, inviting arrest, in the hope of clogging the machinery of justice and causing a labor dislocation. At the police station at Sharpeville, near Johannesburg, the police resorted to shooting at such a crowd, killing sixty-nine Africans and wounding 178. Both the A.N.C. and the P.A.C. called for a day of mourning a week later, and there were widespread stoppages of work, especially in Cape Town, Johannesburg and Port Elizabeth. In Cape Town an impressive demonstration took place on March 30, when some 30,000 Africans marched in orderly procession under the leadership of twenty-three-year-old Philip Kgosana to the center of the city, near the Houses of Parliament, which were in session.[36]

The government struck back fiercely: it declared a state of emergency; it mobilized the armed forces, including the reserves; it outlawed the A.N.C. and the P.A.C.; it arrested 98

[35] On the origins of the P.A.C. see Benson, *op. cit.,* chapters 21-22; Feit, *op. cit.,* chapter 3; Luthuli, *op. cit.,* chapter 18; Segal, *op. cit.,* pp. 433-34; *Survey of Race Relations,* 1957-58, pp. 12-14, 1958-59, pp. 10-16.

[36] Muriel Horrell, compiler, *Days of Crisis in South Africa* (Johannesburg: South African Institute of Race Relations, 1960). Also Benson, *op. cit.,* chapter 23; Luthuli, *op. cit.,* pp. 217-23; *Survey of Race Relations,* 1959-60, pp. 55-68.

whites, 36 Coloured people, 90 Asians, and 11,279 Africans under emergency regulations. It jailed another 6,800 Africans for pass and other offenses, while the police beat up hundreds of Africans and compelled them to return to work. Subsequently, the P.A.C. leaders were sentenced to imprisonment without the option of a fine — Sobukwe to three years, and Leballo and others to two years. These measures broke the campaign. They also deprived Africans of their last means of lawful opposition to the South African political system and engendered in many hearts a hatred which had not previously existed.[37]

After 1960, so far as can be discerned, three main underground revolutionary movements emerged in South Africa.[38] One, the Spear of the Nation [*Umkonto we Sizwe*], was apparently an offshoot of the A.N.C.; another, *Poqo* [*pure,* or *only*], was apparently an offshoot of the P.A.C.; and the third, the African Resistance Movement, was a multi-racial organization, consisting mainly of young white professional men and students.

It seems that the Spear of the Nation was founded by Nelson Mandela and other former A.N.C. leaders in November 1961. Nelson Mandela has said that

> I, and the others who started the organization, did so for two reasons. Firstly, we believed that as a result of Government policy, violence by the African people had become inevitable, and that unless responsible leadership was given to canalise and control the feelings of our people, there would be outbreaks of terrorism which would produce an intensity of bitterness and hostility between the various races of this country which is not produced even by war. Secondly, we felt that without violence there would be no way open to the African people to succeed in their struggle against the principle of white supremacy.

[37] Benson, *op. cit.,* chapter 23; Luthuli, *op. cit.,* pp. 223-28; *Survey of Race Relations,* 1959-60, pp. 68-89.

[38] Muriel Horrell, *Action, Reaction and Counteraction: A review of Non-White opposition to the apartheid policy, counter-measures by the Government, and the eruption of new waves of unrest* (Johannesburg: South African Institute of Race Relations, 1963) pp. 40-55; *Survey of Race Relations,* 1964, pp. 25-33, 83-98.

> . . . Our problem was not whether to fight but how to con-
> tinue the fight. We of the A.N.C. had always stood for a non-
> racial democracy, and we shrank from any policy which might
> drive the races even farther apart than they already were. But
> the hard facts were that 50 years of non-violence had brought
> the African people nothing but more and more repressive legis-
> lation, and fewer and fewer rights.[39]

The Spear of the Nation apparently intended to disrupt communications and power lines and destroy government offices,
hoping public order would gradually collapse, guerrilla warfare would begin and white supremacy would be overthrown.
Poqo was founded at about the same time by former members
of the P.A.C. and appears to have planned some sort of mass
killing of white people and the abrupt termination of white
supremacy in 1963. Of these two, it is likely that the Spear of
the Nation had the more effective leadership and that *Poqo*
created the more effective grass-roots organization, though the
claim of Leballo to 150,000 members in March 1963 is probably grossly inflated.

The African Resistance Movement may apparently be traced
back, under various *aliases*, to 1961 or earlier; but it only became active in 1963, when it committed acts of violence in the
hope of frightening the government into making concessions.

During a three-year period starting in December 1961, there
were over two hundred acts of sabotage in South Africa. Most
of these were attacks in which time-bombs, with imported
ingredients, were used on post offices and other government
buildings, and on railway and electrical installations, in and
near the main industrial centers, especially Johannesburg and
Cape Town. Until 1963, most of these acts were probably committed by members of the Spear of the Nation; in 1964, by
members of the African Resistance Movement.

Poqo was responsible for attacks upon African chiefs and
policemen (three African police were killed in Langa township, Cape Town, in 1962) and for the murder of five whites
near a bridge over the Bashee River in the Transkei in Febru-

---

[39] Nelson Mandela, "Why I am ready to die," *The Observer*, April 26,
1964 (being an abridged version of his speech while on trial in South
Africa on charges of attempting a revolution by violence).

ary 1963.[40] The most dramatic incident attributed to *Poqo* took place at Paarl, thirty-five miles from Cape Town, on the night of November 21, 1962. Corrupt and insensitive local officials had applied the government's policy of limiting the number of African women residents to an absurd degree. A particularly explosive situation resulted and *Poqo* organizers found a ready response in the Mbekeni location, which housed about thirty families and two thousand men. After five Africans and three Coloured women had been murdered in Mbekeni, the police made arrests, whereupon a mob of about a hundred Africans marched into the white town, attacked the police station, burnt shops, damaged houses, and killed a white girl and a white man, before they were dispersed by police, with five deaths.[41]

The most dramatic act of violence in 1964 was committed by John Harris of the African Resistance Movement, who caused a time-bomb to explode in the concourse of the Johannesburg railway station, killing one woman and seriously injuring fourteen other people.

To these acts of violence the government responded by banning the Spear of the Nation, *Poqo* and the African Resistance Movement, by enacting still more repressive legislation, and by further large-scale arrests. *Poqo* was broken by mid-1963; the collapse of the Spear of the Nation was hastened by a police coup in July 1963, when seventeen men were arrested in a house at Rivonia near Johannesburg; and most of the saboteurs of the African Resistance Movement were arrested in July and August 1964. Nearly all who evaded arrest or escaped from detention fled the country, with the result that by the end of 1964 scarcely any active revolutionaries remained at large in the Republic.[42]

REPRESSIVE LEGISLATION

To appreciate the weakness of the internal opposition to the caste system in South Africa, we must understand the techniques employed by the government to maintain the system.

[40] Horrell, *Action, Reaction and Counteraction*, pp. 40-55.

[41] *Ibid.*, pp. 47-51; *Survey of Race Relations*, 1962, pp. 16, 238, 1963, pp. 14-20.

[42] *Survey of Race Relations*, 1964, pp. 25-33, 93-95.

When it came into power in 1948 the Nationalist Party took over a considerable apparatus of suppression: segregationist laws which had accumulated over the previous half-century, including laws giving the administration wide powers over Africans; [43] white police, magistrates and other officials who were almost to a man in complete sympathy with the caste system and were accustomed to using force to suppress the slightest sign of physical opposition; and nonwhite police and African chiefs who were reliable agents, being utterly dependent on the government for support and maintenance. What has happened since 1948 may be regarded, in one sense, as a systematic expansion of the preexisting instruments for the suppression of opposition. However, the expansion has been so far-reaching that South Africa has experienced a veritable counterrevolution.

The caste system in South Africa is supported by vast numbers of statutes and vast numbers of executive orders issued under powers delegated in statutes. The population register determines the racial category, and with it the rights, of every South African; marriages, and carnal intercourse outside marriage, between people of different races are unlawful; the country is divided and subdivided into uni-racial zones for landownership, residence and the conduct of business; specific occupations are reserved for specific races; Africans are excluded from the conciliation machinery for the settlement of industrial disputes; the movements of Africans outside the undeveloped Bantu Areas are rigorously controlled; there are separate educational systems for each race from kindergarten to college; and membership of the authoritative governmental institutions is confined to white people. Most of these laws carry severe penal sanctions. The result is a formidable accumulation of legalized coercive powers in the hands of the executive government. [44]

Over Africans, the legal powers of the government are virtu-

---

[43] Muriel Horrell, *Legislation and Race Relations: A summary of the main South African laws which affect race relationships* (Johannesburg: South African Institute of Race Relations, 1963) pp. 1-10, is a concise, factual statement of racial legislation before May 1948.

[44] *Ibid.*, pp. 10-63, gives a concise review of racial legislation from 1948 to 1963.

ally unlimited. Inside the Bantu Areas the government has always been able to legislate by proclamation (i.e., executive order). The most stringent proclamations in force in 1965 were Proclamations R.400 and R.413 of 1960, which apply to the Transkei. They empower the Minister of Bantu Administration and Development to prohibit any person from entering, being in, or leaving the Transkei; they prohibit gatherings of more than ten Africans (except for church services) without official permission; they authorize the police, without warrant, to arrest and indefinitely detain anyone in the Transkei, without access to a legal adviser unless with the Minister's consent; they authorize a chief to compel any African to move from one place to another within his jurisdiction; they made it an offense to attend an unlawful gathering, to make any statement or perform any action in conflict with the authority of the state or any of its officials, including chiefs and headmen, to threaten anyone with loss or violence, to boycott official meetings, or to disobey a lawful order of a chief or headman; and they prohibit interdicts for the stay of any order issued under the regulations.[45]

Outside the Bantu Areas the government's powers over Africans are the cumulative result of a long series of interlocking laws. These include the Natives Land Act of 1913; the Natives Affairs Act of 1920, with a 1959 amendment; the Native Administration Act of 1927, with amendments of 1929, 1943, 1955 and 1956; the Natives (Urban Areas) Consolidation Act of 1945, with amendments of 1946, 1947, 1952, 1953, 1956 and 1957; the Natives (Abolition of Passes and Co-ordination of Documents) Act of 1952; and the Native Laws Amendment Acts of 1952, 1957 and 1962. Among them is the Natives (Prohibition of Interdicts) Act of 1956, which makes it impossible for an African to get a stay of execution of any order of removal or banishment. These enactments have reached their logical conclusion in the Bantu Laws Amendment Act of 1964, which gives the government absolute legal power to remove any African from any part of any white area at any time. Even if he was born there, has lived there as a law-abiding citizen throughout

[45] *Ibid.*, pp. 57-58; *Survey of Race Relations,* 1963, pp. 93-95.

a long life, and has not been convicted of any offense, an African may only exist in a white area at the government's pleasure; this Act is exercised with the purpose of limiting the African population of the white areas to those who are working for white employers on contracts entered into through official labor bureaux and removing any African as soon as he is suspected of making trouble. It is a simple matter for the government to expel an African from a white area if, for example, he has become politically active or in any way objectionable, and to banish him to a Bantu Area where he has no following and no means of creating one.

The basic law designed specifically to check political activity against the caste system by people of any race is the Suppression of Communism Act of 1950. This act defines Communism and Communists in sweeping terms. Communism includes "any doctrine or scheme . . . which aims at bringing about any political, industrial, social or economic change within the Union [now, the Republic] . . . by means which include the promotion of disturbance or disorder"; [46] and Communist, according to an amendment of 1951, includes "a person who . . . is deemed by the Governor-General [now, the President] . . . to be a Communist on the ground that he . . . has at any time . . . advocated, advised, defended or encouraged the achievement of any of the objects of Communism or any act or omission which is calculated to further the advancement of any such object. . . ." [47]

The Act declares the Communist Party to be an unlawful organization. It creates machinery for the liquidation of the Communist Party and for compiling a list of the names of its officeholders, members and supporters. The Minister of Justice may prohibit any person thus listed, or any person convicted of being a Communist, from being a member of any specified organization. The Minister may also prohibit any person who he is "satisfied" is "advocating, advising, defending or encouraging the achievement of any of the objects of Communism" from being in any defined area; [48] and he may prohibit any

[46] Suppression of Communism Act, 1950, section 1(ii).

[47] Suppression of Communism Amendment Act, 1951, section 1(a).

[48] Suppression of Communism Act, 1950, section 10(1).

gathering or the attendance of any specified person at gatherings in a specified area or for a specified period, when he is of opinion that "there is reason to believe that the achievement of any of the objects of Communism would be furthered." [49] Officers authorized by the Minister may search premises and seize documents without notice at any time during their investigation of an organization suspected of Communism.

These techniques have been given further application in the Unlawful Organizations Act of 1960, which empowered the Governor-General (now, the President) to declare the African National Congress and the Pan-Africanist Congress to be unlawful organizations, and the same applies to any organizations that in his opinion have been established for the purpose of carrying on any of the activities of any organization declared unlawful. Organizations thus declared unlawful become subject to the same liquidation treatment as the Communist Party.

The effect of the banning of organizations is immensely enhanced by a wide range of legislation authorizing the government to take actions against individuals. In reaction to the passive resistance campaign of 1952-1953, Parliament passed the Criminal Law Amendment Act of 1953, increasing the penalties for persons convicted of offenses in protest against any law, making it an offense with heavy penalties to incite persons to commit offenses in protest against any law, or to solicit financial aid for such protest, and authorizing the Minister of Posts and Telegraphs to seize postal matter suspected of containing money or other articles to assist protest campaigns.

To counter the campaign leading to the Congress of the People, Parliament passed the Criminal Procedure and Evidence Act of 1955, and the Criminal Procedure Act of 1955, which increased the powers of judges, magistrates and justices of the peace to issue warrants authorizing police to search premises and to attend meetings, and increased the powers of the police to do such things without warrant. To counter the boycotts and strikes of the later 1950's, Parliament passed the Native Laws Amendment Act of 1957, empowering the Minister of Bantu Administration to prohibit the holding of any meeting in an urban area.

[49] *Ibid.,* section 9.

The Riotous Assemblies Act of 1956 consolidates earlier legislation on the subject and empowers the Minister of Justice to prohibit anyone from being in any defined area when the Minister is satisfied that the person is promoting feelings of hostility between white and nonwhite; as amended by the Unlawful Organizations Act of 1960, it imposes the harsh penalties of five years' imprisonment, or ten strokes, or a fine of $1400, or a combination of any two of these on persons found guilty of intimidating others to stay away from work or to join any association or society, or of breaking a contract of employment in essential services, or of advising, encouraging, or inciting anyone to commit an offense by way of protest against any law or in support of any campaign against any law.

Coercive legislation reached a peak in the devastating General Law Amendment Acts of 1962 and 1963. As the law now stands the President may declare any organization to be unlawful if he is "satisfied" that it "carries on or has been established for the purpose of carrying on directly or indirectly any of the activities of an unlawful organization"; [50] or, more simply still, he may declare by proclamation that "any body, organization, group or association of persons, institution, society or movement described or known by a name specified in the proclamation . . . is in fact . . . an unlawful organization," with the express provision that "no court shall have jurisdiction to pronounce upon the validity of any proclamation issued under this sub-section." [51]

These laws also increase the powers of the executive to harass people who have been "listed" as members of unlawful organizations. The Minister of Justice may order any listed person not to attend: "(a) any gathering; or (b) any particular gathering or any gathering of a particular nature, class or kind, at any place or in any area during any period or on any day or during specified times or periods within any period. . . ." [52] The Minister may also prohibit any listed person from being a member of "any particular organization or any organization of

50 General Law Amendment Act, 1962, section 2(b).
51 General Law Amendment Act, 1963, section 14(a).
52 General Law Amendment Act, 1962, section 7(a).

a nature, class or kind specified." [53] He may also prohibit any listed person "from being within or absenting himself from any place or area . . . or, while the prohibition is in force, communicating with any person or receiving any visitor," except his advocate or attorney.[54] This last prohibition may also be applied to any person who, the Minister of Justice is "satisfied,"

   (i) advocates, advises, defends or encourages the achievement of any of the objects of Communism or any act or omission which is calculated to further the achievement of any such object; or

 (ii) is likely to advocate, advise, defend or encourage the achievement of any such object or any such act or omission; or

(iii) engages in activities which are furthering any or may further the achievement of any such object.[55]

It is also unlawful for anyone to publish any statement that has ever been made by any person who has been prohibited from attending any gathering. Therefore, no statement may be published that has ever been made by an individual listed as a member of an unlawful organization, or by a person the Minister of Justice has prohibited from attending a meeting because he was "satisfied" that person was engaged in furthering the achievement of any of the objects of Communism.

The 1962 Act also provides for the crime of sabotage. Any person who commits any "wrongful and wilful act" damaging "any property, whether movable or immovable, of any other person or of the State," or who attempts to commit such an act, or who encourages anyone to commit such an act, is guilty of sabotage, unless he can prove that the act was not committed with the intent to produce some political effect, such as "the bringing about of any social or economic change in the Republic"; and a person guilty of sabotage is liable to the death penalty, with a minimum of five years imprisonment.[56]

[53] *Ibid.*, section 4.
[54] *Ibid.*, section 8(a).
[55] *Ibid.*
[56] *Ibid.*, section 21.

The 1963 Act empowers postal officials to detain postal articles "reasonably suspected of containing anything which will afford evidence of the commission of any offence." [57] It applies the penalties for sabotage to actions committed outside the Republic. Also the Act empowers the Minister of Justice to have a person kept in prison indefinitely once he has been sentenced to prison under the provisions of several acts, including the Riotous Assemblies Act and the sabotage section of the 1962 Act, provided that the Minister is "satisfied" that the person "is likely to advocate, advise, defend or encourage the achievement of any of the objects of Communism." [58] Section 17 of the 1963 Act is probably as punitive a section as has ever appeared in a law:

17. (1) Notwithstanding anything to the contrary in any law contained, any commissioned officer as defined in section *one* of the Police Act, 1958 (Act No. 7 of 1958), may from time to time without warrant arrest or cause to be arrested any person whom he suspects upon reasonable grounds of having committed or intending or having intended to commit any offence under the Suppression of Communism Act, 1950 (Act No. 44 of 1950), or under the last-mentioned Act as applied by the Unlawful Organizations Act, 1960 (Act No. 34 of 1960), or the offence of sabotage, or who in his opinion is in possession of any information relating to the commission of any such offence or the intention to commit any such offence, and detain such person or cause him to be detained in custody for interrogation in connection with the commission of or intention to commit such offence, at any place he may think fit, until such person has in the opinion of the Commissioner of the South African Police replied satisfactorily to all questions at the said interrogation, but no such person shall be so detained more than ninety days on any particular occasion when he is so arrested.

(2) No person shall, except with the consent of the Minister of Justice or a commissioned officer as aforesaid, have access to any person detained under sub-section (1): Provided that not less than once during each week such person shall be visited in private by the magistrate or an additional or assistant magistrate of the district in which he is detained.

[57] General Law Amendment Act, 1963, section 13.
[58] *Ibid.*, section 4(a).

(3) No court shall have jurisdiction to order the release from custody of any person so detained, but the said Minister may at any time direct that any such person be released from custody.

There is, finally, the Public Safety Act of 1953; this empowers the government to proclaim a state of emergency in any or every part of the country and to rule by proclamation. The safeguards in this law are few. The government may proclaim a state of emergency if it considers that the safety of the public or the maintenance of public order is seriously threatened, and that the ordinary law is inadequate to preserve it; during a state of emergency the government may issue regulations dealing with any subject, except only that such regulations may not alter the structure of Parliament nor suspend its normal sittings, and the regulations require the subsequent assent of both Houses of Parliament.

A state of emergency was proclaimed throughout most of the country on March 30, 1960, and it remained in force until August 31, 1960; the emergency regulations gave the magistrates, the police and the army sweeping powers of search, arrest and detention. At present, however, it would take very unusual circumstances to make it necessary for the government to resort to the Public Safety Act. The other laws in the statute-book, especially the General Law Amendment Acts of 1962 and 1963, give the government all the legal powers it needs to suppress organizations and individuals who seek to oppose the caste system.

The government also has formidable instruments for enforcing the laws. It has a monopoly of modern weapons. Scarcely any nonwhites possess firearms or have had any experience in handling them, for nonwhite police carry sticks and truncheons, and nonwhites are not recruited into the armed forces nor are they given licenses to acquire arms. On the other hand, most white men and many white women possess firearms and are experienced in their use. The army and the white members of the police force are well equipped with the most modern weapons (other than atomic weapons), including up-to-date aircraft, helicopters, tanks and quickfiring guns; they are trained and practiced in the handling of hostile crowds; and they can be quickly augmented by trained reserves. Thus, the nonwhite numerical superiority in South Africa is more than offset by the immense white superiority in the possession of the instruments of violence.

Not the least of the government's agents of law enforcement is the large number of official informers who operate in all the communities in South Africa. White supporters of the government infiltrate into white associations and regard it their duty to search out suspicious activities, while nonwhites, some in the plainclothes branch of the police force and others who are employed for particular assignments, spy upon nonwhite associations. These informers, reporting to police officers, petty officials and chiefs who are vested with wide powers, are a serious deterrent to effective opposition.

THE ELIMINATION OF EFFECTIVE OPPOSITION

All this organized state power is exercised with the primary purpose of eliminating opposition to the caste system. The Communist Party, the African National Congress, the Pan-Africanist Congress, the Spear of the Nation, *Poqo,* the African Resistance Movement, and the Congress of Democrats have all been declared unlawful organizations. Between 1948 and the middle of 1963, 132 African men and women had been banished from their homes to farms belonging to the government or to tribal areas remote from their homes for various periods, and thirty-one were still in banishment in June 1963.[59] In November 1962 the government issued a list of 437 people who were listed as Communists in terms of the Suppression of Communism Act (129 whites and 308 nonwhites),[60] but no lists have been published of persons who have been named as members or active supporters of other banned organizations. Between 1954 and 1962, over 270 people were served with banning orders of various types, and many more such orders have been issued under the General Law Amendment Act of 1962.[61] Muriel Horrell has published an analysis of 202 banning orders

[59] Horrell, *Action, Reaction and Counteraction,* pp. 64-67.
[60] *Star,* November 16, 1962.
[61] Horrell, *Action, Reaction and Counteraction,* p. 72.

which were in effect on October 14, 1963.[62] All of them were prohibited from attending political gatherings; from belonging to thirty-five specified organizations (including all the non-white political organizations, the South African Congress of Trade Unions, the Coloured teachers' organizations and liberal groups like the Civil Rights League); and from being members of any other organization that discusses politics or prepares, publishes or distributes any publication. Fifty of them were also forbidden to attend social gatherings; twenty-four were under house arrest; 104 were confined to specified magisterial districts; and many were subject to a wide variety of special restrictions — for example, one was forbidden to enter any hospital. Several people have also been tried and convicted for contravening their banning orders; others have been subjected to fresh bans directly after a ban expired. In addition, by March 13, 1964, 682 people had been arrested and detained without warrant under the General Law Amendment Act of 1963; while most of them were released within the ninety-day period mentioned in the Act, sixty-nine were rearrested immediately after the ninety days ended, and eight were arrested yet again after 180 days.[63] A further 176 people were in detention in the Transkei in June 1963 under Proclamation 400. Between December 1961 and March 1964, 62 persons were found guilty of murder, 258 of sabotage, and 1,466 of other crimes of a subversive nature, and 562 persons who would have been charged fled the country.[64]

All the effective African leaders have been silenced or have left the country. Albert Luthuli, winner of the Nobel Prize for Peace and the last president-general of the A.N.C., was banned from all political activities and from all South African towns for a year starting in 1952. He was banned for two more years from July 1954; in December 1956 he was arrested and charged with treason and he was released with the first batch in December 1957; he was confined to a small area in an African reserve in Natal for five years from May 1959; and he was confined there for a further five years from May 1964, when he was

[62] *Ibid.*, pp. 73-75.
[63] *Survey of Race Relations*, 1964, p. 65.
[64] *Ibid.*, 1963, p. 52, 1964, p. 83.

sixty-six years of age.[65] Walter Sisulu of the A.N.C. was sentenced to six years' imprisonment in March 1963 for continuing to further the aims of the A.N.C. and for inciting people to stay at home during the demonstration of May 1961. Released on bail pending an appeal, he was placed under house arrest, but disappeared in April 1963 and remained at large until he was one of those persons arrested at Rivonia near Johannesburg on July 11, 1963, after which he was charged with sabotage and sentenced to life imprisonment. Nelson Mandela, who was the principal planner of the demonstrations of May 1961, evaded the police for six months after a warrant had been issued for his arrest, but was arrested in November 1962 and sentenced to five years' imprisonment for incitement and for having left the country unlawfully, and he, with Sisulu, was later charged with sabotage and sentenced to life imprisonment.[66] Robert Sobukwe, president of the P.A.C., was sentenced to three years' imprisonment after the events of March 1960, and immediately the sentence expired on May 3, 1963, he was taken to Robben Island near Cape Town, and imprisoned there indefinitely under the General Law Amendment Act of 1963.[67] Virtually all of the other established leaders of the A.N.C. and the P.A.C. are also under bans or serving prison sentences or in detention without trial, except those who have left South Africa.

The émigrés include many members of both organizations, such as Tennyson Makiwane, Joe G. Matthews, Tom Nkobi,

[65] On Luthuli see Edward Callan, *Albert John Luthuli and the South African Race Conflict* (Kalamazoo: Western Michigan University Press, 1962); and Albert Luthuli, *Let My People Go: An autobiography* (London: Collins, 1962). Callan includes his Nobel Peace Prize address of December 11, 1961, on pp. 55-63.

[66] On Sisulu and Mandela see Benson, *op. cit.*, pp. 104-10; Anthony Sampson, "The men who may hang," *The Observer*, March 1, 1964; Segal, *op. cit.*, pp. 169, 246-47; "Mandela's Defence" and "Why I am ready to die," *The Observer*, November 18, 1962, and April 29, 1964.

[67] On Sobukwe see Segal, *op. cit.*, p. 250. There have been serious allegations of police brutality in South Africa, including allegations of maltreatment and torture of political detainees. Patrick Duncan, *South Africa's Rule of Violence* (London: Methuen, 1964); *Guardian* (London), February 26, 1964; *Star*, weekly edition, January 25, 1964, March 14, 1964.

Duma Nokwe and Oliver Tambo of the A.N.C., and Philip Kgosana, Potlako Leballo, Nelson Mahono and Peter Molotsi of the P.A.C. They also include members of other political organizations, such as Dr. Y. Dadoo of the S.A.I.C., I. Tabata of the African People's Democratic Union, Reg September of the Coloured People's Congress, Patrick Duncan, formerly of the Liberal Party, who later became the first white member of the P.A.C., and several people who were listed as Communists.[68]

Part of the price South Africa has paid for the suppression of opposition to the caste system has been a very general abrogation of the rule of law.[69] The rule of law is now violated in South Africa by many statutes empowering Cabinet Ministers, government officials and police officers to deprive people of their liberty and their property. In many cases the violation is compounded by the fact that a deprived person is not informed of the precise nature of the charge made against him, nor of the persons' names initiating the charges, and is given no opportunity to defend himself, nor to appeal to a court of law against the order of deprivation.

In this connection three points may be noted. One is that the rule of law was generally respected and widely applied in the early years of the history of the Union of South Africa; that the first major inroads were made during the period when the Afrikaner Nationalist Party of J. B. M. Hertzog was in power, by laws such as the Native Administration Amendment Act of 1929 and the Riotous Assemblies Act of 1930; and that the rule of law has been overridden by a mass of legislation enacted by

[68] Horrell, *Action, Reaction and Counteraction*, pp. 33, 95-97. In March 1964, the Minister of Justice said that 562 people who would have been charged with sabotage had fled the country. *Survey of Race Relations*, 1964, p. 75.

[69] The literature on this subject is considerable. See especially Edgar H. Brookes and J. B. Macaulay, *Civil Liberty in South Africa* (Cape Town: Oxford University Press, 1958); International Commission of Jurists, *South Africa and the Rule of Law* (Geneva: International Commission of Jurists, 1960), and the *Bulletin of the International Commission of Jurists*, No. 14 (October 1962) pp. 29-34, No. 16 (July 1963) pp. 37-39, No. 17 (December 1963) pp. 41-48, No. 18 (March 1964) pp. 37-43; Elizabeth S. Landis, "South African Apartheid Legislation," *Yale Law Journal*, LXXI, Nos. 1 and 3 (1961-1962) 1-52, 437-500; K. L. Roskam, *Apartheid and Discrimination* (Leyden: Sythoff, 1960).

the Afrikaner Nationalist Party of D. F. Malan, J. G. Strijdom and H. F. Verwoerd which has been in power since 1948. The second point is that almost all the early victims of violations of the rule of law were Africans and that, though Africans are still by far the principal sufferers, much of the legislation passed since 1948 has also deprived Asians, Coloured people and even whites of the protection of the rule of law. The third item is that the supersession of the rule of law has been so gradual, so insidious, and yet so complete a process that most of the inhabitants of South Africa, especially the white inhabitants, have become conditioned to it and accept it as a natural state of affairs.

Today the property and civil rights of all South Africans are, in manifold ways, subject to the whims of persons who are not judicial officers. The most devastating invasion of property rights is the Group Areas Act, which has led to the expropriation by administrative committees of land lawfully acquired by many thousands of people. The most devastating invasion of civil liberties is, of course, the General Law Amendment Act of 1963. Indeed, section 17 of that Act, quoted on pages 189-90, removes any doubt that may previously have existed concerning whether South Africa was a police state in the precise sense of the phrase, because it empowers police officers to arrest whomever they want without a warrant and to detain them indefinitely without trial and without access to legal advisers.[70] In the government's determination to preserve white supremacy, which it equates with the safety of the state, the South African authorities have replaced the rule of law with the rule of Cabinet Ministers, public officials and police officers.

By 1965 the internal opposition to the caste system was overawed and fragmented. The mainstreams of the Afrikaner and the English-speaking white communities were more united in defense of their privileges than ever before. Though some of

[70] In terms of the General Law Amendment Act, 1963, section 17 was initially in operation until the end of June 1964, after which the President could at any stage reapply it for periods up to twelve months by proclamation. It was thus extended till January 1965, when it was lifted; but it may be reapplied whenever the government thinks it necessary and its substance was incorporated in a new law enacted later in 1965.

the ablest members of both communities had been prompted by their consciences to become radical reformers, there was nothing to suggest that they would ever make significant headway among the electorate. The subordinate castes were more completely subjected than ever before. The legal basis for their subjection had been perfected and the laws were being vigorously applied by the bureaucracy and the police, who were assisted by allies in all communities, including paid informers and other classes of cooperators, such as African chiefs who were on the official payroll. While the whites retained a monopoly of firepower, the government had built up and was continuously replenishing a powerful arsenal of modern weapons for use in suppressing uprisings. All organizations known to have revolutionary potentialities were proscribed, and all known revolutionary leaders were either in exile or were silenced by banning, banishment, or imprisonment. Managing all educational institutions for nonwhites and controlling some communications media and censoring others, the government had a dominant say in the circulation of information. It was also contriving to separate caste from caste and community from community with ever-increasing rigor.

In these circumstances there was no discernible way in which new revolutionary leaders could emerge or new revolutionary organizations could be created. All that remained of the old organizations was a number of rudderless fragments, geographically separated from one another and psychologically divided by past quarrels and present suspicions. The sporadic and, for the most part, trivial acts of sabotage they were able to commit created enough tension to further the process of the consolidation of the white communities and to provide grist to the mill of government propaganda, but were not enough to threaten the stability of the state. Indeed, in 1965 there seemed to be no prospect of a successful revolution being organized from within South Africa.

Whether the revolutionary ardor of South African nonwhites was weakening by 1965 is difficult to determine. On the one hand, more South Africans than ever before were being harassed by petty officials applying repressive laws that lacked a moral basis, so that the incentive to revolution was stronger than ever. On the other hand the government and most employers of labor were trying to improve the living conditions of the nonwhites, provided that this could be done without threatening the living standards of the whites — since the economy was an expanding one this had been possible. Nonwhite real wages were rising, nonwhite death rates were dropping, and some of the nonwhite slums were being replaced by modern housing estates, so that while the disparity between white and nonwhite material levels in South Africa remained conspicuous, the living conditions of most South African nonwhites were improving. Time will show whether advances such as these can be a sufficient substitute for the absence of liberty.

If in the mid-1960's a prognosis was made of the situation, based exclusively on local factors, the prediction would be a long life for the South African political system. However, there are also external factors to consider.

CHAPTER VI

The External Opposition
to the System

Before 1946 the South African political system was not exceptional, nor was it singled out for condemnation by foreign governments. Today it is exceptional. It runs counter to the almost universal renunciation of racist principles and dismantling of racist practices. It is almost universally condemned. And it is in some danger of coercion by the international community.

One factor promoting the growth of this formidable external threat has been the increasing rigidity and severity of the South African system, marked by the advent of the Nationalist Party to power, the unfolding of its policy of apartheid, and its resort to more and more ruthless methods of suppressing internal opposition. But this has not been the crucial factor. Even if the South African system had remained as mild as it was in 1946, in the changed world of the 1960's it would have incurred severe condemnation and its survival would have been threatened.

The essential causes of this development are to be found in the shifts in the distribution of power and influence in the world. The power and influence of the erstwhile colonial states have shrunk; this is particularly true of Britain, which had a major responsibility for the evolution of the South

African system and continues to have the greatest foreign stake in the South African economy. Furthermore, except in Portugal, the official attitudes of the erstwhile colonial powers towards colonialism and racism have been radically transformed. Before 1946 they not only ruled colonies — and in them necessarily applied some measure of racial stratification — but they vindicated the colonial system. By the 1960's they had renounced colonialism and its concomitants, and such power and influence as they still possessed were no longer overtly exerted in support of white supremacy in South Africa or anywhere else.

Second, as the United States assumed the responsibilities that went with its towering strength in the fluid years after World War II, its anti-colonial tradition, emanating from the conditions of its origin as a nation, outweighed its tradition of negro servitude. American pressures upon its principal allies — including the erstwhile colonial powers — were a major factor in the dissolution of their empires. Later, as the negro revolt gathered momentum in the United States, it served as a spur to the American government to promote the completion of the African revolution by denying the validity of the doctrine of white supremacy, in South Africa as in the United States.

Third, whatever their practices may have been in Europe and in Asia where they have longstanding interests and ambitions, Russia and China have not been inhibited by the possession of stakes in the status quo ante 1946 from encouraging the anti-colonial revolution in Africa. They have disseminated Marxist-Leninist propaganda and fostered Communist movements in Africa; these have had the effect of pricking the Western Powers into yielding to the demands of African nationalists, for fear of being outbidden and losing their influence in the new Africa.

Fourth, the African elites throughout the continent have become obsessed by anti-colonial and anti-racist fervor. This has been the psychological force behind the drive towards independence in each territory, and where independence has been achieved, this remains the basic mystique in the policies of the successor states to the European empires. To the rulers of the new African states, South Africa is not just a foreign country with a different way of life: it is an anathema . . . because its government oppresses people whom the other rulers regard as kinsfolk . . . because it blocks the consummation of their dream to liberate all of Africa, from Cairo to the Cape, from alien control . . . and because it is the one sovereign state in the world today which still practices racism without shame and raises it to the level of a philosophy. No assessment of the present threat to the South African political system is complete unless it takes account of this crusading impulse.

Fifth, the prospect that the territory of the Republic might remain sheltered from contiguity with African-controlled states by an intermediate band of colonial territories is being belied by events. Malawi and Zambia have been added to the number of African-controlled states. The Portuguese hold over Angola and Mozambique is being challenged. There is no assurance of a prolonged continuation of white supremacy in Rhodesia. The legal basis of South Africa's control of South-West Africa has been challenged in the International Court of Justice. Britain has become committed to transferring power to the African inhabitants of Lesotho, Bechuanaland and Swaziland. Changes may take place suddenly and soon in any or all of these territories, and this is not the place to speculate about the future of each of them. But one thing is clear: the northern frontiers of Angola, Rhodesia and Mozambique will have formed only a temporary line of division between an African-controlled north and center of the continent and a white-controlled Southern Africa. During the later 1960's the waves of the African revolution will be pounding upon at least some of the frontiers of the Republic.

Finally, the continuous flow of white and nonwhite refugees out of South Africa has led to the creation, in capital cities of tropical Africa, Western Europe and North America, of groups of zealots dedicated to the overthrow of the South African political system. Despite fierce internal disputes, these groups bring passion and a sense of urgency to the interventionist lobbies, as well as invaluable experience of the realities of life for the subject races in South Africa.

THE UNITED NATIONS AND SOUTH AFRICA

Colonialism and racism have been principal targets for criticism at all the conferences of the associations of the nonaligned, the Afro-Asian and the African states. They figure most conspicuously in the program of the Organization of African Unity. In May 1963 at its inaugural conference in Addis Ababa, the OAU started a liberation fund to which nearly every independent African state has contributed, and it set up a nine-member African Liberation Committee with permanent headquarters at Dar es Salaam. In July 1964 at a conference in Cairo, the OAU founded a bureau to coordinate the boycott of South Africa, Angola and Mozambique. During 1964 a Union of Non-Independent States was formed, comprising refugees from South Africa, South-West Africa and Rhodesia, to work in liaison with OAU.

However, if the OAU is to achieve its objective in the near future, it requires the cooperation of others. Alone, the African states lack the resources to conquer South Africa in open warfare, nor can they inflict lethal damage upon the South African economy because only a small fraction of South Africa's external trade has ever been conducted with the area now controlled by African governments. Moreover, the moral advantages would be immense if South Africa were coerced by a more broadly-based international organization, in terms of general principles and a specific document which South Africa itself has recognized. Consequently, the United Nations is the key organization, and the Charter of the United Nations the key legal basis for the coercion of the Republic.

From its birth the United Nations has been a very different organization from its predecessor, the League of Nations, which was always dominated by the colonial powers and tender towards their interests. These differences have increased with the passage of time, largely due to the structure of the United Nations. At its first session the organization had fifty-one members and the balance in the General Assembly lay with the Western Powers. Later, however, with the disintegration of the colonial empires into a large number of (for the most part) small successor states, and the admission of nearly all of them to the United

Nations, the balance shifted towards Asia and, particularly, towards Africa. In the middle of 1965 there were 115 members, of which thirty-seven were African [1] and twenty-four were Asian. In addition, the majority of the African members had been dependencies of the Western Powers as recently as 1960. In the Security Council the balance is different since the permanent seats, with the veto power, are occupied by Nationalist China, France, the United Kingdom, the United States and the U.S.S.R., but even in the Council there has been an increase in the representation of the new states in the non-permanent seats, which in 1965 were occupied by Malaysia and the Ivory Coast, as well as Bolivia, Jordan, the Netherlands and Uruguay.

In the Charter, the powers of the organs of the United Nations and the obligations of its members are cloaked in ambiguity. South Africa has always insisted on an absolutist application of the principle of national sovereignty, as set out in Article 2(7):

> Nothing contained in the present Charter shall authorize the United Nations to intervene in matters which are essentially within the domestic jurisdiction of any state or shall require the Members to submit such matters to settlement under the present Charter; but this principle shall not prejudice the application of enforcement measures under Chapter VII.

On the other hand, interventionists point to Article 2(2), according to which the United Nations and its members are to "fulfill in good faith the obligations assumed by them in accordance with the present Charter," in conjunction with Article 55 in which the United Nations is to promote, inter alia, "universal respect for, and observance of, human rights and fundamental freedoms for all without distinction as to race, sex, language, or religion," and Article 56 in which "All Members pledge themselves to take joint and separate action in cooperation with the Organization for the achievement of the purposes set forth in Article 55."

How is 2(7) to be reconciled with 2(2), 55 and 56? If the absolutist interpretation of 2(7) is correct, then 2(2), 55 and 56 are no more than pious aspirations. If 2(2), 55 and 56 have any effi-

[1] Not including South Africa.

cacy at all, they qualify 2(7). There is also the remarkable vagueness in the phrase "threat to the peace" in Chapter VII, where if the Security Council has determined that there is "any threat to the peace, breach of the peace, or act of aggression" (Article 39), it may then call upon Members to impose "measures not involving the use of armed force" (Article 41), or it may, if it can, itself take "such action by air, sea, or land forces as may be necessary to maintain or restore international peace and security" (Article 42).

In fact, over the years precedents have accumulated for the handling of critical issues, including the raising and employment of United Nations military forces in the Middle East, Korea, Egypt, the Congo, and Cyprus. Over the years the United Nations has also edged step by step towards the coercion of South Africa.

South-West Africa was on the agenda of the first session of the General Assembly, which rejected South Africa's request to incorporate the territory and invited it to place this area under United Nations Trusteeship with the other former mandated territories (1946). Thereafter, year by year, the Assembly has tried to influence the course of events in South-West Africa and, meeting with refusals and obstructions and with the progressive extension of the policy of apartheid to South-West Africa, it has become more and more exasperated.

This process can be traced in the Assembly's resolutions: The Assembly notes that South Africa intends to preserve the status quo and maintains that South-West Africa should be placed under Trusteeship (1947). It notes the intention of South Africa to form a closer association with the territory by giving it representation in the Union Parliament, but maintains its previous recommendations and further recommends that annual reports should continue to be rendered and should be examined by the Trusteeship Council (1948). It requests South Africa to give effect to the findings of the International Court and establishes a committee to consider what procedure should be adopted to implement the findings, and it reiterates its call for South-West Africa to be placed under Trusteeship (1950). The U. N. notes that South Africa is only prepared to negotiate with the committee on the basis of its own proposals and declines to submit reports, and the organization regrets that South Africa is unwilling to fulfill its international obligations (1952). The U. N. recalls with deep regret South Africa's refusal to implement the Court's decision, notes that no reports or petitions have been submitted, appeals to South Africa to reconsider her obligations, establishes a new committee on South-West Africa, and reiterates that the territory should be placed under Trusteeship (1953). It adopts rules for examining reports and petitions from unofficial sources in South-West Africa (1954). It gives hearings to petitioners from South-West Africa, approves of the recommendations of the committee for the transfer of power and the repeal of discriminatory laws, invites the Secretary-General to explore ways and means of solving the South-West African question, and requests the committee to consider what legal action is possible to ensure that South Africa fulfills its obligations under the Mandate (1957). The U. N. urges South Africa to stop imprisoning and deporting South-West African leaders and to ensure freedom of political rights and expression in the territory, it commends Ethiopia and Liberia for instituting judicial proceedings in the International Court, and it considers that the South-West African situation is a serious threat to international peace and security (1960). It calls the attention of the Security Council to the threat to peace that may arise in South-West Africa, it declares the right of the people of the territory to independence, and it establishes a special training program for South-West Africans (1961). It requests the Secretary-General to take all necessary steps to establish an effective United Nations' presence in South-West Africa (1962), and it requests the Security Council to consider the critical situation (1963).[2]

The South-West African question is not likely to be pressed very much further in the General Assembly or the Security Council until the International Court has given its judgment in the case brought by Ethiopia and Liberia, who have asked the Court to rule that the Mandate is still in force, that South Africa has failed to fulfill its obligations under the Mandate and under the Covenant of the League of Nations, and that South Africa must change its racial policies in South-West

[2] South African Institute of International Affairs, *Check List of United Nations resolutions directly concerning South Africa* (Johannesburg: 1963).

Africa. Should the judgment go against South Africa, it may be expected that the two applicants will appeal to the Security Council for the establishment of a United Nations' presence in South-West Africa and also, perhaps, for the revocation of the Mandate. Therefore, a prospect exists that the South African government may be obliged to choose between outright defiance of the international system of law and order, which would be a very grave decision indeed, and surrender of the control of a contiguous territory it has been treating as an integral part of the Republic.[3]

While the South-West African issue has been coming to a head, there has been a parallel growth of exasperation in the United Nations over the policy of apartheid within the four provinces of South Africa itself. This process, too, has been marked by a series of resolutions of the Assembly dating back to 1946. The Assembly first took cognizance of events inside South Africa as a result of complaints by the Indian government that South Africa was ignoring agreements made with India concerning the treatment of Indians in South Africa. Tracing this process we find: The Assembly declares that South African treatment of Indians should conform to international agreements between the two countries and to the United Nations Charter (1946). It invites South Africa, India and Pakistan to convene a round-table conference (1949). It recommends that, if the proposed conference fails, a commission should be established to investigate the problem, and it calls on South Africa not to enforce the Group Areas Act pending negotiations (1950). It notes that the conference has not taken place and that the Group Areas Act has been promulgated, and it requests the Secretary-General to assist in the establishment of the commission (1952).[4]

After that point, the Assembly continued to pass fruitless

3 International Court of Justice, *South-West Africa Cases* (*Ethiopia and Liberia v. the Republic of South Africa*): *Memorials of the Governments of Ethiopia and Liberia* (1961), *Counter-Memorial of the Government of the Republic of South Africa* (1963), and *Reply of the Governments of Ethiopia and Liberia* (1964). Also R. B. Ballinger, *South Africa and the United Nations: Myth and Reality* (Johannesburg: South African Institute of International Affairs, 1963).

4 *Check List of United Nations resolutions directly concerning South Africa.*

resolutions on the specific question of the treatment of Indians, but at the same time it took up the broader question of the effects of apartheid upon all the nonwhite inhabitants of South Africa. Since 1961 the former question has been subsumed under the latter. The Assembly established a commission of three to study the racial situation in South Africa and declared that South Africa's policies were inconsistent with its pledges under Article 56 of the Charter (1952). It noted the commission's conclusion that apartheid was contrary to the Declaration of Human Rights and invited South Africa to cooperate with the commission (1953). It noted with apprehension the adoption of new apartheid laws, declared that apartheid constituted a grave threat to the peaceful relations between ethnic groups in the world, and invited South Africa to reconsider its position (1954). The Assembly called on South Africa to observe Article 56 of the Charter (1955).

Having reiterated these resolutions in 1957, 1958 and 1959, the Assembly deplored South Africa's persistent disregard of world and United Nations' opinion and its determined aggravation of racial issues, and requested all states to take action to bring about a change in South Africa's racial policies, which led to international friction and endangered peace and security (1961).[5] By 67 votes to 16, with 23 abstentions, it asked member states to break off diplomatic relations with South Africa (if they had any), to close their ports to South African ships, to prohibit their own ships from entering South African ports, to boycott South African goods, to refrain from exporting goods to South Africa, and to refuse landing and passage facilities to South African aircraft (1962). In the same resolution the Assembly established a Special Committee to keep the racial policies of South Africa under constant review, and requested the Security Council "to take appropriate measures, including sanctions, to secure South Africa's compliance with the resolutions of the General Assembly and of the Security Council on this subject."[6]

The Security Council first took cognizance of the South African situation after the Sharpeville shootings, in a resolution

[5] *Ibid.*

[6] United Nations General Assembly, *A/5497/Add. 1* (1963) pp. 3-5.

which recognized that the situation might endanger international peace, deplored the policies and actions of the South African government, and called upon South Africa to initiate measures based on equality (1960). Following interim reports from the Special Committee established under the Assembly's 1962 resolution, the Security Council, by nine votes to none with two abstentions (Britain and France), "Being convinced that the situation in South Africa is seriously disturbing international peace and security," called on all states "to cease forthwith the sale and shipment of arms, ammunition of all types and military vehicles to South Africa" (August 7, 1963).[7] On December 4, 1963 following a Scandinavian initiative, the Security Council unanimously declared that the situation in South Africa was "seriously disturbing international peace and security" and requested the Secretary-General to establish a Group of Experts "to examine methods of resolving the present situation in South Africa through full, peaceful and orderly application of human rights and fundamental freedoms to all inhabitants of the territory as a whole, regardless of race, color or creed, and to consider what part the United Nations might play in the achievement of that end. . . ."[8]

The Group of Experts, under the chairmanship of Mrs. Alva Myrdal, reported in April 1964, recommending that

> The future of South Africa should be settled by the people of South Africa — all the people of South Africa — in free discussion. There can be no settlement and no peace while the great majority of the people are denied the fundamental freedom to participate in decisions on the future of their country. We are convinced that a continuation of the present position including a denial of just representation must lead to violent conflict and tragedy for all the people of South Africa. We wish, therefore, to emphasize the first and basic principle that all the people of South Africa should be brought into consultation and should thus be enabled to decide the future of their country at the national level.
>
> In order to give effect to this essential principle, we consider

7 United Nations General Assembly, *A/5497* (1963) pp. 28-29.

8 United Nations, *A New Course in South Africa: Report of the Group of Experts established in pursuance of the Security Council resolution of 4 December 1963* (1964) p. 7.

that all efforts should be directed to the establishment of a National Convention fully representative of the whole population. Such a representative National Convention would consider the views and proposals of all those participating and set a new course for the future.

We believe that the mounting condemnation by world opinion and the growing insistence on positive action should now be directed to the achievement of this purpose. It is only on the road of free and democratic consultation and cooperation and conciliation that a way can be found towards a peaceful and constructive settlement. Only thus can all people of South Africa be saved from catastrophe and the world from a conflagration of incalculable consequences.[9]

THE CASE FOR COERCING SOUTH AFRICA

In June 1964 the Security Council endorsed this main conclusion of the Group of Experts and set up a new Expert Committee, composed of representatives of all members of the Council, to report on the feasibility, effectiveness, and implications of measures which could be taken by the Security Council under the U.N. Charter. The report of the Expert Committee was published in March 1965. The Committee concluded, by six votes to four, that South Africa was not immune to danger from economic measures, but their effectiveness depended on the universality of their application and the manner and duration of their enforcement. France did not participate in the work of the Committee, having made it clear that it regarded the terms of reference as interference in the affairs of a member-state. Czechoslovakia, the Ivory Coast, Morocco and the Soviet Union, on the other hand, voted against the majority in the Committee because they would have preferred more radical conclusions.[10]

By that time the feasibility of coercing the South African government had already been explored in some detail by a conference held in London in April 1964. The conference was convened by Ronald Segal, a South African émigré, sponsored by eleven heads of Afro-Asian states, and attended by official delegations from thirty Afro-Asian and East European states and by individuals and representatives of unofficial organizations

[9] *Ibid.*, pp. 8-9.

[10] *Africa Digest*, XII, No. 6 (London: June 1965) 163-64.

from other countries. It considered papers commissioned from experts — economists, jurists and strategists — and it adopted resolutions in favor of total economic sanctions against South Africa. The papers and the resolutions of the conference were speedily published, and they constitute an elaborate discussion of the problems of coercion.[11]

The essence of the economic aspect of the case for coercion is that since South Africa is dependent on foreign trade to the extent of 20 percent of its gross domestic product, an effective and sustained embargo would rapidly place the country under siege conditions and eventually bring the economy to a standstill, so that at some stage the government would have to cease defying the world. In particular, the South African economy is non-autarkic with respect to its reliance upon gold sales and oil purchases. Gold comprises from 10 to 12.5 percent of South Africa's gross national product, but practically all gold is exported. This forms over half of the total exports, so that an effective stoppage would severely damage the economy. Although the advocates of coercion concede that this might seriously harm some firms in London, England, they contend that it would cause no more than trifling damage to the international monetary system, and might have the beneficial effect of stimulating the adoption of a more rational system than the present one which relies heavily upon gold.

South Africa imports over 90 percent of its oil; though storage capacity may be increased in anticipation of oil sanctions, a complete stoppage of oil supplies would soon become a very serious matter. Advocates of coercion contend that the imposition of oil sanctions would not seriously dislocate the world oil market, since South Africa consumes less than 1 percent of the world's oil. However, gold is in universal demand for private as well as public purposes, and there is a glut of oil, especially of gasoline which is South Africa's principal need, so that in the event of an embargo being declared the vast profits to be made

11 Ronald Segal, ed., *Sanctions against South Africa* (Harmondsworth: Penguin Books, 1964). See also "Sandor," *The Coming Struggle for South Africa* (London: Fabian Tract 345, 1963); Colin and Margaret Legum, *South Africa: Crisis for the West* (London: Pall Mall, 1964); Amelia C. Leiss, ed., *Apartheid and United Nations* (New York: Carnegie Endowment for International Peace, 1965).

by buying South African gold at a discount and exporting it or by importing gasoline into South Africa and selling it at a premium would probably provide irresistible incentives to many entrepreneurs. Consequently, while an effective embargo on South Africa's trade in general, or on its gold exports or oil imports in particular, would sooner or later bring the South African government to its knees, to be effective the embargo would have to be invoked by the United Nations, supported by virtually every government in the world, and enforced by powerful units placed at the disposal of the Secretary-General for a period of a year or more.[12]

Fundamental to the strategic aspect of the case for coercion is the fact that the application of a total blockade of South Africa is well within the capacity of the United Nations, provided there is the necessary political support for it, and that the greater part of the blockading force would have to be supplied by the major powers, since the Afro-Asian states lack naval strength. If Portugal cooperated with the United Nations, it has been suggested that a force of the dimensions of four fleet carriers and twenty-five warships would suffice; if Portugal did not cooperate, then Angola and Mozambique must be included in the blockade to prevent leaks from them into the Republic, requiring a suggested fleet twice as large. The advocates of coercion also point out that a selective blockade would be more difficult to administer than a total blockade in which there would be no need to search ships; nevertheless, if a selective blockade were preferred for political reasons, then the key commodity would be oil, which is bulky and can only be efficiently transported in tankers, which are easily recognizable.[13]

The essence of the juristic aspect of the case for coercion is the idea that the legality of such a blockade could be vindicated by reference to the Charter of the United Nations, to precedents, and to general principles of international law. The most obvi-

---

[12] A. Maizels, "Economic Sanctions and South Africa's trade," Brian Lapping, "Oil sanctions against South Africa," and Roger Opie, "Gold," in Segal, *op. cit.*

[13] William F. Gutteridge, "The strategic implications of sanctions against South Africa," and Neville Brown, "The strategic situation," in Segal, *op. cit.*

ous way in which this might happen would be for the Security Council to decide, under Article 39 of the Charter, that South Africa's racial policies constitute a "threat to the peace"; and then, under Article 41, to impose on all member states the obligation to refrain from trading with South Africa, and to request the Secretary-General to raise a voluntary force to implement a blockade, following the precedents created when forces were raised to operate in Korea and Cyprus.

Alternative modes of procedure are also available. If permanent members of the Security Council did not all agree that South Africa's racial policies constitute a threat to the peace, they might be prepared to coerce South Africa on other grounds, namely, its persistent refusal over many years to comply with the recommendations of the General Assembly and the Security Council, in conjunction with its failure to carry out the fundamental obligations it assumed under Articles 55 and 56 of the Charter. There is also the possibility of circumventing a veto in the Security Council by a resolution passed by a majority of the members of the General Assembly, inviting the Secretary-General to raise a force to blockade South Africa, following the precedents created in the cases of the Middle East and the Congo; this action would have a defect — some major powers would probably not cooperate in the policy and unanimity is most desirable in effecting the plan.

What is clear, however, is that any decision to apply coercive measures is a political decison and not a legal one. It is a decision made by a political entity — the Security Council (or perhaps the General Assembly) of the United Nations — and enforced by political entities — the governments of members of the United Nations. If there is a general determination to intervene, and if no major power deems it expedient to resist that general determination, intervention will take place, notwithstanding the incompatibility of Article 2(7) with Articles 2(2), 55 and 56 of the Charter, and notwithstanding the ambiguity of Article 39.[14]

14 Peter Calvocoressi, "The politics of sanctions: the League and the United Nations," D. H. N. Johnson, "Sanctions against South Africa? The Legal Aspect," and Rosalyn Higgins, "International action and domestic jurisdiction," in Segal, *op. cit.*

The demand for coercive measures against South Africa is obviously no sudden improvisation. It is the product of nearly twenty years of growth, starting with blandly phrased requests, urgings and invitations by the General Assembly of the United Nations, on the comparatively peripheral subjects of the status of South-West Africa and the treatment of the small Indian minority in South Africa, both of which were related to specific international agreements. The demand has developed into a crusade for the overthrow of the South African political system, led by the independent African states and supported by the Asian and Communist states — a crusade South Africa's traditional friends and trading partners are finding increasingly embarrassing to resist and increasingly difficult to divert or delay.

South Africa has already become the most isolated state in the world. Though remaining a member of the United Nations and some of its related agencies, South Africa has had no place in any of the other great international groupings since leaving the Commonwealth in 1961 after criticisms made by the Afro-Asian members at meetings of Commonwealth Prime Ministers. It is no longer a member of two of the most important agencies related to the United Nations — UNESCO and the FAO; its membership in the ILO and WHO is in jeopardy; and it has left the principal technical agencies for the African continent — the Economic Commission for Africa, the Council for Technical Cooperation in Africa, and the Council for Science in Africa. The country has been excluded from several international sports contests, including the uniquely prestigious Olympic Games. Confining its embassies to Western Europe, the Americas and Australia, South Africa lacks diplomatic representation with a single government controlled by Africans, Asians or Communists, has no political or military agreement with any foreign state, except the Simonstown agreements with Britain which are of limited scope, unless there is some secret arrangement with Portugal that, if it exists, would not be a great source of strength to South Africa.

South Africa has also become the target of economic boycotts. Many African and Asian states have imposed trade boycotts; although those have not always been strictly enforced and if they were they would not affect the bulk of South Africa's customary trade, they are preventing South Africa from developing its natural markets in the less developed areas to the north. African states have also denied South African aircraft over-flight and airport facilities, forcing the South African Airways to use a longer and less profitable route to Europe via Luanda and Las Palmas. Partial boycotts on trade with South Africa have also been invoked from time to time by private agencies, such as trade unions in other countries including European.[15]

THE RESPONSE OF THE SOUTH AFRICAN GOVERNMENT

South Africa's diplomatic isolation, the boycotts that have been applied, and the threats of more general coercion might have been expected to evoke in the South African government a willingness, indeed a desire, to negotiate, but they have had no such effect. On the contrary, the government has shown a persistent determination to resist the external as well as the internal opposition to the South African political system with unrelenting vigor.

In the four years following the Sharpeville shootings, there was nearly a fivefold increase in military expenditure. This reflected the serious concern of the South African government over the world reaction to that event. The 1960-1961 budget allotted $61.6 million for defense; the 1964-1965 budget allotted $294 million, and further increases were predicted. The white population is prepared to convert to a wartime footing at short notice. According to a government White Paper published in June 1964, the Permanent Force comprised 14,926 officers and men; the Citizen Force was providing nine months' training for 16,527 men, and three months' training for approximately another 30,000 men who had performed their nine months' training in previous years; and the Commando organization numbered 51,487 men, who were being given part-time training and were also liable to mobilization.

With the addition of some 13,600 white men in the Police

15 On South Africa's membership of international organizations, see *Survey of Race Relations*, 1964, pp. 128-34; on its membership of sports organizations, *ibid.*, pp. 330-45; and on economic sanctions threatened or in force against South Africa, *ibid.*, pp. 119-25.

Force, this makes a total of some 126,500 white South Africans who are trained in the use of modern weapons and subject to rapid mobilization. Furthermore, large numbers of women and children, as well as men, are trained to handle small arms in pistol clubs — 27,250 women were stated to be members of such clubs in 1964. The number of schoolboys who as cadets receive basic training in military maneuvers and weapons was being doubled from 60,000 to 120,000. These arrangements amount to an efficient and flexible use of South Africa's white manpower, and provide ample scope for political indoctrination.[16]

Since the Commandos serve without pay, the cost of wages for military personnel is comparatively low. The greater part of the budgetary increase has been devoted to the manufacture and the importation of arms and ammunition. Indeed, the appropriation for the manufacture of munitions in 1964-1965 was a hundred times as great as the appropriation four years earlier. The result is that South Africa is now self-supporting in a wide range of guns and ammunition. Pending its development of the production of military aircraft, armored cars, warships, and radar and telecommunications equipment, South Africa has been importing considerable quantities from overseas — mainly from Britain, France and the United States. Under the Simonstown agreements of 1955 Britain has been supplying naval vessels, including three anti-submarine frigates, to a cost of $64.4 million; South Africa has also been receiving British Buccaneer and Canberra aircraft, and Westland Wasp helicopters. France has supplied Panhard armored cars, jet fighters and helicopters; Oerlikon anti-aircraft guns and ammunition have come from Switzerland; and the United States has supplied C-130-B transport planes and Cessna 185 Skywagons. In 1963, however, the United States government stopped all sales of military equipment to South Africa, except existing contracts, and in 1964 the British Labour Government did the same; but France continues to sell equipment for defense against external aggression.[17]

As the military build-up has developed, South African Cabi-

[16] United Nations General Assembly, *A/5497* (1963) pp. 119-27, *A/-5497/Add.1* (1963) pp. 64-75, and *A/5692* (1964) pp. 56-59; *Africa Digest*, XII, No. 1 (August 1964) 25-26.

[17] *Ibid.;* also *Survey of Race Relations,* 1964, pp. 121-23.

net Ministers have expressed confidence in the capacity of South Africa to deal with internal revolt and with any attack likely to be launched upon the Republic by Afro-Asian states without the support of the major powers. As the Minister of Defence put it in June 1964: "We need nothing — and when I say nothing, I mean nothing — at all to maintain internal order." He added that extra equipment was still required from overseas "to make us," he claimed, "a reliable force in the Western defence group"! [18]

But the South African government is by no means resigned to war. It hopes to avoid war by conducting a massive propaganda campaign overseas, and in this campaign the State Information receives powerful support from a private agency, the South Africa Foundation. Created in 1961 in response to the shock created by the Sharpeville shootings, the South Africa Foundation is an association of prominent white South Africans, drawn from both Afrikaans and English-speaking communities and both major political parties. Its chairman is Major-General Sir Francis de Guingand, who was Chief of Staff to Field Marshal Montgomery in World War II and subsequently started a new career as a businessman in South Africa. Its trustees include Harry Oppenheimer who, as head of De Beers and of the Anglo-American Corporation of South Africa, wields far more economic power than any other individual in the country. The Foundation is in essence an association of the controllers of the South African economy, drawn together for the purpose of staving off the threat presented by the external opposition to the South African political system. Most businessmen subscribe to the Foundation, many with great enthusiasm, others because abstention incurs suspicion of being unpatriotic.[19]

The declared purpose of the Foundation is "to present to the world a true picture of South Africa"; [20] the picture it portrays gives a very different impression from the one depicted by most foreign observers and from the realities experienced by most South Africans. The Foundation paints the present regime in a generally favorable light by emphasizing the strength of the South African economy and the value of a white-controlled

18 *Africa Digest,* XII, No. 1 (August 1964) 25.

19 Legum, *op. cit.,* pp. 112-16.

20 *Ibid.,* p. 112.

South Africa to the Western World; while admitting there are flaws in contemporary South Africa, the Foundation insists these are susceptible to reform and that the reforming process must be permitted to operate exclusively from within.

The official and unofficial propaganda from South Africa consists of a constant reiteration of a few basic points, in proportions varied to suit the occasion and the audience. There is sometimes a direct appeal to the racial emotions of white people in Europe and America, who are urged to prevent the most powerful bastion of white power in Africa from falling into African hands. Almost invariably there is a play on Western fears of Communism, with an antithesis between the danger of a Communist take-over of black-controlled Africa and the steadfast anti-Communism of the South African regime. With this is often linked a stress on the strategic importance of South Africa, situated at the junction of the Atlantic and the Indian Oceans. Much emphasis is usually given to the growth of the South African economy within the present political framework and the value of South Africa to foreign investors. In a recent report the Foundation showed that the average dividend in South Africa is 12.6 percent compared with 6.6 percent in Western Europe, and that American companies doing business in South Africa are making profits averaging 27 percent per annum. South Africa's critics are said to be paying too much attention to the birth pains of the Bantustan system, and failing to realize that in the long run the system will provide a viable outlet for African social and political aspirations. Two final points used are the reminder that the United Nations nearly overreached itself in the Congo, where the human opposition was negligible, and the warning that if the United Nations were to attempt coercive action its efforts would be resisted by the white South African nation, equipped with the most modern conventional weapons.[21]

Arguments such as these are effective in many quarters. They attract those elements in Britain and continental Europe which

---

[21] For the official propaganda see, e.g., H. H. H. Biermann, ed., *The Case for South Africa as put forth in the statements of Eric H. Louw* (New York: MacFadden Books, 1963); for the unofficial propaganda see the publications of the South Africa Foundation.

regret the passing of the colonial epoch, and those segments of the population in the United States which look with disfavor upon the negro revolt at home. Indeed, in parts of the southern United States Dr. Verwoerd is regarded as one of the greatest statesmen of the century. Such arguments also hold attraction for some (but not all) of the foreign businessmen who have stakes in the South African economy. The South Africa Foundation has national committees in seventeen Western countries. A recent study showed that the anti-interventionist lobby in Britain is coordinated by the British committee of the South Africa Foundation, whose members have large interests in South African trade, shipping, investment and manufacturing industry, and that it is strongly represented in the House of Lords.[22] The American lobby is weaker than the British, because the American stake in the South African economy is much smaller. Nevertheless, there are American industrialists who, having made superficial tours of parts of the Republic under skillful white supervision, have returned to the United States to extol South Africa as a field for investment, to defend the South African political system, and to join the American committee of the South Africa Foundation.

Tied as it is to a system of white supremacy, South African propaganda necessarily concentrates on the nations controlled by Europeans or people of European origin. These are the countries possessing crucial power in relation to South Africa. The United Kingdom, the United States and France have three of the five permanent seats in the Security Council of the United Nations. The United Kingdom, the United States and the Western European countries are South Africa's principal trading partners, so the success of an embargo hinges upon their support, and their naval forces are indispensable to the enforcement of an embargo. Indeed, while the countries under non-white or Communist control have strong incentives to change the South African political system, they cannot easily do this without the cooperation of the white countries of the West. The governments of the United Kingdom, the United States and the countries of Western Europe, therefore, have a crucial responsibility for determining the future of South Africa.

[22] Legum, *op. cit.*, pp. 243-55.

CONCLUSION

By the mid-1960's the Security Council was seriously consider-ing using coercive measures against South Africa. Its members were unanimous in condemning the racial policies of the South African government, and in declaring them to be incompatible with the obligations of the United Nations' constituents, of legitimate concern to the United Nations, and likely to endan-ger international peace and security. As Ambassador Adlai Stevenson said in the Security Council on August 2, 1963:

> We are all agreed, and we have proclaimed again and again, in this body and in the General Assembly, and in many other forums of the United Nations, certain basic views about the issue before us. . . .
>
> First, we have affirmed and reaffirmed that *apartheid* is ab-horrent. Our belief in the self-evident truths about human equality is enshrined in our Charter. *Apartheid* and racism, despite all of the tortured rationalizations that we have heard from the apologists, are incompatible with the moral, social, and constitutional foundations of our societies.
>
> A second basic principle on which we are all agreed is that all Members of the Organization have pledged themselves to take action, in cooperation with the Organization, to promote ob-servance of human rights, without distinction as to race.
>
> Thirdly, we continue to believe that this matter is of proper and legitimate concern to the United Nations. We have often stated, in the General Assembly, our belief that the Assembly can properly consider questions of racial discrimination and other violations of human rights where they are a Member's official policy and are inconsistent with the obligations of that Member, under Articles 55 and 56 of the Charter, to promote observance of human rights, without distinction as to race.
>
> Moreover, the *apartheid* policy has clearly led to a situation the continuance of which is likely to endanger international peace and security. We also believe that all Members, in the words of the resolution passed almost unanimously by the six-teenth General Assembly, should take such separate and collec-tive action to bring about an abandonment of *apartheid* as is open to them in conformity with the Charter.[23]

Nevertheless, it is also clear that the United States, the United Kingdom and France have been averse to taking

[23] United Nations General Assembly, *A/5497/Add.1* (1963) pp. 149-51.

measures against South Africa under Chapter VII of the Charter. These three states have regarded it as their role to go to the very limits in advising, cajoling, admonishing, condemning and even threatening South Africa, but all in the hope that they would thereby cause white South Africans to initiate radical reforms from inside South Africa, and without actually committing themselves to render support for coercive measures under Chapter VII of the Charter. There have been many differences of emphasis among the Western Powers, and their votes in the organs of the United Nations have often been cast on different sides. However, British Ambassador Sir Patrick Dean was probably not far from expressing their common attitude when he informed the Security Council on June 15, 1964 that his government believed in the goal of "freedom and justice for all in South Africa," but considered that the goal could only be achieved by an evolutionary process. Coercion, he said, might lead to results "opposite to those desired"; he insisted that the situation in South Africa did not warrant the invocation of Article 39 of the Charter and the consequential application of measures under Articles 41 and 42.[24]

The aggregate attitude of the United States, the United Kingdom and the Western European Powers towards South Africa has been, therefore, a policy of brinkmanship, with the objective of initiating reform within that country. Will they persist in such a policy, even though the reformative forces within South Africa have been reduced to impotence by the government? Or are they, themselves, to become the principal instruments of change in South Africa? These would seem to be the only practicable alternatives before the Western Powers; the dilemma is awesome, because the effects will be felt far beyond the confines of the Republic of South Africa.

If the Western Powers continue to stop short of imposing effective sanctions, the South African political system is likely to survive intact for a very long time, even through the crises that will arise as consequences of the continuing advance of the African revolution to the borders of the Republic (including the critical situation accompanying a decision by the International Court against South Africa in the South-West African

24 United Nations Security Council, *S/PV. 1131* (June 15, 1964).

case). Afro-Asian and Communist Powers would then put the responsibility for its survival, and for the persistence of man-made suffering in South Africa, on the shoulders of the Western Powers. In time this would aggravate the existing racial tensions within the countries of the West, with specially grievous consequences in the United States with its large and hyper-sensitive negro population. It would retard the growth of confidence in the Western Powers among the new countries of Asia and Africa and assist the Communist Powers to achieve their objectives in those countries. It would also weaken the United Nations — seriously, and perhaps lethally — for the letter and the spirit of the Charter would have been flouted with impunity on one of the most vital issues confronting modern man, and the effects of this would be incalculable.

There are also great dangers in a policy of coercion. Resort to force is the most extreme step that can be taken by a national government or an international organization. In a case where the offender is not actually attacking other nations, force would only seem to be justified where two conditions are fulfilled: first, the policies of the offender must have poisonous effects upon humanity as a whole; and second, there must be good reason to believe that the force employed will eradicate the poison and bring the offender into a healthy relationship with the rest of the world. In the South African case it is difficult to escape the conclusion that the first condition exists, but the second condition does not seem to exist at the present time.

One of the ineluctable facts about the present state of South African society is that the racial polarization within it has reached the stage where the different communities are incapable of genuine negotiation and creative dialogue, without overriding pressure from without. The dominant community, being in a numerical minority, is consumed by fear of the effects of radical change, while the subject communities, having suffered continuously under the existing system, are imbued with a spirit of revenge. Another unavoidable fact is that the expedient of partition, applied as a last resort to warring communities elsewhere, as in Ireland, India and Pakistan, does not seem to be feasible in South Africa because the South African communities have become so intermingled and so interdependent. There has certainly been no serious demand for partition from any section of the South African population.

Consequently, if the United Nations were to embark upon the physical coercion of the South African government without being prepared to assume the responsibility for the follow-up, the results would probably be most disappointing. The intervening force might withdraw before sufficiently weakening the complex power basis of the present regime, in which case, through skillful use of its monopoly of educational attainments and administrative and economic experience, the white minority might contrive to effect a restoration. Or, the intervening force might destroy the power basis of the white minority, hand over the formal trappings of power to African nationalists, and then withdraw, in which case the bitterness and inexperience of the African nationalists might produce anarchy and economic collapse. Or, the states participating in the blockade might fall out among themselves over the policy to be pursued in the follow-up, and vent their ideological differences and power struggles upon the soil and the peoples of South Africa. In none of these eventualities would the use of force have been justified.

Force would only be justified if all the major Powers agreed upon a viable plan for the reconstruction of South Africa — a plan going far beyond the recommendations in the report presented to the Security Council in April 1964 — and if they possessed the unity and the strength of purpose to give effect to such a plan. In a world that was harmonious in other respects, these prerequisites might exist. In the world as it is and is likely to continue to be, they are unattainable; and the governments of the United States, Great Britain, France and the other Western Powers know it. These governments are not to be expected to embark upon a costly enterprise, with unpredictable consequences, against the government of a country remote from their own borders, which is a trading partner, which contrives to preserve law and order, on whatever basis, and which does not threaten to attack its neighbors. For the foreseeable future, therefore, the political system of South Africa seems likely to remain substantially as portrayed in this book — an anachronistic survivor of the colonial era, a continuous source of embarrassment to the West, and one of the most blatant flaws in the body of mankind.

Index

Index